BODIE & BROCK
THOENE

Take This Cup

Jerusalem Chronicles, Book Two

ZONDERVAN

Take This Cup

Copyright © 2014 by Bodie Thoene and Brock Thoene
This title is also available as a Zondervan ebook.
Visit www.zondervan.com/ebooks.
This title is also available in a Zondervan audio edition.
Visit www.zondervan.fm.
Requests for information should be addressed to:
Zondervan, *Grand Rapids, Michigan* 49530

ISBN 978-0-310-33599-3 (hardcover, jacketed)

Library of Congress Cataloging-in-Publication Data

Thoene, Bodie, 1951-
    Take this cup / Bodie & Brock Thoene.
        pages cm. -- (Jerusalem chronicles ; Book Two)
    ISBN 978-0-310-33598-6 (softcover)
1. Jesus Christ--Fiction. 2. Lazarus, of Bethany, Saint--Fiction. 3. Bible. New Testament--
History of Biblical events--Fiction. I. Thoene, Brock, 1952- II. Title.
    PS3570.H46T23 2014
    813'.54--dc23   2013041150

Cover design: Kirk Douponce

Cover photography or illustration: Robin Hanley

Interior illustration: Ruth Pettis

Interior design: Katherine Lloyd, The DESK

Editing: Ramona Cramer Tucker, Sue Brower, Bob Hudson, Anna Craft

Printed in the United States of America

16 17 18 19 /RRD/ 23 22 21 20 19 18 17 16 15 14 13 12 11 10 9 8 7 6

For my prayer warrior stars, with love from Bodie

Every Friday at 5 o'clock we toast one another with these words:

"Here's to the women who went before us, to those who will come after us, and to us . . ."

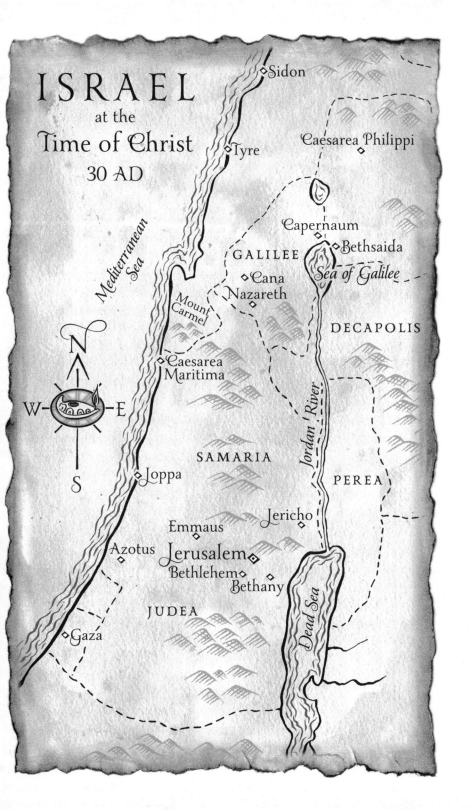

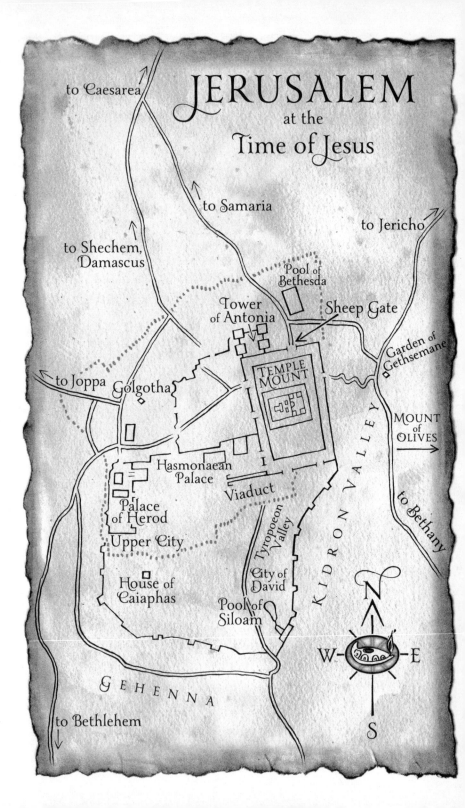

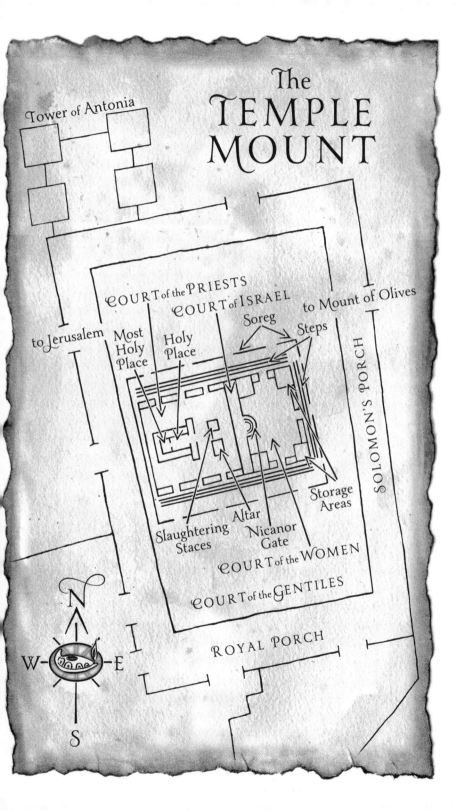

Part One

As a deer pants for water,
so my heart longs for you, O Lord.

PSALM 42:1[1]

Chapter 1

My mother's name was Sarah. She was the fifth daughter of Boaz, a weaver of fine wool prayer shawls in Jerusalem. Sarah was taller than most men, ample hipped and heavy-set, with thick, curly hair, and wide green eyes in a square, practical face. Her teeth were straight and strong. Such things as teeth mattered.

Sarah's weaving of prayer shawls was skilled, her work meticulous. Her shawls were worn by the Temple priests and pilgrims alike.

Sarah's one flaw was that she walked with a limp. But her father was quick to remind everyone that Sarah was a cheerful, loving girl and a hard worker. She would bless any man in search of a good helpmate.

One after another, Sarah's older sisters married. There were, however, no suitors for Sarah. Her limp, though not severe, was problematic. It was not easy for her to ascend and descend the hundreds of steps in Jerusalem. The streets were steep, and a woman's duties of shopping in the souk and fetching water would surely be hindered by her handicap. And men desiring to be head of a household did not want the head of a woman taller than their own.

Year after year she hoped and prayed. But there was not one man in all of Israel who asked for Sarah's hand in marriage.

Sarah resigned herself to remaining an unmarried virgin in her father's house. Content with her life, she helped her mother and father in the little shop, located fourth from the high end of the Street of the Weavers.

Sarah's place was at the entrance of the shop. There, she and the loom were a sort of fixture on the street. Sarah played the loom like an instrument. She sang in perfect rhythm with the movement. Passersby gathered in a half circle to watch and listen as she performed.

Sarah was twenty-three, well past marriageable age, the morning her mother's distant cousin Lamsa ben Baruch entered the shop and fixed his steady gaze upon her as she worked.

"May I help you, sir?" Sarah's mother asked as she braided and tied the knots on the four corners of the prayer shawl.

"Aye. If you are Rebekah, wife of the weaver Boaz, then I am your cousin Lamsa . . . here from the land of Gan Eden."

Sarah's mother squealed with delight and laid aside her work. "Boaz! Boaz! It's my cousin Lamsa! Lamsa, from beyond the four rivers of Eden!" She rushed to embrace him.

"You've gotten plump, Rebekah," Lamsa drawled in his Eastern dialect. "But you are still pretty!"

The *thump, thump, thump* of Sarah's loom continued as she observed the reunion through the screen of warp and woof.

My grandfather, Boaz, rushed from the back room and clasped Lamsa's arms. "Lamsa! And you've gotten lazy! Fifteen years or more since you delivered your wool to Jerusalem personally! Sent a steward to Jerusalem to us every year but now . . . look at you!"

Sarah observed Lamsa. He was tall and strong, but not as tall as she. Lean and muscled, he clearly did not live a life of ease. Though she knew he was in his early forties, his grizzled beard and weathered skin made him appear older than he was. Yet his brown eyes, quick and observant, took in details of the shop.

His expression was pleased as he observed bolts of fine woolen fabric. A rainbow of colors and constellations of patterns filled two walls. Prayer shawls of intricate weaving were priced for rich or humble, a variety of sizes neatly folded on shelves. Finally, he took in the loom and Sarah and grinned.

"My flocks would be flattered that their wool has become such a fine and holy covering. I will tell them next season when they are shorn."

Sarah smiled shyly and looked downward but did not break the rhythm of her labor.

A lock of wild black hair spilled from beneath Lamsa's turban and across his brow like the forelock of a horse.

"There is no wool like the wool of Lamsa's sheep," Boaz praised. "It is the fleece of Eden—that is what I tell our customers. Nothing so thick and yet silky. No fleece like it in the world."

Rebekah clapped her hands in delight. "But you are here with us! How's the family? Your sons? Three of them, yes? And your wife?"

"My sons are well and strong. Ten, twelve, and fifteen." His smile faltered. "But my beautiful Jerusha flew away last spring, trying to give me our fourth child, and I am without my great companion."

Boaz and Rebekah clucked their tongues and wagged their heads in unison at the news.

"Oh, Lamsa!"

"Poor Lamsa!"

"So sorry to hear your news!"

" . . . very sorry. May she rest in peace."

" . . . in peace."

"What's a man without a wife . . ."

" . . . a wife."

"Only half . . ."

"What's life without a woman?"

Boaz's eyes glanced furtively at his daughter. His lower lip extended. Eyebrows rose and fell as he turned his face slightly to one side as a thought passed through his mind and out his ear. "Rebekah, go fetch your cousin something to eat quickly. He has come a long way to see us."

Sarah thought her father made it sound as though Lamsa had not eaten in a thousand miles and that he had come all the way from Eden just to share a meal. Sarah saw that her father and mother had invisibly tattooed the word *widower* across Lamsa's forehead.

Lamsa bowed slightly as Sarah's mother hurried off to fetch refreshment.

"The dust of Eden remains on our mountains." Lamsa laid out his wares on the fabric table to show samples of this year's wool and fine, thick fleeces from his flocks in the North beyond Babylon. "And the glory of Adonai remains in our high mountain pastures. My sheep drink in the memory of it from the waters, and even the grass they graze translates the vision of Adam into this . . ." He swept his hand proudly over the wool.

Boaz ran his fingers over the miracle produced by Lamsa's flock and closed his eyes in pleasure at the quality. "Nothing like this wool anywhere."

Lamsa added, "Ah, brother, you should taste the meat of my lambs. Nothing has such flavor. I dream of it when I am away."

"You must be hungry! Where is that woman?" Then Boaz called to Rebekah, "Wife, where are you? Hurry! Bring the wine and cheese and bread for Lamsa."

Rebekah bustled in with a tray of food and a jug of wine. "I must go prepare a feast for you, Lamsa. So many years since we have served you! Our daughter, Sarah, will help me. She is a good cook. Sarah?"

Sarah tried to maintain her smile but was well aware her mother had already mentally discarded the word *widower* and substituted the phrase *potential husband for lame, too-tall Sarah, twenty-three-year-old spinster daughter.*

Rebekah motioned to Sarah, and the thump of the loom fell silent. She stepped from her chair and towered over the room.

"This," Boaz said, smiling, "is our daughter Sarah. She was a child when last you were here."

Lamsa did not say, "My, how you've grown," but Sarah saw the thought in his expression.

Sarah stepped forward and curtsied. "Cousin Lamsa, I know you by the beauty of the wool I weave, sir."

Lamsa kissed her on both cheeks. "Cousin Sarah, you play the loom as if it were David's harp." He gestured at her father's wares. "And here is the poetry and the melody and the music of your effort."

It was a kind thing for him to say, and a true thing as well. Sarah bowed her head slightly, then left with her mother so Boaz and Lamsa could conduct business.

Sarah limped after her mother through the curtain into the back room of the shop. Rebekah lingered to eavesdrop. Sarah, disgusted, waited, hands on hips. The voices of the two men drifted to her.

"It's a long way for you to travel, Lamsa."

"I wanted to see you. I remembered you have five beautiful daughters."

"Yes. Yes. The four oldest are married with families of their own now. They weave for me in their homes."

"Sarah is a skilled weaver," Lamsa remarked.

Sarah wanted to cover her ears. Her mother was almost vibrating as she panted and wrung her hands at the curtain.

"Mother," Sarah hissed. "Come on. Please! We have to go to the Street of the Butchers before they close." Sarah plucked at her mother's sleeve.

Rebekah came to her senses as Sarah tugged her out the back door of the shop into the late afternoon air. "We must have the butcher prepare a haunch of lamb for us," Rebekah decided.

"Not lamb, Mother. You heard what Lamsa said about his lamb. Anything but his own will be sawdust in his mouth."

"Oh, Sarah, you are so clever. Such a clever girl! Why you have never married . . ."

They trudged up the alley toward the open corridor leading to where butcher shops lined the street known as "Shambles."

Sarah rolled her eyes. "Mother. The man is not looking for a wife!"

"He most certainly is!" Rebekah would not be swayed.

"He's not looking for me."

Rebekah glanced up at Sarah. "And why not you? Why, I ask?"

"And I am not looking for a husband. Not one who lives a thousand miles away."

Rebekah pinched her cheek. "Look at you. Pretty girl. Pretty green eyes. Your eyes are your best feature. What's wrong with you? Such a place he lives. A rich man. Eden . . ."

"I'm no Eve. What's for dinner?"

Rebekah was drawn back to the problem of inferior lamb. "Beef," she declared.

"The best pieces will be gone by now."

"Fish."

"Too late in the day. No fresh fish."

"Then what?"

"A chicken," Sarah answered. "We'll have the butcher slaughter a chicken. Fresh enough."

Rebekah snapped her fingers. "You're so smart, daughter. Yes, you can make that . . . that . . . wonderful dish your father enjoys so much."

❧

And so the chicken was slaughtered, plucked, and roasted as Lamsa hurried to the public baths and returned in time for a sumptuous meal prepared by Sarah. Wine flowed. The best wine. Lots of it.

Lamsa reclined happily and patted his belly. "There are wild pheasant in the hills. Practically pick them up without a snare. But my boys do love to hunt. Imagine pheasant cooked like this."

Rebekah simpered, "Sarah can cook anything. Can't you, Sarah? Tell him your secret."

"Garlic," Sarah replied without elaboration.

Lamsa nodded slowly. "Ah, yes. Garlic. We have garlic. And rosemary and thyme grow wild on our hills." He pressed his fingers together and formed a tent shape. "Two mountain ranges border our grazing lands like this. Climbing and climbing to impossible heights. The snowfall on the peaks never fully melts. On the lower slopes it melts into ten thousand waterfalls and is the source of the Tigris and Euphrates rivers. Eden. You see? And at the very north of the mountain ranges, where my fingers meet, is Ararat, a volcano with two great peaks, where

Noah and his ark came to rest. Noah opened the door of the ark and out they came . . . all the animals. So our mountains and valleys abound with wildlife."

Sarah questioned, "And your flock grazes on the wild spices? Perhaps that is why your lamb is superior in taste to any other." She meant this as a joke.

Lamsa continued to nod as he considered such profound wisdom. "That must be it. Such a clever girl. That has to be it."

Sarah smiled slightly. "It could be nothing else."

"All fruit trees grow wild there. Except orange trees. But every spice grows wild. And asparagus. Just stroll out of your door. Vegetables . . . all kinds . . . wild."

Sarah replied too pleasantly, "A miracle. And so the lamb is seasoned before it is cooked, and vegetables are perfectly ripe and ready on the hillside. A woman has no need to go to the souk . . ."

Lamsa broke his bread and placed a piece on Sarah's plate. "We are never without variety, and every day is beautiful. My town is called Amadiya. It is built of stone and is as old as Jerusalem, they say. Abraham would have known it. Built on a high plateau that overlooks river valleys. Beautiful. A fortress. A safe place for our wives and children. Only one way up. A steep staircase cut in the side of the mountain. Protection for our families from raiders while we shepherds move our flocks from meadow to meadow."

Sarah considered her lame foot and wondered if there were more steps leading to Amadiya than there were in Jerusalem. "But what if the women and families wish to go with their husbands?" she asked.

Lamsa replied, "Then they come. And live in tents among the flocks. Seven or eight months of the year is a long time to stay alone in a stone house in the village. Many families come along with the men. All work together. Children. Women. But only if they do not wish to stay in a fine stone house in the village." He smiled. "It is pleasant. If Father Abraham would come upon us, he would not know how many centuries had passed. The descendants of Noah's wild deer often follow our flocks as we move from pasture to pasture. They drink with the sheep in the dry season. It is written, 'As a deer pants for water, so my heart longs for you, O, Lord.'"[1]

"I have heard something like that." Sarah drizzled honey on her morsel.

"Perhaps it is not the exact quote. But I know the truth of it."

Rebekah, as if fearing that Lamsa would catch on to Sarah's amusement, suddenly interrupted, "Come now, daughter, finish your meal. Lamsa and your father have things to discuss. Business."

The women cleared the table.

Rebekah heated water for washing. "Sarah," she chided, "he is a good man."

Sarah lifted a brow. "He's had too much wine and talks too much."

"Your father knows how to conduct business."

"Business! Do you think I don't know . . ." Sarah exhaled heavily. "Mother, I am content to be who I am and wish to remain where I am. Amadiya! How many steps up the face of a mountain to reach the village? Stop plotting. Not one more word!" Sarah warned.

They cleaned up the rest of the dishes in silence.

Immediately afterward, Sarah retreated to her bedchamber on the rooftop. Storm clouds gathered, and the half-moon shone through the silver vapor. She had been in bed an hour when Boaz and Rebekah rapped softly at her door.

"Enter."

Rebekah's expression was wistful, hopeful, as she blinked at Sarah. Boaz's lower lip protruded as it did when he was negotiating a sale.

"Daughter, are you asleep?" Rebekah whispered hoarsely.

"Not now." Sarah sat up.

"Good." Boaz pulled up a stool and, sucking his teeth, sat down slowly. "The chicken tonight was . . ."

"Just a chicken, Father."

"Lamsa enjoyed it very much." Rebekah leapt in too quickly.

Sarah did not reply at first, but a sense of dread filled her. "Father? What have you done?"

Her parents exchanged a guilty glance. Boaz cleared his throat. "You're no spring chicken."

"Not slaughtered and plucked quite yet, you mean, Father? Not stewed or roasted?" Sarah covered her face with her hands. "Just tell me."

"It's good news, really." Rebekah stroked her back. "He . . . Lamsa . . . likes you."

Sarah sighed. "Mother, everyone here likes me. I have only friends here. I have sisters and nephews and nieces who like me. Who love me. Strangers stop to watch me weave. They like me. I love my work."

Boaz cleared his throat. He smelled of too much wine. "Here's the bargain. Lamsa came here looking for a wife. Here. I mean, to this house. My house. He remembered that I had five daughters. He is looking for a wife, you see, from Jerusalem. He is not finished having children, and he wants a wife from Jerusalem, which will add stature and authority to his descendants, since his people did not return from exile when the captivity ended. He came looking . . . for you."

"No, Father! Not for me. I am the leftover daughter. The only one of five who is unmarried."

"That may be, but that made his choice easier."

"His choice?" Tears welled in Sarah's eyes.

Rebekah glanced nervously at Boaz. "Yes. He is a good man. A rich man."

"He lives eight months in a tent with sheep," Sarah protested. "Is this what you want for me?"

"Here is the bargain," Boaz reasoned. "His choice of my five daughters is you. No matter that your sisters are married. Lamsa chooses you. He came here for you. But he says . . ."

Silence hung in the air like a large spider suspended from a web. Sarah looked from Rebekah to Boaz, then back again. "What?"

Boaz continued cautiously. "Lamsa says he will not force you to marry him. Will not force you to leave your family and go back to Gan Eden unless you are certain you want to go."

Sarah blurted, "Then it's settled. The answer is no!"

Rebekah clasped her hand. "Sarah, your last chance . . ."

"No, Mother."

Boaz drew himself up. His eyes simmered in anger. "He is a fair man. He says you should pray on the matter and ask the Lord if there is some way you might be happy. That is what Lamsa says, and I command you to pray!"

Tears spilled. "What about my work?"

Boaz's chin lifted slightly. "Lamsa will take your loom to Amadiya. You will weave there. Your fabric, your prayer shawls, will be returned here to be sold in Jerusalem. I could not lose my most skilled weaver. For Lamsa, it is less raw wool to be cara-vanned. Thus, more economical."

"What about my limp? The mountains? Walking?"

"He says you may have your own donkey to ride. I would have nothing but the best for my daughter. He is a wealthy herdsman." Sarah could not utter another word. All the details for a marriage contract had been worked out.

So, she pondered, *this is how marriage happens. A distant relative in need of a woman walks through the door, and a bargain is struck. With the one caveat, I must agree.* "All right, Father, Mother. I will consider his . . . business arrangement."

"And pray?" Rebekah clasped her hands in a desperate pantomime of prayer.

"Yes, Mother. I will pray. I promise. I will."

The two scuttled like crabs out of her room and closed the door.

Sarah rose and leaned her chin against her hand on the windowsill. Male voices drifted up.

"My daughter says you are a most excellent man. She considers herself unworthy. You stride the mountains like a lion. She is lame and only useful at her loom."

Lamsa's rich, deep voice replied, "When I was a boy, I owned a pet ewe who was lame. She gave me many lambs. Her wool was the finest grade. Yes, I have many donkeys for Sarah to use. She may choose her own. And I will carry her home riding on my own camel . . . if she will come. But I do not wish for an unhappy companion. It is a long way to my high mountain valleys. She will not likely see her family again."

And so, that night, Sarah prayed about the proposed match. Could she like this man? Could she live in tents among the sheep for eight months of the year? Like the Abraham and Sarah of old, Lamsa's fathers were among those in Israel who stayed behind in Babylon when Nehemiah the prophet returned to rebuild the walls of Jerusalem.

Sarah reminded God that she was happy without a husband. Lamsa was a distant relation, a wealthy Jewish herdsman who lived in the land of ancient Babylon. He was not handsome.

"Abba, God of Abraham, Isaac, and Jacob, you hear my prayers. I do not wish to leave my pleasant life and leave Jerusalem for exile in a wild land unless you have some greater purpose for me. But if I was to have a son, I would dedicate him to serve you. And then I would be pleased to leave my home and kin." She stopped and thought, then continued speaking aloud to God. "If Lamsa says he will stay for a while in Jerusalem, and not leave until after the rainy season, Lord, then I will know. Just after the end of the rains. Tell me, please, Lord, what is your will?"

In that instant, as she finished praying, a flash of lightning split the sky. It divided like forked antlers, and the clouds lit up in the shape of a giant hart. A thunderclap followed, shaking the house. The heavens opened and rain bucketed down, sluicing off the eaves and into the street.

Sarah returned to her bed and lay for a while listening to the pleasant drumming of rain on her roof. Then she went to sleep, believing the Lord would give her a sign.

In the morning over breakfast, Lamsa and Sarah's father spoke about the weather.

Lamsa did not look at Sarah. "Last night I saw a bolt of lightning like the antlers of a great white hart in the sky. And such a rain followed."

Sarah paused. "I saw it too. A great hart in the eastern sky. Beautiful."

Lamsa smiled. "When there is thunder in our mountains, we say it is the sound of two great harts doing battle. The hart is a symbol for us who wander in distant land. Adam's great hart, strong and wise. We will one day all be gathered here in Eretz-Israel, because the Lord promised that even the land where I dwell will be Israel when Messiah comes. I am waiting for that day."

Sarah blinked down at her plate of eggs and bread. "I am also waiting for Messiah. He must come soon."

"When we see him as conqueror, it is written that it will be as lightning flashes from east to west."[2]

"Yes." Sarah swallowed hard as the answer came to her. "We will all see him at the same time. Jerusalem and your precious mountains and pastures."

Lamsa leaned forward slightly and studied her face. "You would love my mountains, I think."

Sarah nodded once. "Yes. I think. I think . . . I will. Yes. I would like to go see such a sight. Asparagus growing on a mountaintop . . . and such things. Thunder."

Lamsa leaned back and laughed loud and hearty. He patted his chest. "Oh, my heart! My happy heart!"

Sarah laughed with him. "All right, then."

Boaz and Rebekah embraced. "Praise be to God! Praise be!"

When things quieted down, Lamsa instructed, "Have the *Ketubah* drawn up, Boaz. I think it would be wise that we would marry here and stay here in Jerusalem with you until the rainy season is over. Sarah, would this please you?"

All was well. The matter was settled over breakfast, and by dinner the contract was signed.

The wedding took place in Jerusalem that very next week. From the first night, Sarah was happy with her husband. He was gentle with her, and she was cherished by him. It was a good match.

16

By the time the rainy season ended, Sarah had intricately woven her husband a beautiful prayer shawl. She was more than content; she was in love. When the rains were over and the camels packed for their return journey to Eden, Sarah told her parents a secret: "I am carrying Lamsa's child. I will send word when the baby is born."

So my mother, with her loom and carrying me, left all her family behind and traveled a thousand miles east and north by caravan.

Chapter 2

*A*ll in the encampment tending my father's herds were asleep, except for the watchmen posted around the flock.

A chorus of summer breezes curled down from the heights, filling the valley with whispers of tall pines and the creaking sighs of yews and junipers.

My mother, heavy with me, had chosen to follow the grazing sheep with my father, rather than stay behind in a stone house in the fortress town of Amadiya to await my birth. There was a midwife in the shepherds' camp and an elderly rabbi named Kagba, a wise man, who knew the secrets of *Torah* and taught the children. If I turned out to be a boy, Kagba would perform the circumcision.

Sarah stood framed in the dark entrance of their tent. Her arms tenderly embraced me, dancing in her womb. "Your father is tending the flocks tonight, my little lamb."

Watch fires had burned to embers that winked and sparkled on the improvised stone hearth. The pleasant sharpness of wood smoke scented the air. Shepherds and vigilant herd dogs ringed the meadow. A psalm of the shepherd boy David came to her: *"The LORD is my shepherd; I shall not want."*

Beyond the circle of guardians, an outer hoop of cedar trees protected the lush grazing grounds. A herd of a dozen roe deer cropped the grass at the near edge of the meadow. For a moment Sarah thought she saw the ghost-like form of a white hart watching from the shadows.

The words of the psalmist continued, *"He makes me lie down in green pastures."*

The crescent of a waning moon climbed over the peaks, and a myriad of stars reflected on the surface of a small, pristine lake. *"He leads me beside still waters."*[1]

Night birds called from the rushes lining the shore. In the middle distance an owl hooted fitfully.

There seemed no separation between earth and sky. Sarah caught a glimpse of Rabbi Kagba standing on a low hill, surrounded by her three stepsons and a half-dozen other children attending his astronomy class. He pointed out constellations and the movement of the stars.

She had never really thought about the constellations or the names of stars when she lived in her lonely rooftop bedchamber in Jerusalem. But now she enjoyed the bits of information in the rabbi's lessons.

"A man will not be lost in the wilderness if he learns the path of the stars," the rabbi told his students.

Sarah whispered, "Stars above and stars shining up from beneath the surface of the water."

Turning, she followed the direction indicated by the silhouette of the teacher's outstretched arm. He traced a waterfall of glittering stars spanning the breadth of the heavens. Kagba's voice drifted across the pond: "The Great Sky River! Other peoples name it 'The Celestial Way.' It is said that when Messiah comes, his authority will stretch . . ."

The breeze reversed its direction, and Kagba's words swirled away toward the west.

A meteor streaked across the sky, followed by another and another as they had done for three nights. Kagba had earlier explained these shooting stars were called the Perseids. They appeared for a month around the same time each year in late summer.

I shifted slightly in my mother's womb, and she smiled.

"You're late arriving, I think, my bright star. Can you hear me? We all wait for you to join us here beneath the stars that shone above Eden."

As if in reply, a brilliant streak flashed across the horizon, and I answered with a rhythmic tapping beneath her right ribs.

"Soon. Is that what you are saying?" She rubbed the bulge. Was it elbow, knee, or behind? "The midwives say you are a big baby. A son, they say . . . ready to be born. Late summer while the Perseids rain down, they told me. Why do you wait? What you have to look forward to . . . You will love living here, little lamb. As I do. I never knew there could be a place on earth so beautiful. Beauty beyond what your father described."

A triangle of mountain ranges framed the valley. There was an opening at the bottom of the triangle so the rivers that watered Eden could flow into the plain. Jagged peaks reared up on her right and left—peaks so stony and so tall they scraped the clouds and pierced the heavens. Waterfalls tumbled from the heights into pools as blue as the eyes of angels.

"Hurry, little lamb, so your eyes will see stars touch earth. You will hear the bleating of your papa's sheep. Oh, when I think . . . what I might have missed if I had not come to Paradise!"

"He restores my soul. He leads me in paths of righteousness."[2]

Sarah knew the path she had taken was the right one. She had not realized how empty her life had been until she fell in love with Lamsa. Her stepsons had accepted her without question and loved her generously. Occasionally the youngest boy, Ezra, spoke to Sarah about his mother. He was the quiet one of the three. How he missed her! She had been a beautiful, fragile woman, and both she and a baby died in childbirth. This fact clearly troubled little Ezra when Sarah's condition became unmistakable. He had lost his beloved mother. Would he also lose Sarah?

Sarah had done her best to assure Ezra that she was as strong as an ox, never sick a day. Lamsa said she was made to bear children with ease. And Lamsa should know such things, since he had spent his life helping the ewes give birth.

The sheep of Lamsa's peaceful flock shone silvery in the moonlight, like a vast field of new-fallen snow. For months since her arrival, she had witnessed the miracle of life as ewes gave birth to lambs in the fields of summer. Sarah was ready now, and unafraid of labor and childbirth.

"Though I walk in the valley of the shadow of death, I will fear no evil, for you are with me."

Sarah had sung the psalm of David daily in Jerusalem as she plucked the strings of her loom, but she had never understood the meaning of the poetry until now.

"Your rod and your staff, they comfort me."[3]

She whispered, "Only let the baby come soon, Lord. So I can send word to my family in Jerusalem before the weather turns bad and none can travel to the west. My mother will worry all next winter if she does not hear!"

As if in answer to her prayer, three meteors drifted slowly from the heart of the constellation. The muscles of her abdomen suddenly tightened in the first sign of labor.

Sarah laughed, gazed up in awe, and stroked her belly. "Well! That was not so bad," she said aloud. Glancing toward the nearby tent of Hepzibah, the head midwife, she wondered if she should fetch her now or let her sleep. Sarah decided she would wait awhile. Hepzibah, who had become her good friend, had explained that labor usually took several hours before a baby was ready to be born.

Sarah returned to her soft fleece bed and propped herself up with pillows so she could view a patch of sky through the open tent flap. She saw the constellation of Perseus with his sword upraised. A meteor shot from the warrior's head. She wondered if her mother could see the same flash of light in far-off Jerusalem. Her eyes brimmed with tears at the thought. For an instant she was filled with longing for her mother. Rebekah had, after all, been present at the births of all the grandchildren. This was one she was going to miss.

Sarah shook herself free from sadness. She counted the Perseids between contractions. About one shooting star every minute. When there were four meteors between contractions, Sarah's water broke. The intensity of the pain suddenly increased.

So this is it, she thought as her belly became rock hard, held for a minute, and then slowly relaxed. *Not so bad. I must tell Ezra not to worry. Not at all.*

Sarah said aloud, "Hmmm. So my sisters exaggerated their pain. Probably to impress their husbands."

Sarah rose from her bed. Yet another contraction seized her. This was much stronger. She groaned and gripped the tent pole for support, panting until it passed.

All right . . . then . . . all right . . . So maybe they were not exaggerating all of it.

Stepping outside the tent, she cupped her hands and called cheerfully, "Hepzibah, wake up, my sister! You'd better hurry. I need your help, Hepzibah. Our little one says he wants to see the dawn with his own eyes this morning!"

Chapter 3

I was born shortly before sunrise. They tell me I was a large, angry, big-voiced baby, with a full head of dark hair and fists that made my father proud. I had an appetite to match my size.

"He's going to be a big fellow." My father smiled down tenderly at me. "A fighter, I think."

According to the tradition of our family, my name would not be revealed until the circumcision on the eighth day. My mother guessed that surely Father would call the boy something that honored a warrior ancestor. She mentioned a dozen names, but my father did not respond to her suggestions.

"Can't you tell me?" my mother asked him the day before my circumcision.

"The Lord has not revealed the boy's name to me yet, wife. Tonight, as is my tradition, I'm going to the waterfall for a *mikvah*. I will pray and ask the Lord to tell me what I should call my son. A name is so important. It sets the course for a life. I will bathe beneath the waterfall and immerse myself in the pool. Then I'll listen for the voice of the Lord. Adonai will speak to me. He will tell me who my son is meant to be." Father gathered clean clothes and a blanket and struck out in the dark up the path to bathe in the cold snow melt.

Mother lay in the tent with me at her side. She says I nursed and then slept. A trickle of milk escaped my full lips. She wrapped my fingers around her thumb, kissed my forehead, and whispered, "I know who you are. Though your father will name you for a mighty man, a great man, you are my little lamb. You will always be that to me."

My father returned at daybreak. With his hair swept back from his face, he looked like a young man as he stood over Mother and me.

"Well?" she asked.

"He is to be a servant of the Most High. The Lord has revealed it to me."

She patted the edge of the bed, eagerly inviting my father to sit. "Tell me."

He grabbed a jug of cold milk and took a long swig, wiping his mouth with the back of his hand. Then he sank down beside her.

Father took her hand. "Nehemiah. That is his name. Like the one who rebuilt the walls of Jerusalem. Look at those hands. The hands of a wall builder, don't you think?"

"Nehemiah. Does this mean our son will return to Jerusalem?" my mother ventured.

"The Lord has spoken. On behalf of all in my family who remained in exile, our son will return . . . for some mighty purpose, it will be. The Lord has spoken this to me clearly."

"For a mighty purpose. Then I will be content."

On the eighth day of my life, my father lifted a calloused palm and squinted toward the brightening eastern horizon. The sun had not yet appeared above the peaks of the Bersheesh range, but he studied the fading stars carefully. When he could no longer distinguish Regulus, the Little King star marking the paw of the Lion of Judah, he muttered, "It's time." Raising his voice he called toward our tent, "Sarah! Bring the child."

My mother, cradling me, stood with Hepzibah in a circle that included my three brothers, a brace of shepherds, and Rabbi Kagba. A chorus of *"Baruch HaBa . . .* Blessed is he who comes," greeted me.

Even though it was the Sabbath, when all ordinary work was prohibited, this particular ceremony was not only allowed to continue, it was required.

Rabbi Kagba explained: "The eighth day . . . always. We stand here in the shadow of Bersheesh, which we remember is the same expression as the first word in *Torah.* Here, beside the Mountain of Beginnings, beneath the same crags that witnessed the dawn of creation, we continue an unbroken obedience to that commitment. A special blessing attaches to a son of Abraham who is joined by covenant to the Almighty on his Sabbath day. Such a one, it is said, is selected by the Lord of the Sabbath for a divine anointing, because the Almighty breaks his own law of Sabbath rest to welcome the newcomer into our people. Please give the child to his eldest brother to hold, on this, the ordained eighth day."

When Mother detached me from her breast, I gave a full-throated yelp of protest.

The rabbi smiled. "In fact," he added, "the only time we do not circumcise on the eighth day is if there is risk to the health of the child. Clearly," he said, indicating how I brandished two clenched fists, "such is no concern today!"

Ezra, my youngest brother, stifled a yawn, and this action spawned a wave of similar motions among the shepherds newly come from the night watches.

"And," Rabbi Kagba instructed, "we perform this ceremony early in the day, because we should always rush to complete a *mitzvah*, a duty, and never delay it or put it off."

A rough-hewn wooden bench had been padded with a fleece and topped with a woven woolen cloth for the ceremony. The group drew nearer together to witness as the rabbi opened a leather case and withdrew a small, sharp blade. My eldest brother unfolded the swaddling from around me.

Without speaking, Rabbi Kagba delivered a message by upraised eyebrow to Hepzibah and received a nod in reply. The midwife stepped slightly behind my mother. The rabbi had seen more than one mother faint at the sight of her son's blood and always made sure someone was prepared to catch her.

"Blessed are you, Adonai, King of the Universe," Kagba intoned, "who has sanctified us with your commandments and commanded us in the ritual of circumcision."

While the last syllable of the blessing still hung in the morning air, the rabbi flicked the knife in its duty and the act was complete. They tell me that, instead of crying out, I frowned and tightened my jaw. This stoicism brought expressions of approval to the faces of the shepherds.

While Kagba staunched the blood, Father loudly bellowed, "Blessed are you, Adonai our God, King of the Universe . . ." When he realized that his shouting was not needed to cover any crying, he moderated his tone and continued, "King of the Universe, who has sanctified us with your commandments and commanded us to make him enter into the covenant of Abraham, our father."

And the witnesses responded, "As he has entered into the covenant, so may he be introduced to the study of *Torah*, to the wedding canopy, and to good deeds." As yet still unnamed, I was rewrapped and cradled by my brother.

Eber, one of the shepherds, poured a cup of wine from a goatskin bag and handed it to the rabbi, who raised it aloft.

"Each time we welcome a son of the covenant," Rabbi Kagba said, "we prepare our hearts for Messiah. 'Blessed is he who comes,' we proclaim, renewing our hope that the Anointed One is coming." Then he added, "And I have seen him."

This announcement caused a stir among the onlookers.

Unwilling to interrupt the ritual, Kagba waved away the buzz of questions. Instead of answering, he prophesied over me, "This son of Abraham will, with his own eyes, see Messiah in Jerusalem. It is time for the blessing of the wine."

When *Kiddush* had been said for the fruit of the vine, Kagba touched his finger to the liquid and placed a drop on my lips. Mother says I sucked the dark red fluid thoughtfully.

"Now," Kagba demanded of Father, "what is his name?"

"He shall be called . . . Nehemiah."

"Nehemiah," Kagba repeated with approval. "Cupbearer to the king and rebuilder of walls. Very good. So, Creator of the Universe, may it be your will to accept this act of circumcision as if we had brought this child before your glorious throne. And in your abundant mercy, through your holy angels, give a pure and holy heart to Nehemiah, son of Lamsa, who was just now circumcised in honor of your Great Name. May his heart be wide open to comprehend your holy law, that he may both learn and teach, keep and fulfill, all your laws. Amen!"

I was returned to my mother and tucked next to her heart. I'm sure I gave a man-sized sigh and snuggled contentedly closer to her.

Though it was barely past sunrise, the feast in honor of my circumcision began. A large tent, its sides rolled up, had been arranged on the grassy plain as a pavilion. It was sizable enough to contain all the herdsmen not on duty. They reclined in a great circle on heaps of hides.

Platters and trays loaded with food were carried around and cups splashed with wine. It was, after all, another *mitzvah* to celebrate the life of the newest member of the covenant, even if I, the guest of honor, was fast asleep.

"So, now, Rabbi," Father demanded, waving a green onion for emphasis, "you must tell us your tale. You say you have seen the Messiah?"

Scratching his beard, Kagba leaned back and stared toward the southwest. "I met him just months after his birth," he said. "By now he would be a grown man, in his twenties. He is somewhere, learning, studying, listening . . . waiting for the call of the Spirit that will prompt him to reveal himself. I'm sure of it."

"Don't be so vague!" Father insisted. "Tell us plainly, who is he?"

"He is called Jesus, the son of Joseph, whose father was named Jacob."

"Like Jacob the Patriarch was the father of Joseph the Dreamer," Mother murmured.

"Just so," Kagba agreed approvingly. "I noticed that connection as well."

"And why haven't we heard of him before?" my father inquired. He counted on his fingers in thought. "If he was born in the time of Old Herod of despicable memory, why are we only now learning of him?"

The rabbi sat up straighter at that. "It is *because* he was born in the days of the Butcher King that you haven't heard of him," he suggested. "But let me tell my story in its proper order."

Father shushed the other conversations around the meal. "Fill your plates," he said, "but listen to the learned rabbi."

The shepherds needed no urging to load their platters with heaps of rice and lamb stewed with tomatoes. Then they settled back to be entertained.

"You know I have some knowledge of the stars," Kagba said modestly. "Many years ago I located something in the fourth book of the law. You all have heard it: 'A star shall come out of Jacob.'[1] Now, many teachers believe this foretells the coming of the Messiah. But I, and others, wondered if his birth was linked to the sight of an actual star in the heavens.

"For many years I studied and pondered, searching the night sky for clues and struggling with ancient texts by day. I was not alone in my quest. There was a great man of our people named Balthasar who lived"—Kagba gestured toward the east—"over the mountains, in Ecbatana. We wrote to each other, sharing knowledge and anticipation.

"And then one spring, we saw it: the wandering star the Romans call Mars, that we call Ma'adim, the Adam. It was joined to the Atonement star that resides as the heart of the virgin. You remember? 'The virgin shall conceive and bear a son'?"[2]

Kagba paused to scoop up some lamb with a piece of flat bread and munched before continuing. "I will not try to recount all that I witnessed over the next year or so, but let me say that there were wondrous sights in the skies: the Righteous King star joined to the Lord of the Sabbath, over and over again, until I became convinced the birth of Messiah must be at hand.

"I traveled from Tarsus, where I had carried out my

studies, to Damascus, and who do you think I found there? My old friend Balthasar, come all the way from Parthia on the same errand as myself. Other scholars assembled too—from Ethiopia, from India—all with the same goal: to greet the newborn king.

"The stars led us to Jerusalem, where Herod was ruling, but he claimed to have no knowledge of a newborn king of the Jews. He said he wanted us to continue our research so that he might worship this child too.

"We were led on to Bethlehem, of which the prophet Micah wrote, and there we found him: a small child, born to parents from Nazareth, but living for a time in Bethlehem. We worshipped him there—Old Balthasar, the others, and myself. We gave him gifts of gold, frankincense, and myrrh."

"But you still haven't told us why no one else knows of him," Father insisted.

Kagba looked grim. Turning toward my mother, he said, "Sarah, child, I wonder if you would see if there are some pomegranates? I'd love to have one."

When Mother rose obligingly, passing Nehemiah to Hepzibah, and was out of earshot, the rabbi explained. "One of our number was warned in a dream that Herod meant to harm the child. So we did not return to Jerusalem, but fled the country a different way. It was right after that when Herod . . ."

Father's eyes saddened as he recognized the tale. "Murdered the boy babies of Bethlehem. I remember hearing of it!"

"But Jesus and his parents, warned by us, escaped into Egypt. Thereafter I lost track of them. But I know," Kagba said forcefully, "that he lives and must be revealed. It is my goal to seek him out and to see him again before I die."

"When? Now?"

Kagba shrugged. "It may not be for years. But I will know when it's time, just as I knew those two decades and more ago. Then I will find him again. And the Lord revealed to me this: your newborn son will play a special role."

Chapter 4

The Perseid meteor shower came around the fourth summer after my birth, marking again my birthday. I had, by then, shortened my name to Nehi, and would answer to nothing else.

My father often remarked that I was a strong child—strong of will and body. I towered over other children my own age by a head, and my shoulders were broader as well.

"Built like his mother," my father remarked to Rabbi Kagba as my mother hefted a large water jar and limped toward the tent. "A crooked foot doesn't even slow her down. And the boy'll be strong as an ox. Smart too, eh?"

Rabbi Kagba agreed. "It's Sarah's doing. She is a good woman. A good mother to all your sons. For a four-year-old to know his letters by sight and sound." He shook his head in awe. "The lad recites the *Shema* and *Kiddush* letter perfect. The lad will be reading *Torah* by this time next year."

All the families in the camp enjoyed my birthday feast. My father chose a woolly, black-and-tan sheepdog puppy named Beni as his gift to me. The puppy was the most aggressive in the litter, and his needle-sharp teeth grasped the hem of the new coat Mother had woven for me. Beni and I enacted a brawl, which ended with me giving him a swift kick. The pup accepted my dominance, but the new coat was already torn.

That night the puppy and I slept together on my mat. My mother repaired the tear and questioned Father about the dog. "Nehi is so young, Lamsa. How will he know what to do? How to take care of the creature?"

"You don't understand how it is out here. Every boy needs a dog. They'll grow up together, those two. Their hearts will be knit. Within a few months, you'll see. Beni will be Nehi's protector. Stand between him and an angry ewe, for instance. Or some wild animal. Beni is bred to give his life for his master, even if his master is only a boy. Later he'll serve Nehi as he learns his duties with the lambs."

My mother bit off the thread and examined the mended hole. "Almost good as new. I had intended it to be like Joseph's coat, you know? Something unique for our son. Special."

My father stooped and kissed her forehead. "Ah, Sarah, what's a little tear in the hands of a weaver? His coat . . . mended now. Not perfect. But it's right for the coat of a herdsman's son to show a little wear."

Within days Beni and I were inseparable.

With the passing months, the young dog assumed the role of protector, just as my father had predicted. Beni remained at my heels as I played with other children. Even though Beni was only a growing adolescent, he placed himself fiercely between me and all other canines. Stiff-legged, snarling, and barking, Beni let the pack know that I was his human lamb to care for, and no stranger could come near without permission.

My father had chosen the right companion for me.

My mother was comforted by the relationship between the dog and me. I could not sleep unless Beni was curled up next to me. This miracle of shepherds and their herd dogs was unlike anything Mama had ever witnessed in Jerusalem. In the city, cats kept as mousers were the only household pets.

By the next spring Beni was no longer a puppy but a lanky young dog. He flashed a white set of adult teeth and was the envy of the pack of herd dogs.

One day clouds had gathered on the high mountain peaks, a portent of an afternoon storm. A massive thundercloud towered above the crags, fiercely bright in its highest reaches while oppressively dark beneath.

A herd of roe deer, with newborn, spotted fawns, grazed near the sheep. I came to my mother and asked, "Mama, I want to take Papa his meal."

She scanned the distance between the tent and the spot where Father sat with his staff in hand, about 150 yards.

She packed the lunch basket, then stroked the dog's head. "Stay on the path," she instructed me. "Don't wander." Then, "You watch over Nehemiah, Beni." The dog wagged his tail, and we two set out.

I held my father's meal with one hand and clasped Beni's tail with the other. We walked the long way round, skirting a pasture dotted with new lambs and their mothers.

Then I noticed the fawns and let go of Beni's tail. I pointed. "Look, Beni! New baby deer! Look at the two tiny ones. Pretty little things."

The dog paused. His eyes traced my gesture across the meadow. Two dozen buff-hued does, and half again as many fawns, grazed at the rim of the forest between me and my father. The route was much shorter to cut through the herd of deer rather than go around. The dog struck out on his own, turning to look as if expecting me to follow him. I hesitated a long moment but remained on the path as my mother had commanded.

I called to my dog, "Come on! Beni, come back!"

Tail still wagging, Beni trotted toward the newborn fawns. After all, his young master had pointed to the fragile creatures. A signal to a stock dog was a command to be obeyed. Did I mean for Beni to herd them, to bring them back?

Dozens of black-tipped ears pricked toward the dog. A score of sable-ringed muzzles lifted to sniff the air.

Suddenly alarmed, one doe wheeled around. Her body became an animated wall, protecting her startled fawn.

The first threat to Beni came from a large, round-rumped doe, the mother of twins. She lowered her head and pawed the ground, warning the canine to come no closer. Oblivious and unafraid, the dog trotted on toward the herd. The doe squealed, preparing to charge. Beni had trespassed into the fawns' nursery.

Beni tucked his tail and, confused by the doe's aggressive behavior, hesitated. A brace of angry mothers encircled him. Sensing danger, the dog bristled and barked. He bared his teeth.

Two does charged, lashing out at Beni with sharp, accurately aimed hooves. Beni yelped and fell. He tried to rise but was knocked back. First one doe struck with powerful front hooves; then a second doe pounced, bringing the full weight of her body onto him. A third pounced again. The young dog was unable to escape repeated blows as he was butted and kicked from all sides.

I froze and shouted, "Papa!" My terrified cries drew Mother from the tent.

My father bellowed and swung his shepherd's staff around his head as he sprinted toward the melee of attacking deer. They scattered. With their little ones, the deer sprang into the forest, disappearing into the shadows of the deep woods.

Bloody and near death, Beni lay panting in the grass. Weeping, I stumbled to the battered body of my friend, then dropped to my knees and began to wail.

My father stooped and with a glance took in the broken body of the dog. "Nehi! Go get a blanket from your mother. Quickly. Go . . ."

Sobbing, I scrambled back up the path toward the tent. My mother met me and scooped me into her arms. "Oh, my boy! My boy!"

"Mama! They hurt Beni," I cried. "The mother deer! Papa says bring a blanket quick!"

Mother returned to the tent and snatched a blanket off a sleeping mat. Neighbors and camp children paused in their chores to shield their eyes against the sun and take in the tragedy.

"What is it?"

"Sarah? What's happened?"

"Nehi's dog got too close to the fawns."

"Stupid dog."

"Young dog. Curious. He's never seen new fawns before."

"Went out to have a sniff and . . ."

"Good thing the boy was not with him."

Rabbi Kagba approached her. "Sarah. The does were protecting their young. It could have been Nehemiah hurt. Aye. Instead, it's the dog. Be grateful."

Sarah nodded grimly and placed me in Kagba's arms. The old man soothed, "There, there, Nehi. It's finished now. We will pray. Come, Nehemiah. We will pray."

"Mama, ask the Lord! Get out the oil of God. Pray, Mama!"

I covered my face and wept bitterly. "Lord, Abba! Save my little friend. Save my Beni!"

As Mother jogged unevenly toward the scene, she guessed the matter was probably already settled. How could anything survive such an assault? She hurried down the path to where a circle of rough shepherds gathered around and offered unhelpful advice.

"Master Lamsa, sir, might as well slit his throat and end it." An elder drew his knife and offered it to my father.

He reached for it but, at the sight of Mother, held back. "A moment, Raphael. Let me check the damage to the little fellow."

"He's broken to pieces."

"Was he protecting the lad?"

"No. Just trotted off on his own, like."

"Still a pup. Curious. They don't know better at this age."

"Should have stayed with his child instead of going off to have a look at the fawns."

Father worked to staunch the bleeding of the dying dog.

Beni's fur was matted and covered in blood. He lay trembling in the trampled grass.

The men parted to let Mother into the circle.

"Beni. Oh! Poor little fellow." The dog blinked when my mother knelt beside him and stroked his head. His eyes were glazed and his breath shallow.

"Oh, Lamsa," Mother whispered. "He's suffering. Oh, what? What to do! Poor boy! Nehi is with the rabbi."

An older shepherd clucked his tongue. "Begging your pardon, sir, I never seen one this bad live. Better to end it."

"No!" my mother protested, and the men fell silent.

"Sarah, look at this." My father swept his hand over the

creature. "Broken ribs, I am certain. Don't know how many. Or if his lungs are punctured. Broken left foreleg."

"Please, Lamsa! Our boy loves him so."

The ring of onlookers did not speak. No one dared to remark on the foolishness of the master's wife.

Father was quiet for a long time. He pressed his lips together and shook his head slowly from side to side. "Sarah . . ."

"Please! We must try!" Mother begged.

My father drew a deep breath. He relented. "All right. But he'll most likely not survive the night. Here . . . the blanket. Let's carry him back to the tent."

The sunset brought on *Shabbat*, but my mother had not prepared dinner. Nor did she light the *Shabbat* candles or recite the blessings. Though the day of rest began at nightfall, Mother and Father had forgotten *Shabbat*.

Exhaustion, brought on by grief, overcame me. I burrowed into Mother's shoulder and dozed, though I was not sound asleep as they thought.

Father cleaned Beni's wounds with wine and oil. The dog was conscious and seemed to be aware but did not stir as my father moved matted fur and assessed the damage.

A smoking oil lamp, casting orange light, revealed the extent of the injuries. There were eight cuts from the sharp hooves of the deer. Starting at Beni's head, gashes covered the length of his body—right leg and shoulder, rib cage and hips.

"They're deep, but I can stitch them up. A clean break of his right foreleg." Father recited the list. "I can set the leg." He shook his head. "But I think his pelvis is broken, Sarah. Look here. When I flex his back leg . . ."

Beni yelped and raised his head in pain.

"What can you do for such a thing?" Mother asked quietly.

Father washed his hands. "If it was any other dog but this . . . well, you know what would have to be done. But for Nehemiah's sake, I'll do what I can. If he lives through the night . . . I don't know. About his hind quarters, we'll have to wait and see."

My father stood, the bit of sacking used as a towel hanging forgotten from his calloused hands as he pondered.

From outside, the familiar *Shabbat* sounds of singing drifted into the tent from the small congregation. Mother and Father exchanged a glance, realizing they had missed the sunset. In Jerusalem, the exact beginning of *Shabbat* was announced by a trumpet blast from the Temple wall. All work ceased immediately. But in the shepherds' camp, the care of the animals continued as needed without fear of God's displeasure.

Father shrugged and lit a second lamp to see by. For several hours he labored over the injured canine. The leg was set with a splint lined with fleece and wrapped with wet rawhide. The cast stiffened as the leather binding dried. Mother later said she wished I was awake to see the care my father poured into the dog, but I was too frightened to move. I remained limp and pretended to be immersed in profound slumber.

"Are you hungry, Lamsa?" Mother asked.

"Aye." Father sat back on his heels and stretched as if to signal that he had done all he could. His robes were streaked with dried blood. "I must get clean for Sabbath. Lay Nehi near Beni, so the dog can see him. Love keeps souls from flying away sometimes." My father left the tent.

Mother gazed at the dog. His breath was irregular. His golden-brown eyes followed her every move as she placed me on his sleeping mat and covered us. Beni blinked at me, his boy, thumped his tail once, sighed deeply, then slept.

Would he ever wake up? I wondered.

"Merciful Lord," Mother prayed, "why should such a thing happen? If it is in your will, O Lord of heaven and earth, spare my son this loss."

Father returned with Rabbi Kagba in tow. "Sarah, the rabbi's here, come to bring us *Shabbat* dinner."

The lamplight cast a glow on the old man's face. He carried a basket of food and a jug of wine. "*Shalom,* Sarah." The rabbi extended the food. "I knew you were too busy."

My mother accepted the gift and smiled at him. "I may never get used to the kindness in the sheep camp. Even on *Shabbat.*"

"So unlike the city, eh, Rabbi?" Father's face and hands were clean, and his hair braided at the back of his neck. He had put on a fresh tunic.

Placing a cloth on the low table, Mother laid out the meal. It was a cold feast of freshly baked bread, hummus, eggs, butter, cheeses, and a variety of dried fruit. She fetched clay cups and poured the wine. She remarked she had not realized how very hungry she was until now.

Father and the rabbi reclined as Mother kindled the candles and recited the prayers, hours late, welcoming the glory of *Shekinah* into her dwelling place.

The ritual completed, Rabbi Kagba asked, "So?"

"He might recover from the wounds," Father said. "But if his pelvis is broken . . ." He inhaled deeply. "If he isn't able to stand in the morning, then . . ."

The rabbi asked, "And if the dog does not die tonight?"

My father replied, "Tomorrow we will sacrifice Eve's lamb." He lifted his cup to his lips and drank before answering the question in my mother's eyes. "In this land where Eden once resided, among us shepherds, there is a secret for healing that is known and practiced still. The life of a lamb is sacrificed to save another life."

Mother studied Beni. I stirred and reached out to touch his muzzle. The dog labored to breathe under his injuries. His bandages showed traces of blood. Would he survive the night?

Chapter 5

When dawn crept over the mountains, I was already awake. I had picked my way out of the wool blankets atop a heap of hides. I crouched in abject misery next to Beni, beside the remaining coals of the night's fire. The fear of the threatened loss of my friend bowed my head down to my shoulders.

And yet the dog still lived, if only barely.

Every few minutes I leaned forward to watch the dog's bound and bloody rib cage for movement. My own breath caught in my throat as I observed each slight and labored inhale. With each additional breath I sighed and sat back, but only for a moment, as if the power of my desire was all that kept my dog's life within its battered frame.

Mother stirred, sat up, and caught sight of me. "Nehi? Is he . . . ?"

"Beni's still alive, Mama," I answered hesitantly, fearful that being too positive might crush my last hope.

"Well then," my mother responded, "the Almighty has answered our prayers."

"But he's still so . . . so hurt!"

"Your father has a plan," Mother said, rising and draping a blanket around my shoulders. "It is the end of lambing season. The flocks are safe. This is the day when the camp will offer a sacrifice to the Lord. Your father was up early, making the preparations. He wants Beni to be present."

"For what?"

"He called it Eve's lamb," she answered. "I don't know what it means exactly, but we will both learn soon. Here he comes now."

Father's heavy tread announced his arrival outside the tent. Taking in the scene within it, he said, "All awake? Good. It's time. Dress quickly." When Mother and I had complied, he added, "The two of you must carry Beni. Take the corners of the blanket he's on. Don't drop him. Bring him and follow me."

Mother and I labored to carry Beni carefully, without jostling him. Mother winced as her bad leg protested the awkward position and bent posture. Biting her lip, she continued anyway.

Beside a blazing fire, a short distance away from the tent, was a knot of shepherds. They and Rabbi Kagba stood above a lamb tethered to a stake. Mother and I gently deposited our charge near the fire.

Bending near me, Father said, "When Mother Eve sinned and Father Adam sinned, they brought death into the world. You know this?"

"Yes, Papa," I agreed. "You taught me this, and Rabbi Kagba talked to us about it too."

"Aye." The rabbi gestured across the landscape. "In this very place the garden of Eden once abided and the Lord dwelt here. It was on this ground the first sacrifice for man's sin was made. The footsteps of Adam and Eve trod in this very dust."

"You know about sacrifice, Nehemiah." My father used my formal name. "Then you know that the price for their sin was immediate death, except the Almighty delayed the penalty so that Adam and Eve did not die that very day." Father raised a warning forefinger. "But an immediate death was still required.

Mother Eve's pet lamb, the darling of her heart, was slain that day. From its hide was fashioned clothing to cover their shame. Its meat was offered up as a burnt offering. Its blood—the innocent blood of the lamb—was poured out on the ground. We remember this event every time our people sacrifice a lamb or a goat or a bull and offer it to the Almighty at the great Temple in Jerusalem."

I looked at my father and frowned. There was no temple here, no altar of sacrifice. What was he talking about?

The rabbi spoke. "One day an even greater sacrifice is prophesied in *Torah* by the Almighty. In the Book of Beginnings the Lord spoke the words of victory here, where we now stand. One day, in the time of Messiah, a 'once and for all' payment will be made, and then, at last, all the power of sin will be broken and death will be no more. But until then . . ." He placed his hands on the head of the lamb. "Father, accept this, our sacrifice, as an atonement for our sins. Forgive us, Lord, we pray."

Father gruffly ordered: "First for our sins. But there is healing in the fleece. Since all humans in our camp are well, we will use this fleece for Beni, companion of Nehemiah and servant to the shepherds of the flock. Now, my son, Nehemiah, lay your hands on the lamb."

I did so. I felt the quaking life beneath my fingers.

"Now say this: 'Merciful Father, please accept this life as a substitution for the life of my friend.'"

As I repeated the words, a knife I had not even noticed flashed out from Father's belt, and the lamb's body fell limply away from my touch. I recoiled in shock.

The rabbi caught the lamb's blood in a cup, held it high, and prayed quietly before slowly pouring it onto the earth where Paradise had been lost. *"Baruch atah Adonai,* may our sacrifice be pleasing and acceptable in your sight. Wipe away our sins and cleanse us from all iniquity."

Before I even found my voice again, the lamb's carcass was stripped of its hide.

"Lift Beni from the blanket," Father commanded Mother and me. "Hold him just so while I wrap him." A moment later, as Father prayed, the lambskin was wrapped about the dog's rib cage and hindquarters, and gently but firmly tied there. The dog was enveloped in a poultice of healing warmth. At its touch the dog opened his eyes, blinked, and wagged—only once, but I saw it. The tiniest hope crept into my heart and curled uneasily there next to my sorrow at the death of the lamb.

"Now carry him back inside the tent and stir up the fire," Father said.

"Will he live?" I blurted.

My father's head bobbed once in agreement. "He will live. And, with the blessing, he will do well enough. You, boy, will remember what it cost."

"I will, Papa," I promised. "I will."

Throughout the months that followed the application of the coat of Eve's lamb, I watched anxiously over Beni. With my mother's help, I carried him and helped him take wobbling steps. I slipped him extra food from my plate, and my mother, bless her, pretended not to notice.

At first he could barely hobble. I bit my lip to keep from crying over his pain, and Father shook his head. For two Sabbaths it seemed that even the application of the costly treatment would not save Beni from being a cripple, unable to follow the flock . . . or worse.

Then one morning I was awakened by a hot breath on the back of my neck. When I turned over, Beni licked my face and pawed my chest, urging me to get up. From that day forward, his recovery was swift.

To quote my father, Beni forever after had "a hitch in his step." Instead of running properly, Beni's back legs moved as one, giving him a curious, hopping sort of gait. Nevertheless, once fully healed, he was almost as swift as he had been before the injury and was more determined than ever not to leave my side.

As the seasons turned, I turned five in the summer. Then, in one night, the warmth of summer slipped away. The sheep camp awakened to autumn. Beni and I followed Father to wash at the pool and pray the morning prayers. The water in the creek was cold against my tender skin. My father's voice was crisp as he prayed. Holy syllables lingered on the air. Across from the camp, aspen leaves danced like a shower of golden coins on the trees.

Sheep were up and hard at work cropping the last inches of the grass that had carpeted the meadow.

That morning Mother cooked a dozen quail. The aroma of the campfire was more pungent, making the meat tangy with a hint of incense, as sap in the wood stopped flowing.

"Good." Father spoke between bites. "I sent the brothers ahead to clear the lower pasture of poison weeds. A week is time enough. The tableland is prepared for the flock. Today I'll move the yearlings. Tomorrow Zeke will follow with the ewes and the lambs."

"When will you be back for the rest?" Mother stirred the fire.

"A few days. A week at most."

"We'll break camp and be ready to move when you return."

I wiped my mouth with the back of my hand. "Can I go with you, Papa?"

My father shook his head. "Not this year, son. You stay and help your mother."

Though I tried to control it, I felt my lower lip quiver with disappointment. "Papa, with the women?"

Father's thick brows met in disapproval. "When you can hear and obey without tears, perhaps then you will be old enough."

Shaking off the emotion, I squared my shoulders. "It was the meat. It was too hot. Not tears."

Father tested me. "I am taking your dog with the others. He is old enough for training. You are going to stay and help your mother."

I looked at Beni. The dog's tail waved in the air as if he knew he was going on an adventure. "But Beni goes and not me?" A single tear escaped and trickled down my cheek. There was no calling it back.

Father's head nodded once. That was the way it was to be. I knew that one tear had cost me an adventure.

※

It was the silence of the sheep camp that awakened me. The usual bleating of the yearlings was absent as the first light of morning crept up the lavender sky and illuminated the tops of the east-facing mountains.

I snuggled deeper beneath my fleece and tried to remember why this dawn was quieter than most. I sat up as Father's journey to greener pastures with the young flock jolted my memory.

"Papa's gone," I whispered. "Beni too." Then I climbed out of my warm nest and planted my bare feet on the cold dirt floor. The blue light of dawn illuminated the tent flap. I watched the stars of the constellations fade. One glance at the mound of blankets on the large sleeping mat told me my mother was still asleep.

This was a good thing, I reasoned as I dressed. While Mother slept, and my father and brothers were gone, I would have the opportunity to be the man of the house. I decided I would begin my day with ceremonial washing and prayers, as my father had taught me. Only this morning I would do it all by myself. By the time Mother awoke, I would be back from the creek, clean and ready to eat. She would be proud of me. She would tell Father that I had behaved well and thus was worthy of making future journeys with the men and older boys.

I stepped from the shelter into the crisp air and drew my cloak tight around my chin. With a peek over my shoulder into the dim interior, I made certain Mother was still sleeping. Then I set out along the well-worn path to the boulder-strewn stream, where a pool served as a *mikvah*. My stomach growled. I would be glad when it was time for breakfast. When I inhaled, the scent of pine boughs mingled with the earthiness of the deserted yearling pasture. A remnant of the meadow grass remained, grazed to stubble, but by spring the sheep manure would nourish the soil, and grass would sprout and grow lush and thick for next year's flock.

I paused at the crest of the path and placed my hands on my hips in imitation of my father. I surveyed the wide meadow. A hawk flew above it, crying.

I thought if I cut across the pasture, the way to the stream would be quicker. I stepped from the path and hurried toward the high pines that concealed the brook. Almost to the rim of the dark forest, I heard the rush of the water and the hush of soft wind in the tree tops.

Then, as I neared the wood, a single doe crept forward from the cover. I felt myself blanch as I halted mid-stride. Six, seven, and then eight deer followed her and ambled cautiously toward me.

A vision of sharp hooves trouncing Beni made me scan for a way of escape. I felt frozen in place. I could not run. The deer were much faster than the legs of a five-year-old. I could not turn to the right or the left. A dozen from the herd now blocked my path and moved to encircle me.

The spots of the fawns were fading now. Their wide brown eyes observed me curiously. A spike-horned yearling came directly toward me, snorted, then turned away.

Within moments nearly fifty deer surrounded me, towering over me, considering me. I had never seen so many deer in the open all at once. They claimed the remainder of the meadow. I was the intruder. The sheep had taken the best of summer grazing, and I must have the smell of those who had guarded the sheep and kept the deer from foraging the tall grass.

I stood with my eyes level with the shoulder of a muscled doe.

Would she charge me, as another doe had charged and struck down my dog?

I was close enough to a weanling that I could have reached out and touched her. But I kept my arms crossed over my chest, lest the mother think I meant to attack her offspring.

Quietly, I spoke. "I only want to wash and pray. Will you let me pass?" But the circle of bodies grew tighter until I could see only legs and hoofs and strong heads for butting.

The sound of teeth tearing off blades of grass filled my ears.

I wanted my mother but fought the urge to cry. It was tears, after all, that had condemned me to stay behind and face the very animals that had nearly killed Beni.

A young buck approached and lowered his head until he was nose to nose with me. The creature could have knocked me to the ground with one quick strike. It snorted, covering me with a spray of saliva.

I wiped my face and stuck out my chin. "I'm not . . . afraid. Not afraid of you."

The creature extended its neck and offered its muzzle to me. I cautiously reached out and touched the velvet nose. The buck did not draw back or flinch. Wide eyes blinked with pleasure. I smiled as I felt all my fear melt away.

Another animal crowded in, as if eager to be touched by a human child.

"You like me." I chuckled with surprise and scratched the ear of a large doe.

It was, I thought, like the story Rabbi Kagba told of Adam in Paradise, when the first man stood in the midst of all the animals God had created. They had come to Adam to receive their names. They had come at the command of the Lord to speak with their master.

"And I like you too." I laughed aloud. "We will be friends, see? I forgive you for what you did to my dog." Solemn, brown-eyed faces were everywhere, all wanting to be touched. "Papa said you thought Beni would hurt your children." My hands went from deer to deer. "But he wouldn't hurt you. He meant no harm. He was only curious. I do forgive you, friends. But you must not hurt anyone in the camp again."

Suddenly the heads of the herd rose in one motion and turned toward the copse of trees beyond the thicket. The herd parted slightly, giving me a clear view to the wood. There, in the midst of the trees, stood the Great White Hart—master, father, and king of the deer. He had a pure white bib on his chest, with a buff mantle like a cape across his broad back. Antlers were so wide they nearly touched the trunks of two trees.

I could not count the points of his antlers. There were too many. But there, in the center, was a curious pattern. The intersection of branches formed a perfect cross.

I had heard stories of the Great White Hart as the shepherds sat around the campfire. He was real enough. He had been spotted two years earlier and had been tracked but never found.

"Aye," the shepherds had exclaimed. "He's one of those who lived in Paradise with Adam afore it was sealed up. He escaped and lives on still in this land. He kills serpents. Where he grazes, we shepherds find dead snakes that were forced out of their holes when he blows water in; then the evil creatures are trampled under his feet. They say the hart's waitin' for the Messiah to come and redeem the broken world and open up the gates of Eden. Legend has it that he carried the sign of Messiah on him, but what that sign might be, no one knows."

I had dreamed of the majestic creature. Few had ever seen him. He was the legend of the mountains where Eden had once been. He had boarded the ark in the days of Noah but returned to this place after the Flood. No human but Adam and Noah had ever come close enough to touch him.

Until now.

I stood rooted while a corridor opened in the herd as does and yearlings and young bucks stepped back to make room for the hart to pass. He stepped from concealment and, fixing his gaze on me, passed through his herd directly to me.

The hart halted and waited. His head towered over me. I squinted up at the blue sky. The hart's crown, with the cross at its center, seemed to me like the branches of a tree. Thick, strong legs could have killed me with one blow, but I was strangely calm in the presence of the powerful creature.

"I've heard of you," I blurted.

BODIE & BROCK THOENE

The massive head lowered until the ancient face was even with mine.

"They say . . . you are the hart Adam knew. You lived in Paradise. You are the killer of serpents, knowing the serpent that caused the fall of men. You rode in the ark and spoke with Noah. You have seen the patriarchs."

The animal touched my cheek with his muzzle and breathed softly on me. It felt like a familiar, loving gesture.

"So you are the same one they tell the stories about?" I questioned. "Oh. My name is Nehi . . . Nehemiah," I corrected. "They don't have a name for you in the story. The Great White Hart or Adam's great hart is what they call you. King of all the deer." I patted the thick, muscled neck.

In reply the buck placed his right leg forward and bowed to me. Chin on knee, the hart held the pose for a long minute, then raised up. I thought I recognized pleasure in the king's wise eyes.

"Some shepherds say you aren't real," I whispered. "But now I know."

The wind sighed through the Great Hart's antlers as if he were a tall cedar tree. Did I hear a hushed voice calling my name? Or was it just the wind?

"Nehemiah . . . cupbearer to the King."

I answered the whisper: "That's my name. Called after the cupbearer who was sent from this land to Jerusalem."

The voice spoke again, more distinctly this time: *"Nehemiah . . . the King's Cup."*

I replied cheerfully, "Yes. Yes! You know my name!"

Suddenly the hushed communication between the hart and me was interrupted by a shrill call. My mother's terrified voice rang out across the meadow. "NE-HEH-MI-AHHHH!"

The hart raised his head to look for the source of the unhappy sound.

"That's my mother. She sees you here. All of you. And she knows, as mothers know, that I am with you. And she's afraid what happened to my dog will happen to me."

The herd stirred uneasily. The king bowed once again to me and backed away several paces. Then Adam's Great Hart turned and trotted back into the forest.

The herd followed as one, after their leader. I found myself alone in the field, staring after them, with my mother's terrified cries at my back.

The nearly breathless voice of Rabbi Kagba called to me: "Nehemiah! Boy!"

Weeping with relief, my mother flung herself on me, touching arms and legs and caressing my face. "Nehi! You could have been killed! They could have trampled you!"

The rabbi's eyes scanned the rim of the forest. The tribe of deer had vanished, but a circle of hoofprints left behind in the dirt surrounded me. "He is unharmed," the rabbi admonished my mother. "Tell us, boy. What happened?"

Chapter 6

Several days later my father returned for the rest of the sheep and heard my startling story. Light and shadows from the fire danced on the faces of my mother, father, and Rabbi Kagba as they questioned me again . . . as if Mama and the rabbi hadn't already asked me enough questions.

Father tossed a stick onto the embers. "A white buck. White, you say?"

"Yes, Papa. Like the very old one in the stories."

Father leaned in close to the rabbi. "See, the child speaks of stories. Stories he's heard from shepherds telling tall tales."

The rabbi held up his hand. "Not so fast, Lamsa. This is not like any legend I've ever heard." The old man fixed his gaze on me. "Can you describe him again? What did he look like? The Great Hart? Pure white?"

I shook my head. "No. Not white everywhere, but mostly. On his back he wears a sort of pale cape. That coat was more tan than white. But very pale."

"And his antlers?" Mother asked.

"Very large. Woven together like a crown. And this was in the center of all." Putting my index fingers together, I formed them in the shape of a cross. "Like this."

Father stroked his beard. "Such detail from a lad." His heavy brows knit together. "But you, Sarah, you did not see the animal?"

Mother said, "He was surrounded by the herd. I couldn't see him, only backs and antlers, in a circle crowded all around him."

"And you, Rabbi?"

Kagba's lower lip protruded. "Nay. There was an entire herd. Acting strange for certain. Surrounding the child and then . . ."

My mother contributed, "We began to walk slowly toward them and—"

I finished the story. "Mama started yelling, and they all got scared. The Great Hart left first and then the others."

"What happened just before your mother shouted?" the rabbi queried. "You said you heard another voice say your name?"

I gave a half smile at the recollection. "Yes. The wind through his antlers whispered, 'Cupbearer, Nehemiah' and 'the cup.'"

"Was it the hart who spoke?" Father asked.

"No. I told you. A whisper. Hardly anything at all. But I heard it."

My father and the rabbi conferred.

"Too much detail for the boy to make up," Father said. "He saw something, all right. But what can such a thing portend?"

The rabbi considered the meaning. "I have told you Messiah is alive at this very moment. He is walking among the men of Israel. The appearance of the white buck, the snake killer, Adam's Hart, means something very significant."

"How can we know the meaning?" Mother queried. "Such a large thing to be given to such a small boy."

The rabbi put his arm around my shoulders. "We will know what it means by and by. Aye. In the future everything will be revealed."

Occasionally we spoke of the Great Hart as we sat around a campfire. Three times over the next summer, when I turned six, the herdsmen found snakes that had been trampled, evidence that the buck was still near. I was comforted by the knowledge of his presence.

In the dead of the following winter, on the second night of Purim, midway through my seventh year, I stood on a rooftop in Amadiya with Rabbi Kagba. The mountain passes were choked with snow, but none had fallen for about a week. The sky was clear and crystalline, with glittering stars.

It was the middle watch of the night. Raucous laughter still emanated from the adults in the dining room below, but the rabbi had gathered up his students by offering us an astronomy lesson. We all wore fleece coats and fleece-lined boots and were enfolded within closely woven woolen cloaks.

Facing east, the rabbi splayed his bony fingers to mimic a bowl-shaped object. He held his hand aloft and invited me to locate that shape in the stars.

It took awhile, but I succeeded. "There!" I said, pointing. "Over the mountain to the east."

"Just so," Rabbi Kagba said approvingly. "Its name is Kohs, the chalice. Many other nations see a drinking cup there as well. What might it remind us of?"

"The Purim feast?" one of the older boys ventured.

"Very good!" Kagba praised. "It is written: 'As they were drinking wine on the second day, the king again asked, "Queen Esther, what is your petition? It will be given you . . . Even up to half the kingdom."[1] It was thus that the brave queen saved our people from evil Haman."

So strongly was the Purim holiday habit engrained in us that at the mention of Haman's name we all hissed and stomped our feet.

The rabbi smiled. "It was truly the cup of salvation for us that day. And Kohs always rises in the east on Purim in honor of that occasion. That's enough for tonight, boys. Go about your business quietly tomorrow morning. Your elders will thank you for it later."

That night I went to bed thinking about the cup in the heavens. I wondered if the image of the chalice was meant to remind us of other stories in Scripture. At first the only one I could recall involved Passover. There were four cups of wine drunk during the Seder feasts.

Then it came to me: there was a cup in the story of Joseph the Dreamer. And his story involved his brother Benjamin.

"Same name as my dog," I said aloud for my own amusement. Then I fell asleep.

Almost immediately I began to dream . . .

I was in a banqueting hall. It was night, judging from the flickering torches in wall sconces around the room. A young man, clean-shaven—Egyptian, I thought, from his appearance—was clothed as a prince in brightly colored silk. The eleven others in the room were all thickly bearded, except one. Each wore the drab homespun robes of shepherds like me.

Though the Egyptian seemed to be of higher rank than anyone else present, he acted as servant. I noticed something else: all the shepherds were seated in order of their ages, from the eldest to the young man whose beard was just beginning to grow in. I sat beside him and saw the light reflecting in his eyes. I was close enough to hear his breath, yet he could not see me. I said aloud, "I'm dreaming, aren't I?" but none of them heard me or looked at the place where I was seated.

This youngest fellow came in for more attentive service from the Egyptian. In fact, he received five times as much food and drink.

When the shepherds were filled to capacity, their host poured one more cup of wine for each, and then poured one for himself, using a shining silver cup. Hoisting the cup aloft, he saluted them. "Have a safe journey to your home in Canaan," he said. "Salute your father, Jacob, for me. In fact, you, young Benjamin, carry my greeting to him."

It was then I realized what story was unfolding in my dream. The Egyptian was Joseph, whom these same men, his brothers, had sold into slavery, but they didn't recognize him.

Because of famine in their land, they had come to Egypt to buy grain.

When the meal was completed, the guests thanked their host and departed. Servants appeared to clear away the platters under the supervision of a steward.

Joseph called the steward to him and handed over the silver drinking vessel. "Tonight, go to where those men keep their provision sacks," he said. "Fill each sack with as much food as you can stuff in. Also, I want you to take the money they used to pay for the grain and divide that among their sacks as well. Finally," he said, indicating the chalice, "place my cup inside the sack belonging to the youngest brother."

The scene I was watching shifted. It was morning. I was with the brothers as they drove a file of donkeys down a road not many miles from the city. A cloud of dust swirling up behind us resolved itself into a host of Egyptian chariots in swift pursuit. Each chariot had a driver and a spearman. In the leading chariot was the steward I had noticed at the end of the banquet.

The warriors overtook the shepherds and surrounded us. The sons of Jacob surrendered without a fight. Their leader asked, "What is the trouble? What have we done?"

The steward said sternly, "Why have you repaid good with evil? You stole from my master."

All of the brothers protested.

Benjamin said, "Why say such a thing? Tell him, Reuben! Tell him, Judah."

And I said, "No! No! I know what really happened," but no one paid any attention to me.

Reuben argued, "We would never do that. We even returned the silver we found in our sacks when we came to Egypt the last time. We still don't know how it got there!"

Judah added, "Why would we steal silver or gold from your master's house? If any of us has it, he will die, and the rest of us will be your slaves."

When the sacks were opened, of course the cup was located in Benjamin's possession.

"Isn't this my master's cup?" the steward said. "This is a wicked thing you did. Take them away."

All the shepherds exclaimed and tore their clothing, but the steward was unmoved. The Hebrew brothers were escorted at spearpoint back to Joseph's palace.

Once more the view in my dream changed. I was inside the palace, watching the confrontation between Joseph and his brothers. The silver cup sat on a mahogany table in the center of the room.

Stalking around it with his hands on his hips, Joseph confronted them. "Why did you do this? Don't you know that a man like me learns things in dreams?"

Judah replied, "We have no way to prove our innocence. We are your slaves."

"No, only the one with the cup shall be my slave. The rest of you, go home in peace."

Judah approached Joseph and spoke quietly to him. In my dream I felt myself lean forward to hear better. "Even though you are the second in command to Pharaoh himself," Judah said, "I must tell you something. Do you remember when, on the other trip to Egypt, you asked us if we had a father or a brother, and we answered that we had an aged father and a younger brother?"

Joseph admitted that he recalled the conversation.

"Even though we said Benjamin was the only surviving son of his mother, and our father's favorite, and that it would kill our father to be parted from him, you insisted we bring him with us this trip . . . which we did."

Joseph listened but said nothing. Judah continued, "If we go home without Benjamin, our father will die. The shock will kill him. Now I, myself, pledged to bring Benjamin back safely. Please, I beg you. Let me stay here as your slave in place of my brother, and let him go home."

I saw Joseph trembling. His brothers may have mistaken it for anger, but I knew better.

The Prince of Egypt, unable to control himself any longer, burst out crying. "I am Joseph, your brother. Is my father still living?"

The brothers shouted in amazement, babbling questions and comments.

"Listen," Joseph said, when he could speak again. "Don't be

afraid because you sold me into slavery in Egypt. God used all of that to save our whole family from starvation. You must go home and bring my father back here with you. Bring all your families! There will be land for you in Goshen."[2]

Something like mist swirled around my vision then, until all the people were obscured. Only the silver cup, shining like a brilliant star, remained in my view, before it too faded.

Chapter 7

*O*n the frosty morning after the Purim celebration, remembering the warning, I tiptoed out of the house. Almost immediately I encountered Rabbi Kagba. He blew on his hands to warm them and greeted me.

I asked, "About the cup in the sky? I thought of another cup in Scripture. The one Joseph the Dreamer hid in Benjamin's sack. What happened to it?"

"What a penetrating question," the scholar murmured. "One I have never been asked in all these years. It is said that the cup remained with Joseph all his days, passing to his children and grandchildren, even down to the times when our fathers were slaves in Egypt."

"What happened to it then?" I demanded.

Kagba spread his hands. "No one knows. It was hidden so it would not be stolen by the Egyptians. Some say it left Egypt with Joseph's body in the time of the Deliverer and was later in the great Temple in Jerusalem. Then, still later, it was carried away from there to be saved from the Babylonian invaders." The rabbi shrugged. "Who can say? What is also known is that it is said the cup will reappear in the Day of Messiah. So, perhaps soon, eh?"

The following night the rabbi and I were again on the roof of my home.

"Aren't you cold?" Kagba asked.

"Yes, but I want to know more. Once you showed me a great hart in the sky. Where is it?"

Grasping my shoulders, Kagba turned me completely around to face west. "Just there. See it? The form the Greeks call Andromeda and we call the Hart is setting behind that peak. In fact," he mused, "this is the only time of year when the Cup and the Hart can both be seen in the sky . . . and only a short while."

"Does that mean something too?"

"You are full of questions again tonight, young son of Lamsa. Yes, I think it does. You see, we didn't talk about it, but I believe the cup also represents the suffering that is required before redemption can take place. When the cup is full, it is as if the hart has laid down his life and so he departs for a season." Then more cheerfully he added, "But he will rise again, when the cup of suffering is poured out."

Chapter 8

When the Passover before my eighth birthday came, I was out in the fields at night, tending the sheep with my father. Rabbi Kagba had joined us, as he often did when the starry host was on display.

"If we were shepherds in Bethlehem," Father said, "this would be our busiest time of year. The herdsmen of Migdal Eder supply most of the lambs for the Passover pilgrims, except for families that have raised their own."

"How many lambs?" I asked.

"One for every ten people." The rabbi paused. "Half a million people in the Holy City for this holiday. Fifty thousand lambs."

I shook my head and whistled softly. A night bird answered from the rushes by the pond. "I've never seen more than five hundred in one place, and only then when we bring all the flocks together for shearing."

Rabbi Kagba squinted at the sky, judging the progress of the waxing moon, then setting in the west. "Nine days more till this year's Passover. Look where Jupiter, the Righteous King, hangs beside the moon. I saw such a sight three decades and more ago now, when I met the shepherds of Bethlehem and the child in the manger."

"What child?" I demanded.

My father shushed me. "Just listen," he corrected.

The rabbi continued, "I mentioned him before. He is more than thirty now, in his prime, and no doubt going about his work. In fact, I hear that he has caused quite a stir."

"Who?" My curiosity did not allow me to remain silent.

"The one I believe to be the Messiah," Kagba said. "The one born of the virgin, born in Bethlehem, as it is written by the prophet Micah. You remember. His name is Jesus of Nazareth, called son of Joseph. I followed the stars to worship him, those thirty-some years ago. Thirty years," he repeated. "I hope I have the strength to seek him again."

"Are there still signs in the heavens about him?" I peered at Jupiter. Sometimes I thought I saw fragments of light swirling very near the Righteous King, like moths around a flame, but I could never be certain.

"Signs still? Of course," Kagba replied. "And they are there before you. What is that bright star?"

"Spica," I replied. "Some say it's a wheat sheaf, but others see a baby—"

"Held by his virgin mother," the rabbi interrupted. "Just like the prophecy in Isaiah."

"Oh!" I responded. "More?"

"What is that outline to the west of the virgin?"

"Easy," I answered. "The lion."

"The lion of the tribe of Judah. You see, there is the beginning and the conclusion of the life of Messiah, all recorded in the stars: both his virgin birth and his destiny to reign as David's heir and the King of Judah."

"And right there," I said, pointing, "the one just below the Atonement star. The one you called the Virgin's Heart. That's the cup you showed us on Purim. Kohs, yes?"

Kagba nodded thoughtfully. "In Bethlehem we met the rabbi who was present at Jesus' circumcision. He told me a story about the baby's dedication and redemption in the Temple. Jesus is a firstborn son, after all. The rabbi told me that Mary, the baby's mother, encountered an old prophet, a true man of God. He prophesied over the child and then he said: 'And a sword will pierce your heart too.'"[1]

"Too?" Father rumbled. "Whose is the other heart to be pierced?"

Kagba said grimly, "That thought has always bothered me as well."

My attention had partly drifted away from the discussion of Jesus of Nazareth but had remained focused on the stars. "Look at where the cup is in the sky. If the virgin's heart were bleeding, it would fill the cup," I said.

Father and Rabbi Kagba exchanged a look, but neither commented on my observation.

The snows melted and the rivers swelled. The foothills were carpeted with red poppies, purple lupines, and frolicking lambs.

Summer arrived, the time of moving the flocks around the meadows and pastures, and the celebration of my eighth birthday. After the shearing season was complete, my three older brothers set out with a caravan to Jerusalem. They would stay with my mother's parents on the Street of the Weavers.

In their cargo was the output of my mother's winter and spring labor over her loom: prayer shawls of the finest cloth in the most eye-catching designs. They were custom orders for the wealthy worshippers of the Holy City. One of which she was especially proud had a wavy edge, bordered with a band of azure blue. The

Hebrew letters around its fringes proclaimed the *Shema*: "Hear, O Israel: The LORD our God, the LORD is one."[2]

Limping painfully as she came out of the tent to display it in the sunlight, she remarked, "The man who ordered it has waited an entire year for it. I hope he likes it!"

Every year Mama dispatched such custom work with the caravan to Jerusalem, along with a carefully wrapped special parcel to her sister in Joppa.

"It's beautiful, Mama," I said.

Then it was the autumn again. I found it lonely and quiet around camp with my brothers and most of the other shepherds away on the caravan to Jerusalem. The intense labor of the shearing season was over, and the excitement of lambing was still months away.

The flock was slowly transitioning back toward winter life near Amadiya but had not yet arrived there. The sheep were moved a short distance every morning to fresh pasture. Every third day the encampment itself had to be uprooted and relocated. I spent as much time helping my mother pack and unpack as I did tending the sheep.

The route we traveled from the high mountain pastures back to the Sapna Valley west of Amadiya was not through pleasant scenery. There had been so much snow the previous winter that the rivers still flowed swiftly despite the lateness of the season. The frequent bends, twists, and turns of the main watercourse meant too many difficult crossings with too few men to assist.

Instead of the usual track, Father directed our herdsmen to follow a smaller tributary. Our descent from the mountains was along a series of small, gorse-choked meadows separated from each other by narrow, precipitous, rocky gorges.

It was a late afternoon between the High Holy Days and the Feast of Tabernacles. The sheep were two days' journey farther downstream. Tomorrow it would be time to reposition our camp again. Tonight, my parents and I would have supper with a handful of herders who had returned for a load of supplies to take to their fellows.

The night was chilly in the high country. I was grateful for the heavy, fleece-lined coat and fleece-lined leather boots my mother had made for me.

My chores completed for the moment, I sat on a boulder on a ledge facing the upstream bend of the canyon. Beni was beside me. Even before we heard the dog growl, I felt the animal stiffen and watched his ears prick up. The fur on the back of Beni's neck stood erect. The dog stared intently up the trail along which the flock had been driven three days before.

Snatching up my shepherd's staff, I leapt upright. Twisting side canyons led into remote and trackless wilderness, home to Armenian leopards and even wolf packs. I glanced down at my friend to make certain Beni was not going to dash off and get hurt, but the dog was plastered beside me.

What had the animal sensed?

Some dust rose over the rock wall separating this pasture from the one upstream. I studied the swirling cloud of grit. It seemed to be moving closer.

The clatter of horses' hooves announced the true nature of the disturbance. A band of riders swept into view around the bend.

As the lead horseman caught sight of our camp, he threw his right hand into the air, signaling a halt.

"Papa!" I waved and called to my father, standing at the entry to our tent. "Riders! Riders coming!"

I saw Father turn in the direction I pointed.

With cupped hands, Father called the four shepherds away from the creek and back to camp. The five men formed a protective barrier in front of the tent. "How many?" Father's voice boomed up to me.

I counted, then pantomimed two handfuls and two left over: twelve. The troop of horsemen remained motionless for a time. They clustered around the one who appeared to be their chief. When they moved forward again, it was at a measured, walking pace.

Rabbi Kagba emerged from his own tent and stood some distance apart from the other men.

The cavalcade approached the camp and drew rein on a sandy shelf across the creek. The leader halted his men again, then rode forward into the water. "*Shalom* to the camp!" he called out.

My shoulders relaxed. They were Jewish travelers. Father stepped forward. "*Shalom* to you. Who are you, with your fine mounts in this lonely place? And what do you want?"

"My name is Zimri," the captain of the troop responded. "We are going to the Holy City to serve the one who will liberate us from the Romans."

My pulse quickened at the words. A band of Jewish warriors going to serve the Messiah! Zimri's words could mean nothing else.

"We planned to reprovision in Amadiya," Zimri continued, "but we have been riding for three days and are short of food. Can we buy some from you?"

"No," my father replied curtly. "We won't sell to you. But we will welcome you to our cook fire and feed you. Turn your horses out to graze and join us. We have plenty of bread and roast meat."

There was ample food. A roasted haunch of mutton was

soon sliced and handed round to the newcomers by Mother and
Hepzibah, along with stacks of unleavened bread. "Will this
leave your other men short of food," Zimri questioned, "when
they get back to camp?"

Father waved dismissively. "We have plenty for them."

I knew no one else was expected tonight. My father's motive
for the lie must be to make the number of attendants seem larger
than it really was.

"For me and my men," Zimri said, "I thank you. It's a long
ride from Ecbatana."

As darkness fell, small knots of Zimri's men coalesced around
our herdsmen, exchanging stories, but mostly eating in silence.
Over my shoulder I toted a goatskin wine bag from which I
filled their cups. One rider wiped grease from his face on a sleeve
while catching me with the other hand. "Not so fast, boy," he
said, draining the cup at a single swallow. "A refill before you
move on. I've been thirsty all the way from Shirak."

I nodded and poured more wine. I was puzzled but kept
quiet. Zimri had said the group came from Ecbatana, which
was to the east over the mountains. Shirak was due north.

Another rider called out and waved a cup for me to fill, so
soon I forgot my question.

"You have a fine camp, brother Lamsa," Zimri praised.
"Your tent is draped with fine cloth, and your dress announces
your good fortune as well."

"I am just a shepherd," Father returned. "My good fortune
is my family." He nodded toward me and toward Mother, who
was carrying around another platter of meat.

My mother's face showed pain. The weight of the serving
tray and the uneven ground made it difficult for her to walk, yet
she did not complain.

"My skillful wife has taught the weavers of Amadiya," Father continued. "Now we ship bolts of cloth to Jerusalem instead of only sending the raw wool."

"So you go to seek the Messiah?" Kagba questioned Zimri.

"Aye!" Zimri agreed. "And we won't be alone either. But I hope we get there soon enough to share in the spoils. I hear he's been catching small Roman patrols in the hills of the Galil and east of Jordan and cutting Roman throats. Soon enough of us will gather to take Tiberias and the armory there, and after that, Jerusalem herself."

Rabbi Kagba's eyes narrowed, and his face twisted into a frown. "Surely you don't mean Jesus of Nazareth? He preaches peace and offers healing and reconciliation with the Almighty. I hope to seek him myself."

"That one?" Zimri said loudly. "I've heard of him, but I wonder if he's still alive." He laughed coarsely. "If you want to find him anywhere but on a cross, you better get there soon! Preach peace to the Romans? Might as well cut his own throat, eh, boys?"

There was a round of laughter amongst all the riders in which our men shared uneasily.

"If the Romans haven't already killed him," Zimri continued, "Bar Abba will. Death to all traitors, I say. Death to all who would offer their backs to the Roman lash."

Leaning toward his guest, Father said firmly, "I will not challenge you about this, but neither will I allow you to insult my good friend, the rabbi. I don't know about such things as messiahs, but Kagba is a learned man and must be respected."

Zimri's sneer was broad, fueled by the wine he had consumed. He clapped his hand to his right thigh, where a short sword hung. "Religion and learning are all well in their place, but not when it comes to getting the Roman boot off Judea's neck! No, bar Abba has it right. And now that I think of it, I must ask you for your contribution to our cause."

"What are you talking about?" Father demanded coldly. "You have been fed. Be on your way."

Zimri shook his head. "Those who cannot or will not fight always hide behind some pretext or other while the real patriots spill their blood. You who are well off must share the load in some way."

Holding the now-empty wineskin, I witnessed Zimri stretch his left arm high above his head. It was an awkward, unnatural movement, as if the Jewish horseman were reaching toward the waxing moon that hung in the sky to the south.

Then Zimri dropped his hand abruptly, and pandemonium broke loose. All of Zimri's rebels drew their swords. The shepherds, wary men at all times, jumped up, staffs in hand, and the battle was on.

Rabbi Kagba was too old to fight and, besides, was unarmed. There were twelve bandits against Father and four shepherds.

"Grab the boy!" Zimri yelled as he slashed with his blade and Father parried with his six-foot-long staff. "Grab him! Then they'll throw down their weapons."

The greasy ruffian lunged toward me but missed when I tripped and fell backward over a heap of firewood.

"No!" Mother shouted, crashing the serving platter against the bandit's head. He warded off a second blow with his upraised arm, then struck my mother across the face, knocking her down.

"Run!" Father yelled. "Run and hide! Kagba! Help him!"

The same bandit who had felled my mother reached across the heap of sticks and seized my ankle. Then Beni, dashing in from outside the firelight, sunk his teeth into the cutthroat's wrist. The man howled and released his hold on me and dropped his sword as well. Beni kept his jaws clamped tight, even when the rebel swung around in a circle, bellowing with pain. He hammered on Beni's skull with his other fist. "Get him off me!" the bandit shrieked. "Help!"

"Run, Nehi!" Father yelled again. "Go!"

My father stabbed with the point of his staff and hit Zimri in the forehead with it, opening a gash. The bandit chief staggered backward, blood smeared across his eyes, and lashed out with his sword.

I fled.

All I could think to do was to run toward the boulder from which I had first seen the bandit troop. It was on a steep slope above the camp. Once there I would be outside the firelight and could even throw rocks down on the rebels.

As I ran, the sounds of battle continued behind me: the clatter of staff against sword, muttered oaths, sharp exclamations of pain. Over it all came shrieking and ferocious growling from the combat between the bandit and Beni.

I had just reached the base of the boulder when there was a single high-pitched yelp and the growling stopped. I almost turned back at that. How could I fly when my father, mother, and best friend were in danger?

I was climbing the rock for a better view when a hand seized the hem of my robe and dragged me downward.

"Down from there. Come here, boy!"

It was Rabbi Kagba. "No time for second thoughts. Your father and the men are giving you every chance to get away. We must not squander it. Up this canyon. All the way up. Hurry! No time to waste."

Into the darkness we ran. Beads of the sweat of fear dotted

my face and trickled into my eyes. I did not know if my mother or Beni still lived, or how much longer my father could hold out with a wooden staff against an iron sword in the hands of a much younger man.

Halfway up the canyon the footing turned to loose gravel, and I fell. My chin collided with a rock, opening a painful gash. I was dazed.

Panting, Rabbi Kagba lifted me. "Come on, Nehemiah. We can't stop yet. Listen!"

Sandaled feet scrabbled up the same path we had recently climbed, echoing from below. How many bandits were in pursuit I could not tell.

Hand in hand, the elderly rabbi and I continued upward into the night.

Part Two

Whoever dwells in the shelter of the Most High
will rest in the shadow of the Almighty. . . .
You will tread on the lion and the cobra;
you will trample the great lion and the serpent.

PSALM 91:1,13[1]

Chapter 9

Rabbi Kagba and I traveled all night, climbing steadily upward. Our path into the mountains was illuminated by moonlight. The trees cast wavering shadows on the rocky crags. I spent the hours casting fearful looks over my shoulder, until while doing so I fell over a dead branch. When I tried to catch myself, I skidded along a jagged edge, which sliced parallel grooves in both my palms.

The old man kept his eyes on the stars as if they were a map that would, in a thousand miles or so, lead us to Jerusalem. The rabbi jabbed a bony finger at the path of the constellations. "See? There is the great lion of the tribe of Judah. He rises in the east and sets in the west. Soon he will be passing over Jerusalem. A thousand miles from where we are yet we will see him even as he looks down on the Temple Mount. The one we seek may be looking up at him even now. Follow the lion in the sky, and you will find Jerusalem. You will also find Messiah . . . Jesus, son of Joseph, son of Jacob."

"I won't follow anything other than you," I protested. Why did the teacher speak as if I must find my own way, alone, to the Holy City? It could not happen! "We will go together, you and I. We will find my brothers and see the Messiah together."

Rabbi Kagba, breathless, did not reply for a long time.

He pointed to the east-west track of the stars in the heavens. "You must learn, boy. You will never be lost if you set your course by the twelve star patterns that recount the story of our redemption. From here caravans make their way to Israel and Jerusalem."

I trudged in thought for several paces, then asked, "Must we still journey by night, Rabbi? I'm so tired."

"Yes. Thirty years ago I journeyed from my homeland, by night. I followed the tale of redemption recorded in the stars. And my companions and I found the newborn King of Israel in Bethlehem. The House of Bread, its name means. Surely by now Jesus is acclaimed in Jerusalem. In his thirties. A fine, strong man. I pray we find him well and soon to sit upon David's throne."

We halted beside a stream just as daybreak lit up the eastern sky. I used the momentary rest and the growing light to pick splinters out of my ravaged hands.

The horror of the battle in the sheep camp was miles behind us but very near and real in my mind. Had my mother and father survived? Were the bandits still combing the hills in search of any shepherds who might have escaped? There was more money in slaves than in sheep.

My teacher's voice cracked as he spoke. "'As the deer pants for water' . . . I understand the meaning of that thirst better now." He was clearly suffering the strain of the climb.

As he rested on a fallen log, beams of light shot through the trees, illuminating the rabbi's ashen face. We had not had water in many hours. There was a limpid pool nearby. I plucked a large, green frond and fashioned a cup. Scooping it full of clear water, I carried it to the scholar. The rabbi drank slowly.

I threw myself on the ground beside the pool and sucked up the water greedily, then returned to face Rabbi Kagba.

"What has happened to my father? To my mother?" I finally had worked up the courage to ask the unthinkable.

"Your father is a warrior," Rabbi Kagba said. "It is written, 'You will tread on the lion and the cobra; you will trample the great lion and the serpent.'[1] Any snakes, crawling or human, foolish enough to battle your father will soon learn their mistake. Don't let your heart be troubled, Nehemiah. Lamsa has killed bears and lions. He has rescued a lamb from the jaws of a leopard. Pity the man who seeks to overthrow your father."

"Then may we not turn back now?" I urged. "Return to camp?"

His grizzled head wagged. "Jerusalem! Lamsa instructed me to take you to find your brothers and see King Jesus. I will not turn back. But I may not be able to go forward if we don't sleep awhile."

The rabbi pointed to the form of a fallen tree. Away from the trail we followed, and not visible until I circled it, the downhill side of the log was propped up by a rock. The soil beneath had washed away, leaving a hollow large enough to shelter us. The outstretched, overhanging bark was shaped like the feathers of an enormous wing.

"'Whoever dwells in the shelter of the Most High,'" the rabbi quoted, "'will rest in the shadow of the Almighty.'[2] See here, boy: the Lord has prepared a nest for us. We can rest here out of sight of any who might be looking for us.'"

My stomach growled and I rubbed it. "Sir, I'm hungry. Will the Lord give us breakfast too?"

"Aye, count on it," the rabbi affirmed, scanning the forest floor. "It is written, 'Call on me in the day of trouble; I will deliver you.'[3] Nehi, my boy, the Lord provides for all his children. Look there, at the base of the cedar: a crop of mushrooms. Big ones, some as big as my hand. Go on, boy. Pick as many as you can eat. Wash them there in the pool. Two of that size is enough to fill me up. When we set out again, we'll take a sack full with us."

I plucked the thick, meaty caps and rinsed them in the clean water. The rabbi made the blessing for the bread, and then we two made a meal. *They are very good,* I thought as I munched, *and filling too.*

A wave of exhaustion swept over me. With the rabbi already in the shelter of the fallen tree and snoring softly, I crept in beside him. In moments I was also fast asleep.

When I awoke, I did not immediately recognize where I was or remember how I came to be there. The wounds in my hands stung, and my chin and jaw ached. Dirt sifted down the back of my neck, and a sharp rock pressed into my ribs. I wanted to move, to stretch, but was overcome with a sense of dread.

Then recollection flooded me: The riders in camp. The attack. The escape into the darkness. The endless struggling uphill into blackness. The ominous sounds of pursuit. The collapse into the shelter beneath the fallen tree and the over-powering need to sleep away the dangers of daytime.

What about my mother and father and Beni? Were they alive, or had all been killed? I refused to believe any of them were dead, even though I had seen how desperate the fight was. I shook away the gloomy thoughts. Surely my father was seeking for me . . . or was it only the murderer Zimri who followed us?

How I longed for the security of our camp! For Father's steady, confidence; for Mother's quiet, peaceful strength; for Beni's exuberant defense. Anguish bit off chunks of my hope. How much had been stolen from me in less than a day!

Lying very still, I listened. A bird chirped across the canyon. Rabbi Kagba's breathing was rasping but steady.

A swirl of air brought the scent of pine. We must have climbed very high indeed to be so near an evergreen forest.

I squinted at the light lancing down outside the shelter. A flat, dark green, knife-shaped leaf, sticking upright in the soft amber-hued soil, cast almost no shadow. *So, it's near noon,* I thought. *The rabbi said we must remain in hiding until nightfall; then we can emerge and decide our next move.*

A towering white thundercloud loomed up above the opposite peak. It spread out across the gorge, obscuring the light for a minute before retreating again.

I reached over my head and patted the reddish-brown roof formed by the fallen yew tree. It must have been a giant before some storm brought it down. Its trunk was at least eight feet across. When the rabbi and I discovered the hollow on the downslope side, I had seen that the log stretched some sixty feet along the hillside.

How long until it was night again? Was there still a reason to remain hidden, or were we fleeing from shadows without substance?

A pair of finches, fighting over a sprig of red berries, fluttered to the ground in front of me. They chattered and argued, tugging against each other until a plump gray-and-rust-colored thrush swooped in and settled the dispute by seizing the twig and flying off with it.

I looked over my shoulder at the rabbi. Still sleeping. I wondered if I should emerge and seek the water I was craving, or imitate Kagba and try to sleep more.

Outside the overhang, a ledge of decomposed granite formed a bench just before the hillside dropped away into the canyon.

A lizard, blue throat pouch pumping rhythmically, stretched his legs in the sunshine.

I envied him and wondered again, *What danger could there be on this pleasant-seeming day?* Imitating the lizard, I half emerged from hiding. It was good to feel the sun on the back of my neck and stiff shoulders.

Across the chasm the thunderclouds built again, threatening an afternoon storm. A pair of stones clicked together somewhere below our perch. That slight sound was followed by the sifting of sand and the crunch of gravel hurtling into the abyss.

A voice called out, "We're still on their trail, Captain. Two sets of tracks—one small, one larger—came up this way."

Despite the warm sun, the gruff words that replied sent a chill down my spine. Zimri's unmistakable voice echoed up the passage: "Good. They can't be far ahead. Let's catch them before it comes on to rain so we can get off this cursed mountain."

Someone posed a question I could not overhear, but Zimri's answer was clear enough: "We'll kill the old man and sell the boy. That way we get something out of this mess."

My instinct was to burrow instantly back into shelter and pull dirt over my head, but I had to know what we were facing. I bellied-crawled to the lip of the ledge, my face and body sheltered from view by a clump of wild pistachio shrubs, and peered over.

Three switchbacks below, about two hundred feet of elevation and a half mile of traversing the hillside, was a single file of eight horsemen and a riderless ninth animal led by a rope. So my father and our servants had accounted for four of the raiders. My spirits rose with that observation, even though it left unanswered my parents' fate. I also noted with grim satisfaction that Zimri's forehead was bandaged, and another bandit had one arm in a sling.

It would take them no more than twenty minutes to climb the rest of the distance to the ridgeline and the fallen yew tree. When the rebels reached there and saw that the footprints stopped, they would scour the area.

Should I rouse the rabbi now? Could the two of us flee ahead of the horsemen to another hiding place?

I felt a sprinkle of water on my head. Wind from the thundercloud spattered me with raindrops. Would the rain come soon enough and hard enough to wipe out our tracks?

Rabbi Kagba was still asleep! His breath was hoarse and his color not good. Even if I could rouse him, could the elderly man move swiftly enough to escape?

Back out onto the ledge I found the choice no longer existed. After the rain squall passed, the trackers were coming on faster now.

Hope and pray and hide were the sole options that remained.

I scrunched as far back beneath the overhang as I could. I resolved to make the bandits dig us out. I would not go easily into slavery or let them kill my friend.

Outside the shelter, storm clouds spilled over the brink of the peaks and tumbled down, misting the gorge with vapor. Above me thunder boomed and rolled, bouncing off the walls of the ravine.

A solid sheet of rain swept toward me, like a gray curtain blotting out sight and sound.

Time passed. A flash of lightning briefly illuminated the underbelly of the storm before the day was shattered by a crash so immense that the ground jumped under my stomach, and I with it. I held my breath.

Rain—soaking, glorious rain—turned soil into mud and erased footprints while forming puddles in every crack and crevice. Maybe the storm was ferocious enough that the riders turned back to seek safety at a lower elevation.

A horse snorted and called. Another answered, sounding nervous amid the clashing peals of thunder and slashing rain. When Zimri spoke again, his voice came from right above my head. The raiders had drawn up alongside the fallen yew tree!

"Well?" Zimri demanded.

"It's not good, Captain," the tracker responded. "Washed out. Their tracks are gone. Nothing since that last switchback."

I felt like cheering until I heard Zimri say, "Maybe they went to ground right around here. We should search."

I lifted my hand to the tree trunk, as if trying to push them away, ward them off.

A centipede, perhaps driven to seek protection from the storm, skittered over my hand. Yet my gasp of alarm and Kagba's tortured breathing were both covered by the stamp of impatient horses.

Another bolt of lightning slammed into a tree across the canyon, making it explode. The thunderclap that followed terrified the horses. I heard several riders shouting, "Hold up!" and "Stupid beast!"

"Captain," the tracker said, "we didn't meet them coming back down, and there's no place to hide around here. It's more likely they went to ground up ahead, where there might be caves to crawl into, not here on this unprotected stretch."

Without wanting to sound cowardly, the man was suggesting it was not wise for men on horseback to remain outlined on the highest part of the ridgeline in a lightning storm.

"All right," Zimri grudgingly agreed. "We'll push on."

When the hoofbeats moved off in the distance, I breathed a sigh of relief. Wiping my forehead, I checked my friend. The good rabbi was still fast asleep.

𝕏

Throughout the afternoon Rabbi Kagba slept while I kept watch. We remained in the shelter. I did not think that if the raiders turned back along the trail they would stop and search the yew tree. Still, I would not give them any chance to catch me unawares, or leave any sign that might give us away.

The thunder and lightning moved off toward the east, but the rain continued to fall, almost without letup.

When there was no more than an hour of gray daylight remaining, a trickle of water managed to thread its way through a crevice to drip into Rabbi Kagba's ear. The scholar groaned, rolled over, and awoke. Rubbing his eyes and coughing softly, he asked, "Nehemiah? Have I been asleep long?"

I smiled. "Nearly the entire day, Rabbi. It's almost sunset again. The storm has lasted all afternoon."

"Ah?" Kagba stared out at the drizzling rain. "So it was good we had cover here, even if there was no threat."

I explained how our hiding place had served a greater purpose than just shelter from the weather.

Rabbi Kagba looked distressed as he listened, then laughed. "Truly it is written, 'He will take pity on the weak and the needy and save the needy from death.'[4] And perhaps it should be added, 'He also pities the ignorant and insensible!'"

"Do you think we could go out now?" I asked. "Since they went up the trail past us, couldn't we turn back toward Father's camp?"

Though I did not speak it, I was anxious about my father and mother.

Aware of what was really being asked, Kagba said kindly, "We should not attempt to go down the dangerous slope in this weather. Besides, as soft as the ground is now, we might not hear riders approaching. No, it's best not to chance it. We should remain here tonight. Tomorrow we'll go out, if the way is clear. I have an idea that should serve us well. Have we anything to eat?"

"I saw some nuts . . . pistachios, I think . . . growing in the bushes near the ledge. I could crawl out and gather some."

"Excellent!" the rabbi praised. "Only wait until after sundown, when it should be completely safe."

When I returned from my expedition, I emptied a half pound of nuts from a makeshift pouch formed in my robe. I had also gathered a double handful of red berries such as the birds fought over. "What about these?" I asked.

The rabbi praised me again. "Here we have shelter and provision both. These are yew berries. The leaves and the seeds are poison." He paused to pat the tree trunk like greeting an old friend. "But the fruit is sweet and can be eaten. Well done, Nehemiah. It seems the Almighty has provided both food and drink for us! As it is written, 'Stay awake and you will have food to spare,'[5] and again, 'Come, all you who are thirsty, come to the waters.'[6] Eat and drink and rest again, boy. Tomorrow we must journey."

Chapter 10

*T*he second morning after we took refuge beneath the yew tree, dawn's curtain lifted on a day that was overcast and chilly. The threat of rain was not great, and the air was sparkling clear. A covey of quail chirping and pecking in the brush could be heard from across the canyon. A hawk screaming above the highest peak to the east made himself known, though a mile and more away. If a group of men, especially a troop of horsemen, was anywhere near, the rabbi and I would hear them at a great distance.

"Now we'll go back to Papa's camp," I said.

"I've been giving that much thought," the rabbi replied. He pointed to the saddle between two peaks to the southeast. "There is a village just over that pass. If we make for that location, there should be no risk at all of encountering Zimri and his men. There are easier routes, so no one will think to look for us there."

Sticking out my lower lip, I also narrowed his eyes. "But my papa and mama will be worried about me," I said stubbornly.

"True enough," Kagba agreed, "but once at the village we can send word to them. Remember, your father instructed me to keep you safe, and I must do what I think he would want."

I nodded slowly. I did not like the plan but I accepted it.

Picking at the tattoo of scabs on my face, I asked, "How long will it take us?"

"No more than two more days if we leave soon. We'll have to shelter on the mountain tonight but tomorrow we should easily reach our goal. Gather more nuts and berries, and we'll eat them on the way."

Descending the first fifty yards into the ravine from the ridgeline was scary. The hillside was steep, and Kagba would not let us use the trail, in order to avoid leaving tracks. We deliberately crossed rocky ground, sliding at times and catching hold of scrub brush to slow ourselves. I gritted my teeth as each precarious handhold dug into the lacerated flesh of my palms.

The creek at the bottom of the gorge was full of the runoff of the storm. We quenched our thirst, then crossed the stream by jumping from boulder to boulder.

It was the hike up the other face that gave us the most difficulty. Even though I located a game trail for us to follow, the slope was precipitously steep. Despite rest and nourishment, Rabbi Kagba was barely capable of the ascent. After the first hundred yards he could manage no more than ten paces at a time without stopping to rest and breathe.

I seized the dried, gnarled branch of a juniper, already bent at one end to form a handle. This I gave to Kagba to use as a walking stick.

"Thank you, my boy," Kagba wheezed. "And give me a handful of those juniper berries. I will inhale their scent. It helps clear the lungs."

Despite the use of the cane and the aid of the juniper aroma, Kagba grew slower and slower until he was barely creeping. It was clear we would not reach the summit of the pass before nightfall, despite our best efforts.

Even worse, we remained exposed to the view of anyone using the switchbacks on the other hillside. Once more I missed having Beni's alert watchfulness of sight, sound, and smell. How I longed for him to be able to give me warning.

It was on another of our frequent halts that I heard it: the unmistakable sounds of a horse snorting and harness jingling. I eyed the top of the ridge we had left and the hillside on which we now stood. It was not good. We would be fully in view from the trail. There was not even brush enough to crouch behind.

"Rabbi!" I said urgently. "Riders! Riders coming. We have to hide!"

"Eh? What?" The scholar returned between gasps for air.

I doubted if Kagba even heard the warning over the sounds of his own labored breathing. Without trying to explain, I grasped the rabbi's hand and tugged him up the slope.

From my sudden burst of speed the rabbi caught the urgency and did what he could to move faster.

A series of rocky ledges terraced the hill like giant steps. They provided no cover, but at their top was a larger clump of junipers. If we could reach that foliage, we might be safe.

After I leapt easily atop a stone block, I then had to haul up my friend. Kagba dropped the cane, which clattered down the slope. No time to retrieve it!

Shooting a glance over my shoulder, I caught the glint of sunlight reflecting off something on the trail across the canyon. We had only moments before we were spotted!

The next rank of boulders was even taller than before. I would have trouble climbing it and much more difficulty hoisting my friend. What to do?

A rocky outcropping resembling squared stones protruded from the rest, making an overhang above the shelf of slate.

Could we possibly squeeze into the narrow space, like rabbits hiding from a fox?

Then I spotted it. Right in front of the overhang there was a gap in the ledge, a crevasse that plunged into the mountain. I peered over the edge. It was a drop about the height of a man, but was wide enough to admit us . . . and there was no choice.

"Rabbi, follow me!" Lying flat on my stomach, I pivoted so my legs hung over the lip of the chasm, then pushed myself into the void.

I landed, sprawling, but picked myself up immediately. "Hurry!" I urged. "I'll help you."

Guiding Rabbi Kagba's toes onto tiny ledges in the rock, I eased the scholar downward until both of us were concealed behind the rock wall. We stood panting with fright and exertion. His words fractured by coughing, Kagba said, "Thank . . . you."

In the expanse of stone at the back of our landing was another small opening. It could not be seen or even suspected from the outside. Only by falling into the crevice, or climbing down inside it as we had, could the entry be discovered.

Once through the arch the cave increased in height until there was room for Kagba to stand upright. The passage stretched upward into darkness, reaching toward the heart of the mountain.

Even when the danger of discovery had passed, it was clear we would not be going farther that night. I foraged for evergreen branches, using pine needles and a thin layer of dried leaves to make a bed for the old man to lie upon.

The rabbi gratefully spread his cloak and stretched out. He was waxy and ashen in the dim light. His cracked lips were parted as he slept, and his breathing labored.

I sat in the shadows in the mouth of the cave and scanned the terrain beyond. No sign of our pursuers. Had Zimri and his men given up their quest for a slave to sell? Had they set out for Jerusalem and the rebellion?

A heaviness settled over me, like nothing I had ever felt. I was homesick. Scared. Filled with dread at the nearness of our enemies. Had my mother and father been killed? What had become of the shepherds we had left behind? What good were shepherd staffs against sword blades?

The old man stirred. His voice trembled as he spoke. "I . . . I must have dozed off. A pleasant dream. You and I set out for Jerusalem to see the great King." He paused.

"It will be dark soon," I said. "Are you cold, Rabbi? Shall I build a fire tonight?"

The rabbi continued as if I had not spoken. "And when we entered the great Temple, there were your mother and your father. And yes, even your dog."

"My mother and father?"

"Yes," the rabbi wheezed.

"Alive?"

"Oh yes. There among thousands who came to greet Jesus. Son of Joseph. Son of Jacob. And you . . . in my dream you were carrying something . . . a gift for the King."

"Shall I search for something for us to eat?"

"Asparagus. I saw some growing beside the path. Ah, this land was truly Eden."

I nodded, but remembered that if this had been Eden, death had still entered here. The old man seemed very near to Paradise. "I'll go find something for us to eat, then. You rest."

The rabbi's arm raised slightly in agreement and then fell back on the bed. "I'm not going anywhere."

I found a plot of wild asparagus and filled my tunic with big, thick stalks. Nearby, a blackberry vine was loaded with ripe berries. A few mushroom caps rounded off the harvest. I discovered a clutch of eight partridge eggs in a thicket. I had seen hungry herders puncture holes in the shells and suck out the raw yolk, but I much preferred eggs as my mother cooked them.

I took only four of the eggs, leaving the others in the nest. Raw or cooked, such nourishment would help strengthen the rabbi.

Clouds like great fortresses heaped upon the heights. There would soon be another thunderstorm. Laden with the bounty of the mountain, I hurried back to the shelter.

Rabbi Kagba was propped up but shivering. I displayed the harvest.

"A man could live here forever . . . if a man could live forever." Kagba smiled. "I don't fancy eating my eggs raw as some do."

"You're shivering. I'll build a fire and dry out the air and . . . we can cook them."

Kagba lay back and stared at the gloomy ceiling as I labored to build a fire on the floor of the cave. As sparks cast by the rabbi's flint and steel caught amid leaves and pinecones, I breathed the flames to life and fed it with sticks and dry foliage.

"My father said a man must know how to make a . . ." My words trailed away as I raised my eyes to the ceiling and I gasped. The walls of the cavern, suddenly illuminated, were alive with painted splendor. Shadows danced upon primitive paintings.

"Well done, Nehemiah." The rabbi seemed cheered as he stretched his hands to the blaze. He chuckled at the visions all around us.

"What are these?" I looked into painted stars and spotted the constellations of the Cup and the Virgin.

Kagba was delighted, but not surprised. "A Jew has been here before us. Look there. The story of Joseph, son of Jacob, in his coat of many colors. Aye. There is the boy, Joseph, in his splendid coat. The coat, a gift of honor from his father. And Joseph dreams . . . the sun and the moon and stars bow down to him. He tells his brothers they will one day bow to him. And there, the coat torn to shreds and Joseph is sold by his jealous brothers . . . Joseph's hands bound as he is led away to Egypt by slave traders. In prison with the baker and Pharaoh's cupbearer."

Every inch of the interior was painted with the biblical account of Joseph's life. And there, in the last frames, was Joseph's silver cup buried in the grain sack of his brother Benjamin to trap him. And, finally, Joseph weeping over his reunion with his brothers.

"Who did such a thing?" I turned round and round in place, examining the panels in awe.

"One who knew the story well, I think," Rabbi Kagba whispered.

"But why? Why paint the story of Joseph here?"

The old rabbi considered. "Here in a cave for hundreds of years? Someone lived here, plainly. Someone who had reason—"

"But who? Why?"

"Whoever he was, he knew the story of the Prince of Egypt. Perhaps he was on the run. As we are, eh? I would think one who was trying to escape the captivity of Babylon. Everything means . . . something." Kagba closed his eyes and smiled slightly. For the first time in days, as warmth radiated in the space, some color returned to his gray-green complexion.

As the old man slept, I searched for stones to use in the cook fire. In the corner of the cavern was piled a heap of rocks. I sorted through them, looking for a flat rock to heat and cook on.

I examined stones and discarded them. At last I found the perfect rock for cooking. When I tugged at it, several stones tumbled down. The top of a clay amphorae protruded from the opening left there.

"Rabbi!"

The old man had dozed off again. His breath was steady and even.

I tore at the heap, revealing four sealed storage jugs. Each was about two spans high.

Should I open them? What if something terrible was in them? I had heard of shepherds stumbling across burial caves and making grizzly discoveries.

Human bones?

Pagan gods?

Some terrible curse written on a parchment?

I decided to wait until the rabbi awakened.

Heating the flat stone red-hot in the coals, I then cracked the eggs and fried them. I waved eggs and berries and warm asparagus on a broad leaf beneath the nose of my teacher.

"Rabbi? Wake up. I have dinner for you."

His eyelids fluttered open. "Well." The rabbi inhaled deeply and struggled to sit. "Well, now. My boy. Look at this. A feast."

"It will make you strong."

He accepted the leaf plate. "How did you manage this, Nehemiah? Fried eggs." He prayed the blessing without waiting for an answer.

"Amen." I jerked my thumb toward the rubble heap and the four containers. "I found the stone over there . . . see? On top of the clay jars."

The rabbi plopped a whole egg into his mouth and turned

his head to follow my gesture. "What!" he exclaimed around his food. "What are those, boy?"

"Under a heap of stones. I was looking for a cooking stone. I didn't mean to uncover them, but you see, there they are."

The rabbi swallowed and waved a stalk of asparagus in the air. "What have you found?"

Weighed with remorse, I sat back on my heels. "I'll put everything back, sir. I was only looking for a flat rock, you see, and . . . I can put it all back as it was. I . . . was afraid."

Kagba's eyes gleamed. "No. A Jew like ourselves lived here for a very long time. He would not live in a place of desecration. Eat. Such good food. You are a fine cook. Finish your meal, and we will see what treasure our friend left for us."

Chapter 11

A flash of lightning illuminated the world outside the cave in monochrome shades. Thunder followed, opening the heavens with a torrent of rain. Water sluiced off the rocky ledges and streamed down the embankment, but the cavern remained dry. The previous occupant had chosen his home well.

The fire burned low. The rabbi reached out from his bed and touched each clay jar as if they were old friends. "Something very good, I think. I heard of a man . . . ah, well. No use speculating until we know, eh? We need more light, I think."

I heaped dry wood onto the embers and stood back as the flames caught hold and blazed up. The branches crackled. The old man's skin took on the color of parchment. He made an attempt to stand but winced and gave it up. "You'll have to be the one, Nehemiah."

I licked my lips and picked at the red wax that sealed lid to base. The wax was brittle and broke in pieces with the digging of my fingers. Within minutes the first lid was free.

I hovered over it, with my hands encircling the neck of the jar. Waiting for the rabbi's instruction, I glanced up to see an almost childlike eagerness on the face of the sage.

"All right, then," the old man whispered hoarsely. "Open it."

I nodded once and pried it open. It made a popping noise

as air trapped for centuries rushed out. The sweet aroma of lavender scented the space, overpowering the wood smoke. I sat back. The rabbi must be first to see.

The old man leaned forward. "Tilt the opening toward the light, boy. I cannot make it out."

I obeyed. A soft sigh of pleasure escaped the rabbi's lips. He smiled as he reached in and took hold of the contents, pulling out a scroll wound in supple sheepskin and tied with strips of leather.

On the exterior of the scroll were Hebrew letters spelling out the name of the author.

The rabbi extended it, face up, toward me. "You must read it."

I squinted in the light. The ink was distinct, undimmed by centuries. "'Within is the SCROLL OF BARUCH BEN NERIAH, SCRIBE OF THE PROPHET JEREMIAH. Written in his own hand. Various writings of Jeremiah about the exile.'"

"So." Rabbi Kagba cradled it like an infant. "As I rest and recover here, the good Lord has given us something to read and study. You know of the scribe Baruch. Companion to the prophet."

I exhaled with relief that my teacher had been correct. The jars were not full of evil, frightening things, as I had feared. "He helped Jeremiah hide the Temple treasures. I am happy there were not bones inside."

"Only the flesh and bones of history." Rabbi Kagba mopped his brow. "What was, what is, and what will be." The rabbi swept a hand over the Joseph murals. "There is a legend concerning a treasure that Baruch carried away. Hidden until the day when the Messiah will come to Jerusalem." He frowned. "Well then. Open the others. Hurry!"

The second container held the complete scroll of the prophet

Jeremiah and the book of Nehemiah, as well as a number of short documents containing an inventory of Temple treasures.

The old man scanned them quickly, running his finger down the list. "Ahhhh. Here it is! As I thought it might be."

He laid the list aside. The third jar held a tightly rolled copy of the five books of Moses—all protected in the exact same manner as the first scroll.

The last jar remained to be opened. I plucked at the red wax seal and pried the lid off, welcoming the *whoosh* of ancient air. I peered in. This time there was no scroll, but a fleece-wrapped package.

"Rabbi Kagba. It's not like the others," I said, some nervousness returning.

"Fetch it out, boy. My hand is too large."

Reaching in elbow-deep, I grasped the prize and brought it into the light. Beneath thick wrapping, with smooth leather on the outside and fleece on the inside, I felt something the size and shape of a cup. Three strands of knotted leather bound the hide to it. On the exterior of the skin the label read, BEHOLD THE SILVER CUP OF JOSEPH, SON OF JACOB, PRINCE OF EGYPT.

A message inscribed on sheepskin fluttered to the floor at my feet.

The rabbi picked it up, read it, and passed it to me. "Nehemiah. This was written to you, I think."

The comment startled and confused me. Written to me? How could that be? What did he mean? At the rabbi's urging I read the letter aloud.

"INSTRUCTION—
CUPBEARER GUIDED BY THE HAND

OF THE ALMIGHTY,
FEAR NOT,
YOU OF CHILD'S HEART WHO DRAWS FORTH
THE CUP OF JOSEPH'S SUFFERING.
TAKE BENJAMIN'S COINS FOR PASSAGE
AND BEAR JOSEPH'S CUP HOME TO JERUSALEM.
THE CUP OF SUFFERING,
JOSEPH'S INHERITANCE
FOR THE ONE WHO IS TRUE KING OF ISRAEL.
HIS NAME IS SALVATION,
WONDERFUL,
COUNSELOR,
SON AND HEIR
OF HOLY PROMISES,
AS FORETOLD WITHIN THESE WRITINGS.
AS JOSEPH'S LIFE A PROPHECY PORTRAYED,
THE SUFFERING
SAVIOR OF ISRAEL'S CHILDREN,
SO THE LORD HIMSELF,
CONCEIVED BY THE HOLY SPIRIT,
BORN OF A VIRGIN,
WILL BE BORN AS A BABE
AND SUFFER FOR OUR SAKES,
THE TRUE REDEEMER OF ISRAEL.
CUPBEARER TO THE KING,
GO FORTH TO HIM WITHOUT TREMBLING.
FOR THE SAKE OF HIS BROTHERS
MESSIAH
MUST DRINK THIS CUP.
HE WILL PARTAKE OF SUFFERING
AS JOSEPH

SAVED HIS BROTHERS,
WHO SOLD HIM AS A SLAVE.
THEREFORE WATCH AND WAIT HERE
FOR A SERVANT CLOTHED IN WHITE RAIMENT
WHOM THE LORD WILL SEND TO GUIDE YOU
THROUGH THE MOUNTAINS
AND LEAVE YOU WHERE THE PLAINS BEGIN.
IT IS WRITTEN 'WHAT MAN INTENDS FOR EVIL,
THE LORD INTENDS FOR GOOD.'

The rabbi whispered in awe, "The cup. From the Book of Beginnings. It was for you these instructions are given."

"Not me. I'm just Nehemiah, son of Lamsa and Sarah."

Rabbi Kagba wagged an admonishing finger. "But named for the cupbearer of the King who rebuilt the walls of Jerusalem."

"But not me, sir."

"You drew it forth. You hold the silver cup of Joseph the Revealer of Secrets, dreamer of dreams. The cup Benjamin carried away in his grain sack . . . could it be? The cup Baruch the Scribe spirited off to hide during the exile! Nehemiah, break the strings. Open it!"

Urged by the rabbi to haste, I tore at the leather, finally slipping it off the package. Joseph's cup, black with tarnish, tumbled out onto the rabbi's bed.

We stared at it a long moment without speaking, neither of us moving to touch it.

It seemed unremarkable—the size and shape of a *Kiddush* cup, blackened inside and out. Time and tarnish had concealed any beauty of Joseph's ancient chalice. It seemed not only ordinary but common and ugly. It was not even worthy of a thief to steal such a thing.

I began to rub the tarnish with my cloak, much as I had learned to clean dishes for my mother without being told to do so.

The rabbi stopped me. "No. Leave it tarnished, boy. It is a disguise. Concealment and protection. It appears a thing that no thief will value. Unpolished. Black and worthless in the eyes of men. But when you see him, Messiah, Jesus of Nazareth, then you must clean the cup and present it to him."

"You must come too! You'll know what to do, Rabbi. I will carry it, but you must—"

The old man wagged his head wearily. "No, my boy, I cannot. This task has been given to you. I will stay here awhile."

"Zimri and his men . . . what if they find you?"

"Listen, now. Don't interrupt. I will rest here in the cave. Look about. You will gather food for me. Bring firewood. There is water in the pool just there. When I recover, I will return home. I will find your parents, if they live, and tell them the task the Almighty has given to you."

"But how can I go without you?" My voice quaked with panic. "Jerusalem?"

"Our footsteps were guided to this place, and we were hidden from the eyes of our enemies. It was you who moved the stones and found the scrolls and the ancient treasure." The old man blinked at the fire.

I waited, knowing that some important thought had struck the rabbi. "What is it, sir?"

"The note said . . . in Benjamin's sack there was the cup and also money. Twenty pieces of silver. The price for which Joseph's brothers sold him into slavery. Aye. The instructions speak of coin for your passage to Jerusalem. Draw out the silver that is there for your journey."

Reaching deep a second time, I found the heavy money pouch in the bottom of the jar and held it up triumphantly. "Look!"

"No need to count it. It is said Joseph's brothers sold him for twenty pieces of silver. And Joseph put the same amount of silver into Benjamin's sack and sent him on his way. Money is nothing. But the cup you hold is the sign of God's love and mankind's redemption."

"The real treasure is . . . this?" I frowned at the black, remarkably unremarkable thing. Hard to believe it had any value.

"The cup . . . but not just any cup. Nehemiah, you will wait here with me. Wisdom now will visit you in dreams. It is written: At the proper time the Lord will send a servant clothed in white to guide you to safety through the mountain passes."

"But how long, Rabbi? What if he doesn't come?"

"He will come." The rabbi closed his eyes with a contented exhale. "Aye. This was all seen and known long afore you were born. He will come."

"And after he leads me out of the mountains? And I am left alone at the plains? What then? How will I get safely to Jerusalem? I am a boy. Zimri will catch me and sell me if he can. The route is full of men like him. How can I know who is safe?"

The rabbi considered the question. "I know of a place. You will come to a caravansary along the great caravan road. Take one coin to the master of the inn. Tell him you were sent ahead to prepare a place for your family. He will give you a chamber. You must stay and watch all those guests who enter. There will be many rough sorts, indeed, happy to steal a boy and sell him. So watch the travelers until you see Jews who gather for morning prayers and rest on the *Shabbat* Day. While they are adorned with phylacteries and prayer shawls, approach them with one silver coin. Tell them you are separated from your family. That your brothers are in Jerusalem and your brothers will pay them if they deliver you safely to Jerusalem, to your family. Do you hear me, boy? Obey my every instruction."

I drank in the words. "And you will find my mother and father? And tell them everything?"

"Aye. If they are alive."

"And if they are . . . dead?" I could not conceive of such an outcome. Whatever manly courage I had gained at being divinely appointed to an important task threatened to evaporate.

The rabbi continued, "Then you alone will find your brothers. And your mother's parents on the Street of Weavers. But most important, remember: you are Nehemiah . . . cupbearer. Before all else, you must first seek and find Jesus of Nazareth. He is son of Mary, and Joseph is his foster father. Bring this, Joseph's cup, only to Jesus."

"When? How?"

"When you see Jesus enter Jerusalem, proclaimed as King. Then allow no one to take this from your hands but Jesus. No one but you is anointed to present the cup to the King. Reveal the cup's identity to no one. Speak of its discovery to no man or woman along the road, lest they slay you and steal the treasure. Let everyone you meet believe the cup is a black, worthless thing, the last possession of a lost boy who seeks his brothers in Jerusalem."

Chapter 12

As Rabbi Kagba pored over the manuscripts that had been freed from the clay storage jars, I set to work foraging for supplies. I hauled an improvised broom behind me with which to brush away my tracks as I walked.

From time to time I heard the insistent whine of horses across the canyons or above our hiding place. Was Zimri still on the prowl in search of a valuable slave?

I felt the nearness of the enemy. I lived as though my enemy were right around every bend in the trail.

The mountains were thick with wild crops sown by some ancient unknown hand. Apricot trees grew from craggy outcroppings. Mushrooms the size of fired clay platters provided the main meat of our meals. I toasted these over smoky coals, infusing them with flavor. A lifetime of helping my mother dry the wild fruits and vegetables had given me the skill and knowledge to preserve food. I prepared a packet of supplies for my travels and packaged the rest for the rabbi's journey home.

Daily Rabbi Kagba grew stronger. Perhaps he would be ready to travel at the same time I set out for Jerusalem. The old man made certain my soul was well fed for the journey as well. For ten days and nights the rabbi read aloud the prophecies about the Messiah from the scrolls of the prophets. He told again the story of what he had witnessed in Bethlehem: the stories of shepherds, of angels, of the infant king pursued by the brutal soldiers of the usurper Herod.

"The babe is grown up now, boy! How I long to speak with him of heavenly things come down to earth!"

At night I lay my head on the pillow and gazed up into the flickering shadows, half expecting a white-robed character to step from the paintings and call me to come away.

But each night I slept a dreamless sleep and awakened as dawn crept through the entrance to our shelter.

On the eleventh day a great storm swept over the peaks and howled at the mouth of the cave. Water dripped into the pool inside the cavern. The rabbi slept deeply in spite of the crash of lightning against the boulders above us.

I crept toward the portal to see the fury of the gale. Rain fell slantways. A jagged bolt fractured the blackness as it blasted a gnarled pine tree. The ground shook. Bark and limbs exploded and burned. Not even the torrent of rain quenched the embers.

Gradually the downpour slackened, and the wind was tamed.

Silence was broken only by water dripping from the trees. In the east, the full moon rose, outlining thunderheads in silver. The clouds seemed like the mountains of a distant world.

Chin in hand, I lay for a long time at the mouth of the cave, expecting God to walk up the hill and call my name. At last I could not keep my eyes open. I rose and tossed a few more sticks onto the coals and stretched out my hands to warm myself. Then I staggered back to bed and lay down.

Perhaps the servant of the Lord was not coming after all. The letter had been written hundreds of years before. Maybe the Almighty had forgotten. Maybe he had even forgotten where he had put Joseph's cup, as very old people sometimes forgot things.

Ah well, what was one more day in this place? The rabbi was growing stronger, was he not?

I yawned and closed my eyes. The warmth of the fire flowed over me like a blanket pulled up around my chin. I remembered my mother tucking me in. Soft fleece and soft words. I smiled, almost feeling her nearness. Sleep came over me.

The fire had burned low when I heard the wind whisper my name: *"Nehemiah. Cupbearer to the King."*

I replied to the rabbi without opening my eyes. "Yes, sir? Do you need something?"

The rabbi did not reply. While I waited, I dozed and again heard my name distinctly. *"Nehemiah. Get up."*

Now I rose and went to the rabbi's side. "Yes, sir. What is it you need?"

Rabbi Kagba turned over and blinked up at me in confusion. "What is it, boy?"

"Did you call me, sir?"

"No. What is it?"

"There was a fierce thunderstorm. I watched until I was too tired. When I lay down, you called to me," I explained.

The old man said, "Not I."

"But I heard your voice."

The rabbi put a finger to his lips. "Shhhhh. Go lie down. And if you hear the voice again, answer in this way: 'Here I am, Lord.'"

I returned to my mat and waited, all sense of drowsiness lost in expectation. Water dripped into the pool. The embers crackled and hissed. Hours passed, but now there was no call. I drifted back to sleep at last.

"Nehemiah . . ." The voice was deep and resonant, as though it came from a deep well. *"Nehemiah! Cupbearer to the King."*

"Yes, yes, that's my name." I recalled the rabbi's instruction. "Here I am, Lord."

The voice replied, *"Nehemiah, get up. Put on your cloak and sandals. Take up your provisions and the cup. It is a long journey. My servant stands outside the portal. He waits for you."*

I glanced toward the entrance.

Someone . . . or something . . . glowed white in the moonlight.

I stammered, "T-tell him I . . . am coming."

I gathered my things without waking the rabbi. I heard movement—the crunch of gravel and a treading underfoot of fallen leaves. My own voice seemed like the voice of a stranger. "Yes, I'm coming!"

For a moment I stood above the sleeping form of the old man. Would I ever see the rabbi again?

Rabbi Kagba opened his eyes. "So, Nehemiah, the one you have been waiting for? He has come, as the Lord said he would?"

The luminescent being passed before the portal.

"Yes. He's there," I confirmed. "Yes, look. See how he moves! White like a candle."

The old man sat up and nodded. "Hurry. And the Lord be with you!"

I turned away as my teacher spoke the benediction at my back. I hesitated as the hope of a holy destiny became a reality. Stepping forward out of the warmth of cave, I croaked, "It is me. Nehemiah."

Something like a sigh replied. Suddenly the familiar, beautiful face of the Great White Hart peered at me.

"You!" I exclaimed.

The thick neck bowed deeply, presenting to my view the sign of the cross at the center of the antlers.

Stretching out my hand, I touched the crown of my old friend. "You! Clothed in white! Who better to lead me? Adam's beloved hart!"

The hart knelt in the mud and, with a turn of his head, indicated that I should climb onto his back. Grasping the thick base of the antlers, I mounted, swinging my leg over the withers and settling in.

The creature swayed and rose to his full height.

I clung tightly to the antlers. "All right, I'm ready!"

Facing west, the hart took a few paces. And then, as if he had wings, he leapt up the embankment and entered the dark, trackless forest.

Fireflies danced in the brush as if to light the way for us. The rhythmic chirp of crickets accompanied the song of nightingales and hoot owls.

The hart's warm back and rocking motion lulled me to a pleasant drowsiness. Hovering on the border of slumber, my head jerked up. What if I fell to the ground? What if I dropped the sack containing the treasure?

A myriad of stars shone through the branches of the trees, in imitation of the dancing fireflies. I adjusted the shoulder sling and held tightly to the fleece bag containing Joseph's cup.

Even if I fell and the beast continued on without me, I hoped I would not lose the treasure.

As if sensing the unsteady seating of his passenger, the hart halted on a stony precipice overlooking the plain. A vast valley spread out beneath us. Reflected moonlight on the waters turned the rivers of Eden into silver ribbons.

I unfastened my belt, then wrapped it around my waist and

secured it to the rack of antlers. Once I was safely tied on, the great animal set out through the forest again.

There was little sound to accompany the swift movement of the hart. His hooves seemed to barely touch the ground. Only an occasional cracking of twigs was heard. The hart's steady breath rose in a vapor from flared nostrils as he flew onward.

Near sleep, I squinted toward a bright gleam on the far side of the mountain slope. Fire and smoke meant humans were near. Humans meant danger to me and my mount.

Were these the same men who had hunted me for the bounty of a slave? And how much would the magical hide of a white hart fetch in the court of some potentate of the East? I guessed that every piece of the mythical beast would fetch a high price in the dark arts marketplaces, where sorcerers and court magicians searched for ingredients for potions.

I stroked the hart's thick neck. "Did Adam teach you how to carry a man on your back? Did you fly with him over the mountains of Paradise?"

The hart snorted and effortlessly leapt over a fallen tree.

Hours passed. My head bobbed forward. I began to slip. The hart turned his muzzle and nudged me upright onto his back.

At last I could not keep my eyes open any longer. My head fell forward, and my fingers released the strap of the sack containing Joseph's cup. The hart evidently did not notice the clank of the precious cargo as it tumbled out of the bag and onto the ground.

It would be many hours before I realized I had dropped the treasure somewhere on the trail.

Chapter 13

Morning dawned, lighting treetops like a stand of verdant candles. I burrowed deeper into the warmth of the hart as we lay side by side in the sage. The steady drumming of the hart's heart pounded in my ear. I opened my eyes to see that I was in the center of the hart's harem. Does and yearlings dotted the gentle slope of the hillside where they slept at night. How many were there in the herd? Perhaps as many as fifty, I guessed. Their tan hides concealed them from the eyes of any human or other predator traveling the narrow track below.

As if on cue, the clumsy clopping of a troop of horses echoed from the trail, disturbing the peace. Yet the does did not stir from their hiding places. I tried to sit up, but my protector gently placed his chin over me in warning: Stay down! Keep quiet!

A gruff human voice spoke. "I think it's time we push on."

Another answered, "You were stupid, Gomer. We could have had the woman, too, if you hadn't let her do herself in."

"Not my fault, Zimri! I turn my back, and she's off the cliff."

"Do you know what she was worth?"

I gasped as I recognized Zimri's gruff chiding.

My fingers gripped the strap of the pack containing the cup. I pulled the bag against my chest and discovered it was limp, without shape, empty. I moaned softly, "Gone!"

The bandits' conversation fell silent.

Zimri demanded, "What was that?"

"I don't know . . . sounded like . . . like . . ."

"Sounded human. Like a groan." The bandit chief pulled up his mount. "You sure we got them all? None escaped?"

"Sure. You seen as good as we did."

Where had the cup gone? I slid my hand into the pouch and searched. My mind reeled in disbelief as I buried my face into the sack in horror.

The precious cargo must have fallen to the ground during last night's journey!

I fought the urge to stand and run back along the trail we had traveled. The warm golden eye of Adam's hart observed me with a kind of comprehension.

Below the resting herd Zimri shouted, "Hey! Who's up there?"

As if by command, a covey of more than a hundred quail erupted from the dense undergrowth above the trail. They flew across the path of the bandits, drawing their attention away from the herd, away from me and the white hart.

I resisted the need to cry out in anguish, but silently screamed, "Oh God! The Cup of Joseph is gone!"

Zimri commanded, "All right, then. Let's get along. The pilgrims will be like those quail, flocking on the pilgrim road. All headed to Jerusalem. Easy prey."

The riders moved on.

Magpies chattered in the trees. Tears escaped my eyes and coursed down my cheeks. I turned the bag inside out. "It's gone. Gone." I moaned again.

One by one the herd rose and shook sand from their coats. The hart studied me with what seemed to be curiosity. The animal did not rise, as if awaiting some signal from me.

"You see?" I held the bag beneath the hart's nose. "See here? I lost it! Somewhere along the road last night, it fell out. I don't even know how we came to be here. I don't know where we are. Don't know where to look." Once more I buried my face in the empty sack. "I don't even know . . . when it could have happened!"

Gripping the fleece container, I jumped to my feet. My guardian remained curled on the soft earth, his legs tucked beneath him.

"What am I supposed to do now? It was given to me to carry! I was the cupbearer to the King. Now look—one night out and . . . just look!" I tore at the bushes around me and turned useless circles. "Gone. What am I supposed to do? Cupbearer to the King. I could not even care for it for a single night! Gone. How can I ever find it?"

The hart gave a deep groan, then slowly unfolded himself and rose to his full height. He nudged me with his muzzle, nearly knocking me to the ground with his suppressed power.

"What?" I sniffed. "What?"

The hart faced the forest and the wild half trail over which we had journeyed last night. He ambled toward it, gazed back at me, then strode very deliberately toward the broken brush.

I shook my head, hands hanging limply at my sides. "Crazy. What are you doing? What? It's . . . gone! That's all."

Still the hart walked on calmly. Where the brush parted, the beast turned and lowered his head. He looked a question at me.

Slinging the empty bag around my neck, I said, "All right. Hopeless. But show me the way back. Show me if you can, so I can look for the rest of my life."

112

The search was tedious on foot, exhausting and dispiriting. My legs ached. My sandal rubbed a blister on my heel. Sweat dripping from my forehead hurt my eyes.

"It's the hart's fault, God. It is his fault the Cup of Joseph is lost!" I muttered blame in the desperate breath of a half prayer as I retraced the route from the long night ride.

Hours passed. The hart, his legs strung taut like the strings of hunters' bows, could have leapt over me and vanished in a breath. Instead, he trailed patiently behind as if waiting for something.

Waiting for what? I wondered. Why does he stay with me? I am cupbearer to the King, and I have lost the cup!

I scoured the bushes and the ground for the treasure but was uncertain this was the path we had taken. Here and there a broken twig or branch gave sign that something big . . . and ancient and wise . . . had passed this way.

Black and ugly under ages of tarnish, the divinely appointed cup could be buried in the sand. It could look like a stone. It could hang like a fallen pinecone caught in a gorse bush. Safety, yes, for who would notice such a thing? But its disguise could also make it impossible for me to spot and recover.

What if it was buried in sand?

What if the black shape was concealed in a shadow?

The trail wound up and up. The hart's brow was almost against my back, urging me onward.

At last we came to the bank of a river that ran deep and swift from the recent rains. Impossible to cross, nor did I remember crossing it in the night. Where were we? Where was the cup, hidden for long ages only to be lost by a foolish boy?

I sank down on a stump, buried my face in my hands, and groaned. Then I shouted at the hart, "Did you carry me across this water last night? I don't remember! I don't remember crossing!

What if I lost it there? What if the water's swallowed it? Oh, I am lost! Lost! How will I ever show my face at home? How can I say to my brothers I have lost this thing I was meant to carry to the King?"

The beast stepped forward, wading up to his knees in the torrent. Pausing, he glanced over his shoulder at me. Sunlight glinted in his golden eyes.

"Then take me back if you can." I leapt to my feet. "Carry me if you will!" Plunging into the icy water, I plastered my face against the side of the hart. The animal dipped low and positioned his antlers like a ladder for me to grasp and climb.

Scrambling up onto the hart's neck, I slid over the withers and onto his back. And the search continued.

We moved at a slow but steady pace, retracing the path from the night before. I clung to the base of the antlers and leaned over the hart's right shoulder. I squinted, searching the ground.

For seven hours we followed a thin, shallow tributary of the river. Gaudy butterflies with wings as broad as my hand fluttered beside me. Lizards scrambled up boulders. Squirrels bustled out of the great hart's way. Startled flocks of partridge and quail rose in clouds.

The cup was nowhere to be seen.

In the late afternoon I noticed something large and ominous skulking just out of sight. I caught sight of coarse gray hide that appeared for an instant, then vanished in the brush.

I was suddenly aware of movement behind us: a wolf. Perhaps there was more than one stalking the lone buck, waiting for nightfall. The hart must have known we were being pursued, but he moved on steadily without sign of alarm.

How many miles had we retraced because of my careless-
ness? The sun began to sink low on the western horizon.

Little gray owls with white-ringed eyes perched on the
branch of an ancient oak tree. A thick patch of wild wheat grew
on a gentle slope near the brook.

At last the buck paused. He knelt low, and I slid onto the
ground.

"Are you tired, old man?" I asked. "I haven't seen you take
even a single sip of water. Nor graze neither. I bet you're hungry
and thirsty. If you say so, we'll stop here."

Was the wolf watching us? I peered over my shoulder as I
stooped by the water to drink from the pristine stream. I cupped
my hand to scoop up the cool liquid. Raising my palm to my
lips, I let out a cry. There, before my eyes in a patch of wheat,
was Joseph's cup. It stood upright beside a flat stone as if it had
been carefully placed there for a thirsty traveler to use in drawing water.

I laughed and snatched it up, then held it aloft for the hart
to see. "Look. Look what I found! Look where it was, all
along!" The hart calmly grazed as I filled the cup and drained
it, then filled it again and poured the water over my hands and
head.

The hart was likewise thirsty from our journey. He bowed
his head and drank deeply.

I sighed, kissed the cup, and said aloud the Scripture the
rabbi had taught me when I first met the hart so many years
before: "'As the hart pants for streams of water, so my soul pants
for you, my God.'"[1]

I held the treasure to my cheek and closed my eyes, as
though embracing a brother. "Of course you would be found
on a journey amongst the grain. I should have known."

Sitting back on my heels, I slipped the cup into its sack and then slung the strap over my neck.

I was in the shadow of the hart. For the first time I noticed jagged scars on the animal's legs and shoulders. Evidence of fierce battles both ancient and recent etched the hide like tributaries flowing to a river. A pattern of teeth marks crisscrossed the hart's throat and shoulder.

"Wolf!" I said aloud.

Heads of dry grain hissed in the wind. The hair on the back of my neck prickled with fear of an unseen threat. But what?

Perhaps sensing danger at the same instant, the hart's head jerked up. His nostrils flared, searching the air, and golden eyes fixed on a distant point. Ears twitching, he turned this way and that to locate a sound.

"What?" I whispered.

A low growl answered.

A massive wolf crouched a few yards away. Yellow eyes gleamed, and saliva dripped from its jowls.

On the opposite side of the stream a second snarl replied.

The hart seemed to grow even larger as his muscles hardened in anticipation of combat. He snorted and tossed his head. Instantly, he placed himself as a wall of protection between me and the ravenous wolf pack.

Clasping the cup, I dashed to the oak tree. The little owls screeched and fluttered away. Tearing at the bark, I clambered up the trunk and into the limbs. At the same instant two wolves leapt, snarling and barking, onto the back of the hart.

Suddenly four more dashed from the cover, tearing at his flanks and legs. Drops of blood splattered his white coat.

"Run!" I shouted to the hart, but the great buck did not run. He held his ground. Bucking fiercely, he tossed the attackers off. They crashed into rocks and tree trunks. Stunned and confused, they scrambled to their feet and circled unsteadily.

Then the buck turned on them. He attacked, striking with sharp hooves and powerful legs. Bellowing with rage, he swung his antlers right and left. Impaling the leader, he lifted and tossed its body hard against a boulder. The wolf whined, raised its head once, then collapsed. It did not get up.

Now the pack wove their approach warily. The hart backed his rump against the tree. Using the tree as protection for his hindquarters, he lowered his head and positioned his antlers at a deadly angle. He was directly beneath me.

A brash young wolf darted in, attempting to sink its fangs into the hart's leg. One hard kick to the head sent the creature sprawling into a heap. It did not rise.

Now the enemy band pulled back and skulked at the edge of the clearing. The hart did not move away. For just an instant he lifted his head as if to signal me that this was our chance to escape.

I climbed down until I was in range of the hart's broad back. Holding to a branch, I lowered myself until my toe touched the hart's shoulder. The buck snorted impatiently.

Three of the wolf pack crouched in order to attack.

What if I missed the mark? What if I fell to the ground and was pounced on?

My fingers were slipping. It was now or never.

The bark cut into my palm, reopening the recent wounds.

"Oh, Lord!" I cried. Releasing my grip, I fell heavily, slipping to the right of the hart's broad back. Lunging, I grasped the antlers and pulled myself onto the deer, finding my balance.

In a flash the hart leapt into the air. Soaring over wolves and fallen timbers, he tore through the woods. I shouted with exhilaration as we outran the baying pack. The hart jumped the brook easily and bolted up a steep embankment, leaving the pursuers in the dust.

We ran for miles, the hart never tiring. The howling of the pack fell away. After a time we were alone in the wood. The wind rushed in my ears and the voice whispered, *"Take this cup! Nehemiah! Cupbearer to the King . . ."*

The enemy was defeated, far behind us, yet still the hart and I galloped on.

The hart's pace slowed to a measured, steady tread, but the travel continued a very long time. Finally the great buck entered a narrow passage between an overhanging pair of thorn bushes.

We emerged from the tunnel in a meadow enclosed on all sides by a thicket of acacias so closely planted their branches were interwoven to form a spiked fence.

The hart's herd already rested in the clearing. An outer ring of bucks, hail and strong, protected an inner ring of older animals. In the very center of the two circles were the does and fawns.

The buck carried me into the heart of the herd and stopped. Gratefully, I slid from the beast's back to the soft grass. As the buck moved away to graze on tender shoots, I recognized I also was extremely hungry.

The herd watched me for a moment, then accepted my presence.

Turning out the contents of my pack produced plenty to eat. I brushed the remaining dirt from a wild carrot and took a bite. Selecting from the other items collected, I cracked, shelled, and enjoyed a handful of nuts, then tried an onion.

An inquisitive fawn approached. Stretching a velvety nose close to my hand, the young deer sniffed the onion, then sneezed and backed up a pace. I coaxed it to return by offering a chunk of carrot, which the fawn accepted, while I ate two apricots and enough berries to stain my hands dark red.

When the feast concluded, I was thirsty. Once again, the hart showed the way. At the far end of the enclosure, beneath the boughs of fragrant myrtle trees, a spring of clear water bubbled up to fill a rock-lined pool. The antlered head bent as the hart drank, then the buck sidestepped out of the way, allowing me to approach with Joseph's cup.

The sweetness of myrtle blossoms surrounded me as I dipped the cup into the pool. "The scent of Eden," Rabbi Kagba called the oil of myrtle. "It's why myrtle is one of the things we wave to celebrate Tabernacles. It takes us back to a time of innocence, a time Messiah will first embody and then restore."

It had to be Tabernacles by now. The attack on Father's camp had been between the Day of Atonement and the start of this, the next feast. We shepherds spent much of our lives dwelling in tents like the children of Israel in the wilderness. But here I was, on the Feast of Tabernacles, sheltered in a booth made by the hand of the Almighty from the very outgrowth of Eden. It was on such a night that all devout Jews invited the exalted wanderers—the patriarchs and the prophets who had gone before—to join us for the feast.

I filled the cup to the brim, swallowed a mouthful of cool water, then drained it. Back on the dense matting of springy grass, I was satisfied. Now exhausted, I curled up with the cup under my arm and fell asleep . . .

Almost immediately I heard someone call my name.

"Nehemiah?"

The sound alerted me but caused me no anxiety. "Who's there?"

"My name is Zaphenath Paneah," a pleasant, youthful voice announced.

"I don't know anyone by that name," I returned. "Not a Hebrew name. Sounds Syrian?"

"Farther south."

"Egyptian?"

"Bravo," the voice applauded. "You guessed it."

"Where are you? I can't see you. Is this a dream?"

"Perhaps. I am a Dreamer of Dreams myself."

"That's what Rabbi Kagba called Joseph the Patriarch."

"A brilliant man, your rabbi. A scholar and a good teacher. The two are not always the same. So, I am Zaphenath Paneah, which means Revealer of Secrets . . . but I was born Joseph, son of Jacob, the son of Isaac, the son of Abraham. Abraham," he repeated. "My great-grandfather."

"I dreamed about you before, only I couldn't talk with you. So this *is* a dream!"

"Again, perhaps. Or perhaps I was sent to you, cupbearer to the King, to reveal secrets to you and to answer your questions. You do have questions, don't you?"

"About the cup? Of course! Many! And why can't I see you?"

A slender, dark-haired, clean-shaven male form wavered slightly, then snapped into focus. "Better?" Joseph asked. "Now, a few questions for you. First, do you know why I hid my cup in Benjamin's grain sack?"

"The rabbi says it was a test. You wanted to see if your other brothers would leave Benjamin to save themselves, or if they were truly sorry for having sold you into slavery. Had their hearts been changed?"

"And they passed the test," Joseph agreed. "Why is my cup now in your possession?"

"Rabbi Kagba says I am to take it to the Messiah. He believes a man named Jesus of Nazareth is the Anointed One, and he wants me to deliver your cup to him."

"Why?"

I was puzzled by the query. "Because he told me to."

"You misunderstand me," Joseph the Dreamer corrected. "Why should Messiah receive it?"

I thought for a moment. "I don't know. To honor him?"

"Truly, but there is more. Do you remember how I was freed from prison in Egypt?"

"When Pharaoh's cupbearer remembered how you could explain dreams and brought you to Pharaoh."

"And the cup came to me in gratitude from both Pharaoh and the cupbearer. But it is more than that. It is the symbol of my redemption. It represents the faithfulness of the Almighty in redeeming my life from the pit . . ."

"Yes."

"From slavery . . . from false accusations . . . from imprisonment . . ."

"All those," I acknowledged. "Yes, yes, and yes."

"And since Pharaoh made me the authority in Egypt, second only to himself, the cup came to represent how I was honored. Now pay attention."

"I'm ready for you to go on." Somewhere nearby a deer snorted and moved in the darkness. How much of this was only a dream?

Joseph resumed his tale. "When famine came to all the land, I was able to save my family because I was then in a position to help them, you see? I was able to redeem them from death, just as I had been redeemed from death myself."

"So the cup is important?" I offered.

"Exactly. It is first a cup of suffering, because of what I went through in order to receive it. Next, it is the cup of redemption. And it is also the cup of God's faithfulness."

"Explain that bit."

"All the way back when my brothers tossed me into the pit and then sold me, God knew that many years later I would be able to save my family. And I am a shadow."

I frowned. "I was right. You are a dream."

Joseph continued as if I had not interrupted. "I was a shadow of things to come. I was betrayed by my brothers because of envy. Sold for pieces of silver. Carried away in chains. Falsely accused. But I rose from there to save my entire family. From before I was thrown into the pit, God already knew what the end result would be. Remember this: The Almighty is never taken by surprise. And his plans always succeed. No matter how desperate a situation may appear, he is working constantly for your welfare."

I summed up: "This is what Rabbi Kagba said: 'What man means for evil, God means for good.'"[2]

"Well done, cupbearer," Joseph praised. "Your rabbi will be proud. Just remember what I have said. Think on it as you go to meet Messiah, because he is the final revealer of secrets." Joseph's form began to shimmer like a reflection in a pond when tiny ripples mar the surface.

"Wait!" I asked. "Don't go. I have many more questions."

"Don't worry, cupbearer," Joseph the Dreamer replied as he faded from view. "You will see me again. We have many miles to travel and many secrets to unfold before you reach the goal of your journey. Sleep, Nehemiah. Sleep."

Chapter 14

It had been a day since I had last drunk water, and my throat and mouth were parched. I knew the hart was also thirsty, yet he did not slow his pace or stop to rest.

He carried me through a narrow canyon of rich red sandstone. Its course ran north and south. Stone buttresses were worn smooth as glass from the water of an ancient river. Though the path was something men would not follow for fear of becoming lost, the hart seemed familiar with this secret route.

The sun had risen hours ago in the east, but I could not see it, and the wadi floor remained in deep shadow. As the sun climbed higher, daylight dripped slowly down from the top of the wall like a waterfall. Etched into the stone I saw a pattern shaped like a cup, tipped as if to pour out golden liquid onto me.

At high noon the sun appeared briefly as it reached its zenith. For a few minutes it beamed directly down on us. Then, as suddenly as it had appeared, it vanished over the western rim of the canyon. Among the shadows on the east wall thorn bushes grew, and I saw a shape something like a crown.

There were no other footprints in the fine white sand of the dry bed—only the hart's. I thought perhaps this course had held Eden's pure head waters. And when the hand of the Lord had lifted Paradise into the sky beyond the reach of mortal men, the spring had also been lifted.

I looked up, certain now that the sky was not the sky at all. Heaven's cobalt blue stream flowed above me. If only I could mount up on wings like an eagle, I would drink from those heavenly waters and never thirst again.

Removing Joseph's blackened cup from its pouch, I held it up to the sky river and cried, "Please, fill this cup, Lord. Let me drink. I am thirsty!" My voice echoed and the walls resounded with my complaint.

The hart did not pause but continued on as darkness descended and the river above me became dark and sprinkled with stars. I fell asleep as Orion stepped across the gulf . . .

When I opened my eyes, it was nearly dawn. We had emerged from the canyon, and the hart knelt beside a spring of fresh water. I stepped from his back and dipped the cup into the cold, bubbling liquid. I drank deeply and sat beside where he lay. We watched together as dawn pushed back the darkness from a valley far below us.

Again, I slept.

It was dawn when I roused. Not yet fully awake, I said in a drowsy voice, "Mama. I've been having the strangest dream. Mama?"

My eyes and my awareness both snapped open at once. Instead of being in the shepherding tent or in my bed in Amadiya, I was on a hard slab of rock. The pillow under my head was the leather and oilcloth-wrapped parcel containing the Cup of Joseph. Tucked against my right side was the leather pouch containing the silver coins. Pulled up around my ears was the fur-trimmed woolen cloak.

If so much of what I thought was a dream was in fact real, was it possible the rest of the memory was also true?

The white hart stood at the edge of a precipice, gazing into the distance. When I raised up, the hart turned toward me. The beast raised his muzzle and swung it toward the land spread out below our perch, summoning me to join him.

In the morning haze it was at first difficult for me to distinguish what I was seeing. Gradually, as the sun warmed the valley, a veil of mist cleared. The light increased, revealing a sizable town no more than a handful of miles away from the bottom of the slope. The unknown city was a pendant glistening golden, strung from a thread of highway that ran east and west, disappearing from view in both directions.

"Is that where I'm supposed to go?" I asked.

The antlered crown dipped briefly in acknowledgment.

I had a sudden chill of realization. "You have brought me over the mountains, but this is where you're leaving me." I tried to picture traipsing into a caravansary beside the majestic hart while stupefied onlookers marveled and pointed, but I could not. Such a picture had more air of unreality than to be standing here, having this conversation with the creature.

I shrugged my clothes into order and secured the cloak around my shoulders, taking care to have both cup and coin purse safely fastened but out of view. "Thank you," I said to the hart. "Am I right to think that we have both been given orders to carry out?"

Once more the glorious corona of antlers bobbed in acknowledgment.

"Then please carry a message for me: Thank the one who sent you to me. Will I see you again?"

This time there was no answering response.

"Then, may Almighty bless you," I said and began the descent toward the village.

Halfway down the gentle incline, I turned to look back. The Great White Hart, nose raised into the west as if both scenting danger and pointing the way, stood outlined against an azure sky.

When I reached the bottom of the slope, I looked again. This time the rock ledge was bare. Scan as I might the expanse of dark green brush and brown earth, I spotted no white form moving against the backdrop.

Chapter 15

*B*efore I could enter the city, I had to cross an arched bridge over a small river. The structure, built of squared stone shaped to form slender, graceful pillars, looked ancient and much more attractive than the squalid, flat-roofed buildings I had glimpsed of the town.

Halfway across the span I met a man leading a donkey who waddled beneath the weight of stuffed saddlebags. "Please, sir," I said politely, and with some fear of meeting a stranger. "Can you tell me the name of this place?"

The portly man paused in gnawing a pomegranate to ask suspiciously, "How can you not know that, boy? Where are your parents? Aren't you very young to be wandering alone so early?"

"I was sent ahead to make arrangements for my family to follow," I said in a matter-of-fact tone. "I am Nehemiah bar Lamsa, but I will ask someone else if it's too much bother."

The man revealed a gap-toothed grin. "My pardon, son of Lamsa. I know your father, and your mother's workmanship in cloth. I am the traveling peddler, Obed of Zakho." Over his shoulder he jerked a thumb stained red with juice. "From which I am just leaving. May I offer directions?"

"The caravansary?"

"There are two, and right you are to ask. The one on this

side is owned by a pig of a Parthian. He overcharges, cooks with pork fat, and his beds all have fleas. What you want is the inn on the far side of town. Its proprietor is my brother, Asa. Mention your father to him and say that you met me, and he will take good care of you."

"And how will I find . . ."

Obed waved his hand and tugged the donkey into forward motion. "You can't miss it. Straight through town, just past the synagogue. *Shalom*, Nehemiah bar Lamsa. Remember me to your parents."

I passed the rival caravansary without stopping. The acrid stench of a muddy swine pen warned me away. There was a brace of pigs corralled right outside the innkeeper's home, alongside a dozen camels.

The town of Zakho was waking up by the time I reached its center. A pair of Jewish men, fringes of their prayer shawls flapping and phylacteries bouncing in their haste, hurried toward morning prayers. A half-dozen Parthian stonecutters passed by. I recognized their floppy, Parthian headgear and the hammers and quarrying tools they carried.

At the synagogue the late arrivals were pushing in to join the *minyan*. Past the building's ornately carved entry stood a wooden stockade. The main double gate for beasts of burden was still barred, but a smaller portal in one panel offered entry for me. I hammered on the door, and it was opened by an elderly porter. "What is your business, young sir?" the servant said.

"I am to arrange a room for my parents, Lamsa and Sarah of Amadiya," I said. "I was told to ask for Asa. Is he here?"

"Indeed he is. I'll take you to him."

While the peddler Obed had named his brother, he had failed to mention that it was his *twin* brother. Identical to Obed in face, stout build, and medium height, Asa's head was bald and almost spherical. Since Obed had been wearing a turban, I wondered if the similarity was exact.

I repeated my requirements.

"Welcome to Zakho, boy," Asa said. "Welcome to the Jerusalem of the North."

"Sir?"

"Don't you know your people's history, boy? When King Shalmanezer carried away Israel into exile, this became our home. Seven hundred years ago that was, but we remain here still. Or don't they teach you that in Amadiya?"

"I'm a shepherd, sir, and I've never traveled, that is, until now." I drew myself up even straighter. "I am told I should offer you one silver coin for half a week's lodging, bread, and suppers. Within that time my parents and I will join a caravan bound for Jerusalem."

The terms were agreeable and, after handing over a silver shekel, I was shown to a room on the second floor of an adjoining building. The lower floor did not contain rooms but rather open stalls filled with straw for animals. It was also shelter for people too poor to afford better accommodations.

The room was small but clean and serviceable. Once inside I sat down to think. I was overwhelmed with loneliness. I had always been surrounded with those who cared about me: Father, Mother, older brothers, Beni, the good rabbi, the other shepherds, my mother's weavers who treated me like an extra nephew. Now I was completely alone. With the immediate danger over and time to reflect on what I had lost, I felt crushed and ready to cry. I wanted to run home to Amadiya and beg for help.

Three things stopped me: the idea of finding my brothers in Jerusalem as soon as possible, the commission I had been assigned by Rabbi Kagba to take the Cup of Joseph to the Messiah, and the mystery of the White Hart.

I lifted my chin. "I will take a bath and wash my clothes," I said aloud. "I will have a good meal. Then I will be ready to locate a caravan and go to Jerusalem."

I wasted no time setting out to locate a caravan bound for the Holy City. The afternoon of my arrival in Zakho, I made my way around the compound, hunting a suitable group. I did not forget to secure the sack of coins and the bundle containing the cup to my waist under my clothing before leaving my room.

There were two bands of travelers within the fences of Asa's caravansary. The first group I approached looked weary and their clothing travel-worn, as if they had come a long distance. Even the camels appeared gaunt, their eyes hollow and staring and their humps shrunken.

The caravan leader, a man named Eram, was a perfect match for his charges. His face was as scored with the crevices of age and rough living as the canyons back of Amadiya.

"My family and I want to go to Jerusalem," I said. "We can pay."

The travel master tilted his head and tugged thoughtfully on an earlobe lengthened by several decades of such abuse. "And I would love to take you," the man replied. "But we are returning from there, heading east and not west." He shook his head glumly. "It was not a profitable trip."

"But you were there? In Jerusalem? Can you tell me about it?"

Eram shrugged. "News is cheap and gossip free. But later. Right now I must see which of these spavined beasts will live to cross the mountains and which I must sell here. Go see Jehu over there. He is heading west." Eram indicated a younger man with a pointed beard who leaned against a heap of bolts of silk.

"Jerusalem?" Jehu said, stroking his beard. "How many are you, boy? And can you keep up? I have a load of fine cloth, spice, and amber I am eager to sell in the markets in Damascus and Caesarea before I go on to Jerusalem."

This was beginning to sound promising. The animals looked healthy and the fittings well cared for. Eagerness to arrive was also in my thoughts. "How long does the passage last? Two Sabbaths?" I guessed.

Jehu roared with laughter, calling to a drover, "Did you hear that? Boy, do you see wings on these animals? Two Sabbaths? The best crossing we've ever made is forty-five days. And we are the fastest. What do you say? Will you join up with us?"

I was taken back. Rabbi Kagba had not told me the length of the journey. A month and more before arriving, and then I still had to locate my brothers?

"I . . . I'll have to think about it," I said. "And you stop for Sabbath, of course."

Hooking his thumbs in a wide silk sash tied around his middle, Jehu burst into another gale of laughter. "We are not religious pilgrims, boy. This trip is all about profit! Stop for Sabbath? Weren't you the one who was just in a great hurry?"

"I have to think," I repeated, and I retreated to my chamber.

Chapter 16

*T*he following morning I went to Sabbath service at the synagogue with Asa and Eram. Jehu did not attend. His caravan was preparing to leave Zakho and would not wait for the end of Sabbath to depart.

I sat in the women's gallery beside Asa's wife. The reading was from the Book of Beginnings: "Now the Lord had said to Abram, 'Get thee out of thy country . . . unto a land that I will shew thee.'"[1]

I was curiously pleased at the scripture. It made me feel that I was doing the right thing in embarking on the trip to Jerusalem. This was further confirmed for me when the rabbi, offering his commentary on the passage, mentioned that Abram had passed through Zakho on his way from Haran to Canaan. "Then as now," the rabbi said, "we were a resting place for travelers."

Eram, shuffling his feet with some show of embarrassment, was called up to read the Scripture portion that followed. It was from the prophet Isaiah: "Lift up your eyes on high, and behold, who hath created these things, that bringeth out their host by number: he calleth them all by names by the greatness of his might."[2]

It was just like Rabbi Kagba said: The Almighty not only created the starry host, but he had a name for each of them and each name meant something. The recollection made me wonder about the scholar's fate. It caused a catch in my throat and a sniff of homesickness until I caught Asa's wife watching me. Then I straightened my back and squared my shoulders.

Eram concluded with, "They that wait upon the LORD shall renew their strength; they shall mount up with wings as eagles; they shall run, and not be weary; and they shall walk, and not faint."[3] Then Eram rolled up the scroll, handed it back to the attendant, returned to his place, and resumed tugging at his ear.

It was still another confirmation for my pilgrimage. Jerusalem might be far away to the south and west, but the promise I heard was that I would be strong enough to make the journey.

It was time to tell Jehu my decision: I would be going with the caravan to Judea, even if they were not properly devout Jews.

When I returned to the corral area of the caravansary, I found it more than half empty. Calling to the aged porter, I asked, "Where is Jehu?"

Brandishing a wooden pitchfork in a wrinkled, age-spotted hand, the servant replied, "Gone! Gone to Jerusalem."

"So soon?"

"I tried to tell him it was bad fortune to flaunt the Almighty so, but he went anyway." The old man made it sound like a personal affront as well as an impiety.

"Did they have other provisions to get?" I inquired. "Somewhere else to stop nearby?"

The porter was already shaking his shaggy locks before the question was completed, "Over the hills and gone," he said, indicating the road. The highway was devoid of travelers as far to the west as I could see.

"Could I catch them? How far to the next stopping place?"

"Boy!" the servant said sternly. "They will make twenty miles before they stop again. Farther and faster than you could manage on foot. Twenty miles," he repeated, then added, "if they make it that far."

"What do you mean?"

"Bandits," the porter said gruffly. "Left on a Sabbath and made too much show of wealth. Bragging about his load of silk and how much it was worth. Word of it got all around Zakho."

"Do you really think they're in danger?"

Grudgingly the porter admitted, "Jehu took some thought about it. Signed on three more men to go along as guards." Dropping a leather water bottle at the end of a braided horsehair rope into the well, he added, "Though what good one of them may do, I'm sure I don't know. Had his arm in a sling. What good'll that do in a fight? But they insisted: 'Sign us all or none,' their leader said."

After offering to tote the skin to water a pen of donkeys, I asked, "How long will I have to wait? I want to get on the road soon."

"Who can say?" the porter said, laying his arm across my shoulders. "Tomorrow or next week? Who can say?"

It was not the answer I hoped to hear.

❦

I was back in the Zakho synagogue for the evening *Havdalah* service. By this rite Sabbath ended and the new week inaugurated. I tasted the wine and savored the aroma as the box of spices was passed around. The sharp sweetness of cinnamon, cloves, and myrtle pepper mingled with the penetrating tang of laurel and the exotic allure of orange peel.

Making sure I used all five of my senses, just as my mother taught me, I admired the entwined flames of the braided candle. Extending my hands, I sensed its warmth while I listened to the blessing:

"Blessed art thou, God, our Lord, King of the Universe,
  who distinguishes
  holiness from the everyday,
  light from dark,
  Israel from the nations,
  the seventh day from the six work days.
  Blessed art thou, God,
  who distinguishes holiness from the everyday."

When the candle was extinguished in the last of the wine, the end of the *Havdalah* service brought Sabbath to a close. Some of the men dipped a fingertip in the wine and touched their eyelids with it for good luck. Neither Rabbi Kagba nor my father had ever followed that custom, so neither did I.

Outside the synagogue a pair of torches lighted the entry. There was no illumination between the religious building and the caravansary, but the latter was only a few paces away.

I had only stepped into the darkness when I heard shouts of alarm and hoofbeats approaching at high speed. From the direction of the bridge came a horseman at full gallop.

The mounted man was upon me almost before I had time to react. I looked up and saw a black-cloaked figure on a black steed bearing down on me. Flinging myself out of the way, I had only a second to spare as the rider thundered past.

Flashing hooves dug sharply into the soil exactly where I had been standing.

But the nearness of sudden death was not what made me quake with alarm.

In the momentary glimpse of the mounted man's face provided by the torches, I recognized Zimri! Had the bandit chief also noticed me?

The assassin hurtled through Zakho without pausing and dashed away into the countryside beyond. There was no sign I had been spotted, no signal that the rebel was returning.

Yet still I could not stop myself from also bolting into flight. Ignoring calls from Asa, asking what was wrong, I sprinted across the stable yard. Up the stairs I charged, taking the steps two at a time.

There was no authority in Zakho to whom I could report, no one I trusted with my complete story, nothing to be done.

All of my anxiety centered on the cup! Unreasonably, I was suddenly fearful for its safety.

Inside my room I tore the covers off the bed and gasped with alarm. It wasn't there! The Cup of Joseph was not at the head of the bed. I rummaged through the fleece and coverlet, hoping I had tossed the sacred object aside without meaning to do so.

Down on my knees I went, handling and squeezing each bit of fabric. It was then that I saw it: a dark bundle, partly unrolled, lying between the wall and the bed frame at the head of the bed.

I snatched it up, feeling the comforting solid form within the folds. Even then I was not fully reassured until I unwrapped it completely and cradled the black, nondescript chalice in my arms.

The parcel had merely tumbled off the pallet, probably when I slammed the door on my way to the synagogue. I vowed to never leave it behind again.

The vision of Zimri galloping past slammed again into my thoughts. The bandit was still out there, somewhere. He had not been after me this time, but if we met again I would certainly be in danger.

I could not stay in Zakho any longer. The need to connect with a safe caravan and leave this part of the world behind was stronger than ever. I prayed earnestly for the remainder of my stay in Zakho to be brief. I wanted to travel with the right companions in a caravan to Jerusalem, but mostly I felt an urgent need to get the journey underway.

I bolted the door securely. Reknotting the fabric, I patted the sacking around the cup into a more comfortable shape. Using it for a pillow, I fell asleep.

Chapter 17

It wasn't even dawn when the bawling of camels and the shouting of drovers woke me. A new caravan had arrived at the caravansary.

Standing on the balcony, I studied the new arrivals. I counted forty beasts of burden, a good number for safe traveling. I saw family groups come in together and be assigned quarters beneath my room.

The man who strode about giving orders to everyone must be the master. He was of medium height and build, with sturdy shoulders and muscular forearms. The fringes of his prayer shawl proclaimed him to be an observant Jew. In fact, all the men in this caravan appeared to be respectable Jews.

Emerging from the inn, Asa greeted the newly arrived chief by shouting across the yard: "Hosea! Welcome! We looked for you these three days past."

"Had a new baby born on the crossing between here and Ecbatana," the leader called back. Hooking a thumb over his shoulder, he gestured toward a baby camel lurching unsteadily beside her mother. "Had to stay over a day, and that put us too late to get here before Sabbath. But here we are. Food ready?"

"Fresh bread, butter, and dates. Come inside and eat."

"I will, soon as I see all the families properly disposed and the animals fed."

"Sir," I called down to Asa, "might I join you for breakfast? I'd like to speak with the caravan master."

"Hosea?" Asa returned. Then, guessing at my purpose, he added, "You could not do better than him, lad. Come down and welcome."

Hosea was even more muscular up close than he had seemed from a distance. The caravan captain had a puckered scar on his brawny right forearm. He was gruff but not unkind when he spoke to me. "What's this about joining the caravan?" he asked. "Where are your parents, boy? Is it true they sent you to make arrangements?" Hosea lowered his chin and looked down a long, crooked nose. "The truth, now, mind."

"Yes, sir," I agreed. "I am supposed to go to my grandfather's shop in Jerusalem, in the Street of the Weavers. My brothers are already there. My parents will be joining me later." It wasn't really a lie so much as a hopeful utterance, I told myself.

Asa, seated beside me on a wooden bench next to a smoldering fire, turned, and looked at me. "Why the story, then? About you being sent here to set things up?"

"My good friend, Rabbi Kagba, said I should tell people that my parents were coming soon. He said then no one would take advantage of me. He said when I found observant Jews I could trust them and then I could explain."

I still did not make reference to the cup, nor to the special mission that had been assigned to me. I had told enough of the tale to get me to Jerusalem. The rest was no one's business.

"When I heard that you keep Sabbath," I added to Hosea, "I was sure God had sent the right caravan for me."

Hosea laughed, exchanging a glance with the innkeeper. "So I'm an answer to prayer, am I? There's few would make that claim about me."

"I can pay." I explained the bargain the rabbi had insisted was fair. "You will be paid the rest when we reach the Holy City."

Hosea waved away the reference to pay. "I believe you, lad. That's not the issue. I cannot take you, alone as you are. Someone must be willing to be responsible for you. See that you're fed. Doctored, if needed. Assign you your duties. On my caravans everyone works if they want to eat."

"I'm a good worker," I maintained stoutly, looking to Asa to back me up.

The caravansary owner nodded.

"All right, let me locate the family I think will serve your need. If they agree, then I'll take you on. Mind, now," he said sternly. The bench legs squealed on the wooden floor as he stood and pushed away from the table. "It's no easy task you've set for yourself. We walk from sunup to sunset, six days a week, and then tend the animals before we rest ourselves. And there's no turning back. This time of year it'll take six Sabbaths with the blessing of the Name . . . eight if we're unlucky. You still want to sign on?"

I nodded vigorously.

Hosea expressed his approval. "You will be able to help this family, I think. They are making this journey because of some healer they heard of. Jesus, I think his name is. One son is going blind, and the other son's wife is barren." The caravan master shook his head. "It's a long journey. I hope they find what they're looking for."

Hosea returned with an older man and his wife and two children younger than me. "This is Raheb and his good wife, Reena. They are traveling west with their sons and daughters-in-law, and these, their two grandchildren."

"Pleased to meet you, Nehemiah," said Raheb, a pleasant-seeming man, nearing sixty, broad of build and face. "Here are Beryl"—he tapped a small girl of about four on the shoulder—"and Michael." He lightly thumped the head of a boy a year or two younger than me. "These two require a lot of looking after," Raheb said. "And they're a bit small for their chores. But you look strong. Shepherd, I hear? Would you help them in exchange for your meals?"

"Gladly, sir," I agreed.

"Then it's settled," Hosea offered. "We leave day after tomorrow at daybreak. You can start helping by watering the camels today."

By the time we were a few days' journey out of Zakho, I had learned a great deal more about Raheb's family. They were loving, pious, close-knit, and diligent. Raheb was a hard worker, his advice sought as frequently as his muscular strength, and he made both available in a cheerful, modest way. Reena was a good cook, caring and unflustered by life amid dirt and sweaty camels, never shirking her labor but always finding time to hug Beryl or tell Michael a story.

They were both a comfort and a grief to me. My guardians represented a place of plenty and safety after all my running and hiding . . . and also a constant reminder of how much I missed my own parents.

I learned more about my temporary family than just their

character. I came to understand their motives as well, much to my surprise.

Going on pilgrimage to the Holy City was something all pious Jews aspired to accomplish. *Torah* enjoined three pilgrim festivals each year: Tabernacles, Passover, and the Festival of Weeks that culminated in Pentecost. Among devout Jews living far from Jerusalem, it was a custom to pay a substitute to appear at the Temple. This allowed distant believers to participate in the sacrifices by proxy in those years in which they could not travel. Ever since my mother moved to Amadiya when she married Father, my Jerusalem grandparents had performed those ceremonies for us.

This year I would be going myself.

But the circumstances that took Raheb and his children to Jerusalem involved more than fulfilling a religious obligation. Raheb's son, Tobit, father of my friends Michael and Beryl, had an eye disease that was robbing him of his sight. His eyes watered constantly and were often glued shut in the morning when he awoke. He was so sensitive to the glare of the desert sun that he kept a headscarf wrapped about his face by day, peering out at the world through narrow slits.

Raheb's other son, Yacov, was wed six years earlier, but he and Dinah had no children. She was barren. She doted on her niece and nephew, but a lurking sadness never fully left her face.

What shocked me was learning the cause of their deciding to make *aliyah* this year: the presence of Jesus of Nazareth.

Stories were swapped around a community campfire. It seemed that everyone had an opinion about the rabbi from Galilee. "I heard once there was a crowd so great it was impossible to get near him," one traveler reported. "So four companions tore off the roof of the house where Jesus was and lowered their crippled friend down to him. This Jesus told him to get up and walk . . . and he did."

"That's all?" a scoffer challenged. "No magic words? No special prayers?"

"No, but he did say the man's sins were forgiven."

Mutters of "Blasphemy!" and "Who does he think he is?" swirled around the leaping flames.

"Perhaps he's a madman, deluded," another remarked.

The original reporter continued, "Jesus asked them if it was harder to forgive sins or to heal a paralyzed man. He said making the man walk was the proof he could forgive sin too."

I did not know what to make of that tale. How could I understand a man who claimed to be able to forgive sins? Didn't that authority belong to God alone? Wasn't Messiah supposed to be a leader who would be like Moses? Or like Joshua? A man who would free us Jews from the power of Rome and restore David's kingdom?

My doubts were echoed by the next speaker. "He's a charlatan! Mark my words: he's just another swindler, claiming to be a messiah . . . right up until he and all his followers get themselves crucified. We don't need a healer, or a smooth-talking liar, or a philosopher! We need a strong military leader. We need another Judah Maccabee."

There were murmurs of agreement at these words. We were hoping to arrive in Jerusalem by Hanukkah, celebrating the rededication of the Temple after the famous Judah the Hammer defeated our foes two hundred years earlier.

Tobit stepped forward into the firelight. Since it was night, his eyes were unbound, but they were red and inflamed all around them. He squinted painfully in the flaring brilliance and wiped away tears that coursed down his cheeks. "I have heard he gave sight to a man born blind. Born . . . blind! No one has ever heard of such a thing. Perhaps it isn't true. But if it is, if he will touch me and keep me from losing my sight, I will follow him, warrior or not."

"I heard," Hosea rumbled, "that he even raised the dead."

"Now you've gone too far," someone sneered. "Is he supposed to be Elijah or Elisha?"

Hosea said, "I have a cousin in the synagogue in Capernaum. He's the one who told me the cantor's daughter was dead and Jesus brought her back to life." Then, speaking very carefully and deliberately, the caravan leader pronounced each of these words: "Or are you calling *me* a liar?"

The one who issued the objection retreated immediately. "Spoke hastily . . . please forgive me . . . some misunderstanding."

When we went to bed that night, I found the Cup of Joseph to be more uncomfortable than usual as my pillow. How would I know whether Jesus was worthy to receive it or not? If he was not who Rabbi Kagba hoped, what would I do with it? Why was I carrying it across a thousand-mile journey away from home, if it turned out to be all wrong?

Then I thought about Tobit's eyes and Dinah's weary sadness. "Almighty, for all their sakes, make the stories be true," I prayed. "And let me know the truth without mistake." I remembered the White Hart and my vision of Joseph the Dreamer. I was sent to Jerusalem for a purpose. The cup had come to me, out of all those who had carried it or who might have found it over the centuries. I was the one appointed for this reason, even if I did not yet understand it.

Chapter 18

We journeyed across the Land between the Rivers—
Mesopotamia, as the Greek-speakers called it. Despite the
promise of abundant water in its name, the area was in the grip of a
prolonged drought. Dry, dusty plains stretched for miles, punctuated by all-too-rare clumps of trees and occasional muddy pools.
Wells, some of them dug back in the days of Father Abraham, still
furnished the life blood of the trade routes.

Hosea urged us to use our water sparingly. "I plan each day's
journey to take us from watering hole to watering hole," he
lectured the group. "But there are no guarantees. A sandstorm
or a greedy caravan that gets there first . . . either of these can
upset the plan. If we are forced to go a second or a third day on
just what we can carry, then so be it, we will."

"And what happens if it's four days?" someone asked.

"Then those who have not been careful will either beg or
begin to die," Hosea said.

The very next morning we rehearsed Hosea's warning. Raheb
made certain every waterskin for our group was completely filled
before we left the well. It was my duty to haul the bulging, dripping bags out of the water source. Tobit and Yacov saw to it that
they were secured to the packsaddles of the camels.

During the very first week of our journey, we experienced the truth of Hosea's words.

Before dawn the camels began bawling as if jackals ran amid their lines. Raheb and Yacov dashed about with drawn swords but found nothing.

Just as they returned to the remains of the previous night's campfire, the tremor struck. The earth rolled and pitched beneath my feet. A tent collapsed on Reena and her daughters-in-law, but they were not hurt.

We sorted ourselves out and resumed our travel.

When it was almost evening, we arrived at a place Hosea called Beth Mah-buwah, the House of the Spring. What we expected to find was a sheltered spot with water seeping out of a rock face. Our leader said the spring filled a pool to overflowing.

Instead, we found the cliffside fractured, the spring dried up, and the pool split, drained and empty.

"The earthquake," Hosea muttered. "In ages past one tremor broke the rock and started the fountain. Now another has closed it again."

"Could another reopen it?" Raheb asked.

"Not soon enough to help us," the caravan leader responded. "Nor would you want to be close by when it did." He gestured to a heap of boulders that had fallen from the top of the precipice. "That would have crushed anyone too close. Still, we camp here tonight anyway," he ordered. "Well away from the cliff, in case the earth is still not comfortable. Use your water carefully. With the blessing, we should reach another well by tomorrow night . . . but we cannot know until we reach it."

On the next day's march Raheb's family was at the front of the caravan. Michael trotted along beside me. My new young companion kept up a constant chatter about whatever popped into his head: what he named each of the goats we herded, what he would see in Jerusalem, the earthquakes he had felt when home in Ecbatana . . . and water. Often he talked about water.

"My father has been on caravan before," he said. "They weren't careful with water like we are. Once they got lost and went a week without finding a well. Two men were driven crazy, Papa says."

Michael's list of the horrors of being without water increased my own anxiety. I was relieved when we reached the edge of the barren tableland and spotted a cluster of trees near its base. I saw bronze sunlight glinting off a pool. The oasis was anchored in place by a large hawthorn tree, but palms and junipers were dotted around it too.

"We're there, and the water is there." I shaded my eyes against the glare. Then renewed worry struck me. "But another caravan is already there," I said, noticing human forms in the grove.

Raheb, leading a camel, arrived alongside me. "It's all right, Nehi. This is the best water for a week, Hosea says. There'll be plenty. Besides, I don't even see any animals."

He was right. As we descended the slope and drew nearer to the camping place, there were no camels, no horses, no donkeys anywhere in sight. I saw people resting against the trunks of trees or reclining beside the water, but no beasts of burden.

Suddenly Raheb stopped me. "Nehemiah," he said tersely, "stay here with Michael. Reena," he called to his wife, "go no farther. Keep together. Yacov, stay with them."

"Grandfather," Michael said, "why are we stopping? There's the water. Why can't we—"

Raheb sounded angry when he repeated, "Stay here!"

Raheb, Hosea, and a party of men, spread out in a line like scouts approaching enemy territory, moved cautiously toward the grove. They advanced among the nodding palms, swords or spears in hand. Hosea called them together for a brief conference, then they trudged back up the hill toward us.

Raheb reported to our family, "Bandit attack. That's why there are no animals."

Reena whispered a question I could not hear, but Raheb answered by saying, "All of them. None escaped. You stay here. We'll get done as quickly as we can."

Raheb told me to stay with the children, but I had been struck by a burning question. "I'm a shepherd's son," I said. "I've seen dead men, and I've seen bandits. Please let me come."

There were fifteen bodies scattered among the trees. All were men. All had been stripped of their clothing.

The caravan had defended itself, but bodies tangled in blankets near campfire ashes told the tale: they had been attacked while they slept. Their guards had failed them.

Or betrayed them.

I found Jehu locked in the embrace of death with his assailant. He had plunged a knife into the heart of his opponent even as a curved dagger slashed his throat.

The dagger had been wielded by the bandit I saw on the trail with his arm in a sling when the rabbi and I were hiding. *One of Zimri's men.*

I trembled. I had almost joined Jehu's company. I would have been in the camp when Zimri's men attacked.

Wielding shovels or using our hands, we buried the bodies well away from the oasis. We dug a trench beneath a sandy knoll, loaded it with the dead, then collapsed the overhanging brow of earth onto them.

Then we brought our caravan into camp.

There was little conversation that night. We realized that crossing the desert exposed us to many dangers besides being short of water. I was glad the Almighty had led me to Hosea and Raheb. I prayed fervently that as we kept the Sabbath, so the Almighty would keep us.

It was four Sabbaths before the start of Hanukkah—four more weeks until our caravan would arrive in Jerusalem. Miles from any town, we kept Sabbath night in camp and worshipped during the following day.

When the service was held, Raheb was called up to read the words of the prophet Malachi. It was a grim passage, I thought, about how the priests stole from God and defiled their worship with theft and trickery. Raheb read God's accusation to the wicked priests: "A son honors his father, and a servant his master. If then I am a father, where is my honor? And if I am a master, where is my fear? says the LORD of hosts to you, O priests, who despise my name."[1]

After the service the assembly scattered to their individual camps. A traveler named Saul of Hebron, passing in the opposite direction, had shared a meal and the worship service with the caravan. He trudged alongside us.

"Things must have been bad in Malachi's day," Saul said, "but they have not gotten any better since. High Priest Caiaphas lords it over the people, because he is backed up by Governor Pilate. His priests cheat the people when they change money for Temple coin. They charge outrageous prices for sacrificial lambs. It is a rotten business, stinking to heaven. No one stands up to them." Then he brightened. "No one except one man . . . Jesus of Nazareth."

My wandering attention refocused at the sound of that name.

"I've heard of him," Raheb said, "but he's supposed to be a man of peace. Meek, they say, and kind."

"Not on this occasion," Saul argued. "Some time ago it was. I saw it! Made a whip and scattered the moneychangers left and right. He may be the very king of peace for all I know, but at the time of which I speak, he was a Prince of Righteousness! Consumed with righteous anger for the One God, whom he called Father."

"A madman, then," Raheb responded.

Saul shrugged. "A brave and righteous madman. No one else challenges the high priest . . ."

"And lives," Raheb concluded drily. "He can't last long, can he? Not after challenging the Levites and the hypocrite merchants right in their lair."

"Perhaps not, but I'd pay good money to see him do it again," Saul concluded. "So would you, I wager. Not since the Maccabees did anyone stand up to the corrupt priests like this Jesus."

That night I worried as I tried to fall asleep. What would I do with the cup if Jesus was arrested . . . or even killed . . . before I met him? How could I complete my mission?

I wrestled so with these concerns that I was relieved when a voice I recognized as belonging to Joseph the Dreamer called to me . . .

"Nehemiah? Will you go on a journey with me?"

"Yes, please," I responded.

There was a crashing noise followed by billows of air. It was like when a tent's guy ropes are released and the shelter collapses with a rush. Just like that, night collapsed to become day. I no longer slept on a sandy trailside. Instead, I stood next to Joseph on a rocky ridge hemmed in on both sides by deep valleys. Above it loomed another rocky outcropping.

Built on the point of the lower ridge was a citadel. In front of the fortress a conference was taking place. A rank of tired-looking warriors with notched swords and tattered bowstrings faced a man dressed as a priest but wearing a circlet of gold atop his head.

"The one speaking is Abram, my great-grandfather," Joseph said, indicating the leader of the warriors. "Facing him is Melchizedek, the king of Salem, where we are now. As to the rest, just listen."

"We pursued the Elamites as far as Damascus," Abram said, "the ones who kidnapped my nephew, Lot, and his family." Abram paused to rub his hands up and down his blood-stained robe. "We attacked the enemy camp by night and routed them. When they fled, we chased them. We rescued Lot and all my kin and all his possessions. We also took spoils of war from the enemy. Now we have returned from the fight, but before we go home, I ordered that we turn aside here. You, Melchizedek, are king. You are also priest of the Most High God. Since we serve the same God and he has helped me, I am here to offer him thanks."

"You have done well, Abram," the priest said. "And wanting to honor God also does you credit. But you are tired. You have traveled and fought, so here is refreshment for you." Snapping his fingers, Melchizedek summoned a row of servants bearing trays of bread and jugs of wine. Moving down the row of Abram and his allies, Melchizedek broke the loaves and handed some to each man. Then he poured wine into a silver cup and carried it down the row of parched combatants for each to drink from. As the king offered the wine, he touched the foreheads of Abram and his men. Melchizedek spoke words for every warrior pronounced too softly for me to overhear. A blessing spoken over each man?

I stared at the cup. It was polished silver that gleamed in the sun. "That looks just like your cup," I said to Joseph. "Except shiny and new-looking."

"That's because it is my cup . . . before it was mine. Listen."

When each man had received the bread and the wine, Melchizedek spoke loudly again. "Abram, you are blessed by God Most High, Possessor and Maker of Heaven and Earth. And blessed, praised, and glorified be God Most High, who has given your enemies into your hands."

Now it was Abram's turn to summon a column of servants. Each bore a pack on his back. At Abram's command the attendants unrolled the bundles at Melchizedek's feet. The contents displayed contained gold coins, jeweled necklaces, bracelets and rings, gold and silver plates. "For the service of the Most High," Abram said. "A tenth of all the spoils, for a thank offering."

Melchizedek nodded gravely. Walking directly toward Abram he extended the silver cup from which the king of Salem had dispensed the wine and his blessing. "For you. A memorial of this day. Whenever you eat bread and drink wine from this cup, you will remember that you honored the Most High and that he has blessed you."

The two groups of men parted. While Joseph and I watched them go, the Dreamer said, "So here is a true and honorable priest of the Almighty. And what does his name mean, Nehemiah?"

"King of Righteousness."

The Dreamer concurred. "And since he is the Master of

Salem, which means 'peace,' he is also the Prince of Peace. Do
you know where Salem is located?"

"Salem is . . . the same as Jerusalem!" I realized. "And so that
rocky cliff," I said, turning and pointing, "that's where the Temple
is now."

"No moneychangers or corrupt priests here today," Joseph
said. "But here were more shadows of things to come. Now let
me take you home."

The Dreamer swirled the edge of his robe around my shoulders. Daytime and Salem disappeared. A cup of jewel-like stars
spilled across the night sky from the constellation called the Cup.

Chapter 19

A herd of goats traveled with our caravan, providing fresh milk for the youngest of our pilgrims. Extra milk, curdled in goatskin bags, became cheese. The animals also furnished a supply of fresh meat we would not otherwise have enjoyed.

Part of the work assigned me by Hosea was to move the small flock along parallel to the plodding camels. The duty was not hard. The shaggy goats naturally followed their four-footed leader, a rangy wether wearing a bell around his neck. All I had to do was prod those that lagged behind and keep track of any injuries they suffered. Raheb praised me for noticing when a ewe scratched her udder on a thorn bush, or if a young animal turned up lame from a stone caught in the cleats of his hoof. Keeping a flock healthy was something I had learned at my father's side and through the skill of my mother. Doctoring with olive oil, in which mint, lavender flowers, and sulfur had been steeped answered for most of their hurts.

At the beginning of our journey, Raheb, or one of his sons, assisted me with the flock. I was proud when, after a week of travel, my guardian recognized I was an experienced herdsman and left the goats in my care.

Michael often walked with me, but only for part of each

day. He was too small to keep up without running, so wore out quickly. Still, I was glad for the company.

He told me stories about living in Ecbatana, within sight of the tombs of Queen Esther and Mordecai. I responded with tales of facing down wolves and leopards in the canyons of my home. (I may have exaggerated slightly.)

One afternoon, as the shadows were drawing in, Michael's uncle Yacov brought us the word that we would be stopping for the night in another hour or so. Bending toward his nephew, he offered, "I'll carry you back with me now, Michael."

"Please," my friend replied, "let me stay with Nehi. I'm not a bit tired. Let me stay till we bring in the flock."

Standing erect, Yacov appeared to judge the distance to the procession of the caravan: about a quarter of a mile. The camels trudged along the flat plain while my herd, and others like it, grazed amid the brush that fringed a serpentine line of small hills. Squinting at the horizon, he agreed to let Michael remain with me. "But as soon as the sun touches those peaks," Yacov said, stretching one hand toward the west, "bring the flock up quickly. I don't want you out here after dark."

"We will," I said.

The dark orange disk of the solar coin was merely a handsbreadth over the peaks when I counted the flock one final time in preparation for bringing them down the slope. "Nine, ten, eleven," I recited, before stopping in consternation. Beginning again brought me to the same conclusion. "We're missing one."

"It's Beulah," Michael remarked with assurance.

He was right. The ewe he named had been more trouble than any of the rest, sometimes butting me in the back out of sheer contrariness. She often found the most awkward, brush-choked gullies in which to wander. Beulah seemed to take delight in hiding her scraggly brown-and-white blotched hide amid matching shrubs and rubble.

"She can't have gone far," I reasoned. "I'll start the leader back toward camp, and the rest will follow. You go with them, to keep them moving, while I go find her."

"I'd rather stay with you," Michael said.

I judged the heavens. Half the sun was below the distant rocky ridge, but the clear sky was still full of light. The flock was grazing contently amongst the scrawny hawthorns, wild olive shrubs, sickle grass, and yellow bedstraw. "All right. We'll make it quick."

I was certain Beulah was no farther than the sharp spine of a limestone outcrop fifty paces away. As I trudged up the incline, I prayed she had not tumbled down the other side into a ravine.

The Cup of Joseph, tied in its covering around my waist and slung behind my back, clunked against my shepherd's staff as it swung with each stride. When I reached the jagged array of boulders forming the backbone of the knoll, I clambered atop it in order to see better. The other side of the ridge did fall sharply into a narrow defile . . . and Beulah was nowhere in sight.

Panting from the climb, Michael joined me at the summit.

"I can't see her," I said. "Let's go back to the others."

"We can't leave her out here," he objected. "Something will get her for sure."

Over our heads a vast flock of cranes, flying south to their winter home, swept past. They soared above us, a living river in the sky, like a stream of clouds flowing downwind.

"Her own fault," I argued.

"There's still plenty of light. Look, there's a path."

It was generous to call it a path. A game trail, no wider than one of my feet, snaked downward by way of a long, slanting plunge into the gulley below.

"Bet there's a pool of water." Michael sniffed. "Don't you smell it? Bet that's what she's after."

I considered what my friend said. The air wafting upward from the shadowed gorge was noticeably cooler and moister feeling than that of the exposed hillside. Tracing the descent of the narrow track with my eyes, I spotted a brown-and-white form darting around a curve. "You're right. There she goes."

With that we also plunged headlong down into the canyon. At each bend in the trail I spotted Beulah for an instant, just before she disappeared again behind a screen of brush or a dusty limestone cornice.

When we reached the bottom, the goat was still bouncing ahead of us toward a goal only she knew. The floor of the gorge was filled with deep sand that made harder walking than the rock-strewn slope had been. It was barely wide enough for two horses or donkeys to pass side by side.

There was no water in the ravine, but we were definitely heading in an upstream direction. The dry creek bed wandered into the heart of the mountain. Side branches appeared along the way. Beulah darted left or right as her mood took her. There was no longer any main channel. All the ravines looked alike: constricted and choked with grit, mere threads of gravel flanked by sheer stone precipices.

I was angry at the goat and determined to catch her. I would tie the sash from my robe around her neck and drag her back to camp. I was sure that soon she would dash into a dead-end canyon, and then her game and this chase would be over.

Soon stretched into a very long time. The pale blue light reaching into the depth of the gully changed to azure, then cobalt, and then to purple. The lateness of the hour had just penetrated my thinking when I turned a final corner to come face-to-face with a blank rock wall . . . and no Beulah.

"Where did she go?" Michael wondered aloud. "Even a goat can't climb that," he said, gesturing toward the cliff. "She disappeared."

Thinking of an explanation, I suggested, "At that place where the last two canyons came together? We thought she followed the left, but she must have ducked into the other way." I saw Michael shiver. The night was growing cold, but with our cloaks and fleece-lined leather boots, his shaking must be from fear too. "Enough," I decided. "It's late. We're late. And we've wasted enough time on one stupid goat. Let's go back."

"But, Nehi, . . . which way is back?" he queried.

"It's easy," I said with assurance. "It's this way." After three steps I looked at my feet and stopped.

"What's the matter?"

"No footprints," I mumbled. "We didn't come this way after all." Facing about, I added, "Silly mistake. Here we go. Follow me."

Three dead ends and five wrong turns later, I admitted we were lost.

"If I could just see the stars," I lamented. "But down here in the bottom of this ravine I can barely see any bit of sky." Michael's bottom lip trembled, and I feared he might cry. "Don't worry," I reassured him. "All we have to do is climb out of here—it doesn't matter where—and as soon as I can see the stars, I can get us home."

My friend sniffed and wiped his nose with the sleeve of his robe. "Is that the truth? Or are you just making up another story?"

"Truth," I insisted. "My teacher, Rabbi Kagba, taught me."

The canyon walls were so sheer that finding an incline we could ascend was not easy. Two more box canyons provided no outlet. As it grew still darker, I began to fear we would have to spend the night in the gully.

"What's that noise?" Michael asked, then answered his own question. "Hoofs. I hear hoofbeats. They're coming to find us! Over here!" he called.

"Wait!" I said urgently, catching him right before he ran toward the sound of riders. "Wait! No one in our caravan has a horse. Camels and donkeys don't sound like that."

"But it doesn't matter," he protested. "They will help us."

I was not so sure. "Just keep quiet. Remember when we found the caravan that had been attacked by bandits?"

Michael's voice squeaked. "And murdered?" Now he looked like he wanted to run the other direction.

"They won't turn into this draw," I explained. "Get behind me. Crouch down and keep still till we see who it is. They won't see us if we stay below this ledge."

The clopping beat of horses being slowly ridden in file echoed off the canyon walls. I did not have to see them before scooting as far back into the shelter as I could. I recognized Zimri's voice. Clamping my hand over Michael's mouth, I hissed, "It's them— the bandits! Don't move!"

He gave a trembling nod, and I released his mouth but kept a hand on his shoulder.

Leading a troop of six riders, Zimri was in advance. The chief murderer did most of the talking, plotting an attack on a group of pilgrims heading west. He spoke of how they would launch the assault when the camp was asleep and the fires burning low. He talked of knifing the men in their bedrolls and carrying away the women and children as slaves.

I realized with a shudder he was speaking of our caravan. Biting my lip, I squeezed Michael's arm. We were almost safe. Half of the riders were already past our position.

Michael tapped me in the back of the head, then on my cheek. Was the boy trying to give away our position? Angrily, I shrugged away his touch. A moment later he tapped harder, drumming my face with his fingertips.

Pivoting away from the annoying slapping turned my face to the rock wall . . . and brought me eye-to-eye with a horned viper no more than three feet from my nose. The snake's tongue darted in and out, testing the air. He must have emerged from his den for a night's hunting.

Horned vipers are deadly poison.

The broad, fat, arrow-shaped head lifted from the stone shelf and swung slowly back and forth, as if deciding what to do about me. The serpent was three feet long. Father taught me they could strike more than half of their body length. I was safe for the moment . . . and then the snake slithered another foot forward.

The last rider in the line of bandits clucked to his mount. Lagging behind the others, he trotted to catch up. The snake heard the change in the rhythm and turned his ugly, evil snout toward the noise.

I waited, holding my breath, as the horsemen retreated down the canyon.

When the snake again fixed his unblinking gaze on me, I could not wait any longer. Seizing Michael, I lunged away from the rocks. We tumbled together onto the sand as the viper struck at empty space where my chin had been a moment before.

Now our line of travel had been decided for us: we scrambled quickly in the opposite direction taken by the bandits. By following the hoofprints in the sand, I knew we would emerge from the ravines eventually.

And, soon enough, we did.

"But we're still lost," Michael whimpered.

"Not for long," I corrected, inhaling the expanse of the heavens the same way I enjoyed breathing the open air. "Look," I urged my friend, "there's where the sun set. That star is the jewel on the forehead of Ophiuchus, the Snake Handler."

"Snake handler?" Michael repeated nervously.

"It's all right," I reassured him. "He's winning. I'll tell you that story some other time. But look, there's Mizar in the handle of the Plow. Halfway between Mizar and the jewel is our camp."

"How do you know?" Michael sniffed suspiciously.

I shrugged. "I just know. Besides, can't you smell the smoke of the cookfires? It's coming from that same direction. Hold my hand. We'll be there in less than an hour."

We spotted the dots of the campfires in only a few minutes and arrived safely well before my allotted time was up.

When we told of our near encounter with the bandits, and what we overheard, Michael's mother hugged him fiercely and gave me angry looks, but Hosea thanked me. The caravan captain ordered the guards to be doubled. Then he brought me more praises, together with my supper. I understood that I was not going to be punished for my foolishness.

Yacov brought in the flock of goats. Not one was missing. Even Beulah had somehow rejoined them, wagging and bleating like the picture of innocence.

Two Sabbaths later the mood around the caravan's cookfires was upbeat. So far the trip had been unusually easy, free from bad weather, bandits, and illness. There had been the normal difficulties of life on the trail: animals that pulled free of their pickets and wandered off in the night, straps that broke, dumping supplies and trade goods into the dirt, but nothing major.

"Tomorrow we reach the river," Hosea announced to a circle of families, traders, and drovers. "And the Almighty permitting, we will cross it."

"The Euphrates," I whispered to Michael. "It's the border between the Parthians and the Romans."

"Since Sabbath begins at sunset tomorrow," Hosea continued, "we will rest the night, the Sabbath day, and perhaps one day more. We reached here three days ahead of the best crossing I ever made, and we need to resupply and do mending. An extra day will do us good."

I slept next to the remains of the fire, beside Michael. Reena and her granddaughter, Beryl, snuggled together just beyond Michael. Raheb was snoring close to me. Sons Tobit and Yacov and their wives rested in a pair of canvas shelters one rank farther back.

Raheb's snoring awakened me. I blinked up at the panorama of stars, trying to recall what Rabbi Kagba had taught me about the sky this time of year. To the south the pale orange dot hovering above my big toe was Mars, what the rabbi had called Ma'Adim, the Adam.

I examined the starry pattern surrounding Mars. An owl hooted in some rushes off in a dry wash while I pondered. The constellation in which Mars hung was the Sign of the Two Fish. Some said its name linked the two kingdoms of the Jews: Israel and Judah.

But Rabbi Kagba, while agreeing with that position, also taught something more. He said the image of the fishes, their tails connected by a ribbon, was also a reference to the Jews and the Gentiles. The rabbi quoted the words of the Almighty about his anointed Messiah, as recorded by the prophet Isaiah: "It is too light a thing that you should be my servant to raise up the tribes of Jacob . . . I will make you as a light to the nations, that my salvation may reach to the end of the earth."[1]

Another owl called from the opposite side of the camp. An errant swirling breath of wind tugged a handful of sparks from the dying fire and tossed them aloft to glimmer beside Mars.

The bandit assault came from both sides of the camp at once. A dozen men, faces wrapped in scarves up to their eyes, wearing dark robes and brandishing short swords, charged in. They attacked in silence from the pitch-black surroundings before bursting into the pale light of the glowing embers.

I shouted and, in so doing, saved Raheb's life. A bandit slashed downward at Raheb's head but missed when my protector rolled out of the way. Jumping to his feet, Raheb parried a second blow with a stick of firewood.

Others in the camp were not so fortunate. Cries of pain echoed in the night.

Then the air was split by a trumpet blast. Hosea, an antelope horn to his lips, sounded the alarm. "Bandits! Up! Up and fight!" the caravan master shouted.

Now the night rang with the sound of blows given and received. Across the fire from me, Reena gathered Michael and Beryl to her.

Tobit and Yacov flanked their father, engaging the lone assailant with their swords, while their father hammered away at him with the chunk of wood. The bandit gave ground before their combined onslaught. The echoing alarm and the speed with which surprise had been lost disconcerted the attackers.

They were outnumbered by the men of the caravan by three or four to one.

A pair of camels, their ties slashed by the marauders, blundered into the scene. They trampled directly across the fire, scattering it and plunging the battle into even greater darkness.

Driven apart from Raheb and his sons by the animals, the bandit seized the moment to escape, but not empty-handed. Knocking Reena down with his shoulder, he grabbed Beryl and began to carry her away with him while the child kicked and screamed.

I launched myself at the kidnapper, tackling him around the knees and bringing the man down. Beryl rolled free and ran back to the protection of her grandfather.

The bandit raised his blade over my head. I winced and cried out, flinging up my arm to ward off the blow. Raheb's improvised wooden club pinwheeled across the intervening space, smashing into the attacker's head and his sword at the same moment, and felling him.

"Away! Get to the horses!" one of the bandits shouted.

In the next instant the assailants disappeared into the countryside, their black robes allowing the night to swallow them up. "Don't follow!" Hosea bellowed, then repeated himself to Tobit and his brother, who wanted to continue the battle. "I say, don't follow! Give them no chance to pick you off in the night. Stir up the fires. Post guards. Tend your wounded."

Of all of us in Raheb's camp only he had sustained any injury, and it was a slight cut on his arm. Our attacker, nose driven back into his skull, was dead.

Beryl, in the arms of her mother, was still whimpering with fright, but quieter now. All Raheb's family gathered around me. "Boy, I am in debt to you for two lives tonight," Raheb said. "For my own and for my granddaughter's. Command me. Anything of mine is yours."

❧

The souk outside the walls of Damascus was a sprawling city in its own right. Camel-traders attempted to outshout grain merchants. Dealers in silk or spice or silver necklaces competed with each other for the attention of passersby from every corner of the Roman Empire and beyond. Next to Antioch, Damascus was the most important city in the Roman province of Coele-Syria, whose borders included the Jewish homeland of Judea.

Hosea spat noisily when he shared that fact with me. The idea that from an outpost of pagan Assyrians, a pagan Imperial Legate held authority over the Jewish Holy City was worse than distasteful to pious Jews. Then he shrugged. "Of course the Romans have great disdain for all things not Roman, not just Jewish. The present appointee, one Lucius Aelius Lamia, has never been to Syria, much less Jerusalem. They say he never leaves Rome."

Damascus existed at the juncture of the highway called Via Maris, which connected the lands of the East to the Sea of Middle Earth, and the King's Road, leading to the spices of Arabia. The mingling of Syrian dialects with the tongues of Cypriots, Armenians, Nabateans, and Ethiopians was overwhelming to the ear. A form of Greek was used as the trade language, but the sons of Abraham with whom we dealt spoke Aramaic and Hebrew as well.

Equally confusing to the senses were the sights and smells of the place. I stood in one spot, revolving slowly and gawking. "If Damascus were the ark after the Flood, Noah just opened the gates," I marveled. "Look at all the strange creatures."

"And pickpockets," Raheb observed wryly. "Don't forget them. Keep your coins and your wits about you, or someone will make off with them both."

At that instant a cry of "Stop! Stop, thief!" resounded from the direction of a dealer in dried fruit, proving Raheb's point. Few of the other tradesmen even bothered looking up. Most resumed their patter as soon as the disturbance faded into the distance.

I hitched the parcel containing the cup around so that it rode at the front of my waist.

The Roman authorities had little concern for either commerce or crime outside the walls. Inside Damascus, it was another story. Tramping squads of Roman soldiers scowled at everyone they met, as if daring us to resist their might.

"Damascus has a kind of independence," Raheb told me. "It is the northern-most city of those ten states called the Decapolis. The emperor likes the tax money he collects from here, so Rome's boot is lighter on its throat."

The emperor had even made an effort to show the regard Rome had for the local deity. An earlier temple to the god of the Assyrians, a storm god named Ba'al Hadad, had been dramatically expanded with Roman arches and columns. The structure was then rededicated under what the emperor said was Hadad's Roman name: Jupiter. Of course the statue dedicated to the worship of Caesar himself was larger and grander than Jupiter's.

"Rome is happy to appease the religious sensitivity of conquered people," Raheb observed with heavy sarcasm. "High Priest Caiaphas would probably let them do the same in Jerusalem if he thought he could get away with it."

Outside the pagan temple, merchants sold clay models of a squatting, bearded figure wearing a conical cap and bull's horns and holding a lightning bolt. It made the Assyrian god look like an angry dwarf. "Unless that's supposed to be Caesar," Hosea muttered under his breath.

I was relieved when we got back to our own circle of camels and tents and away from the clamor. I felt guilty somehow, as if carrying the Cup of Joseph into such an unholy place had further tarnished it.

I said as much to Raheb around the supper fire that night . . . leaving out the part about the cup, of course.

"Just remember," he warned me. "The Almighty cares for the Gentiles too. Didn't he send the prophet Jonah to warn Nineveh to repent? It was, by all accounts, an even more wicked city than Damascus."

Seated with our group and several other families for a supper of fragrant saffron rice and mouth-watering minced lamb, Hosea asked, "Does anyone have a story to share? About Damascus, I mean."

To the surprise of everyone, including myself, I waved my hand. "My teacher, Rabbi Kagba, told me a story of Damascus."

Bushy eyebrows raised, Hosea gestured for me to proceed.

"It was thirty-three years ago, he said. My rabbi, who studied the ancient writing, learned Messiah was about to be born in Judea. My teacher came through here on his way to Jerusalem."

I stopped, suddenly shy at the way the entire group, adults and children both, were silently, attentively listening.

"Is that all?" Michael said. "That's not a story."

I resumed. "It was here . . . in Damascus . . . that the rabbi met all the other scholars who were seeking the newborn king. Rabbi Kagba told me they all saw the sign of his birth in the sky while they were still on their journeys, before they met in Damascus."

Everyone glanced upward into the heavens. The blazing torches of the souk blotted out all the stars, except for a triangle of bright beacons hovering in the southwest . . . in the direction of Jerusalem.

"But at Jerusalem they found King Herod ruling still."

Hosea and Raheb both made sounds of derision at the mention of the Butcher King.

"After escaping Herod, they were guided by the star to a house in Bethlehem where they found him . . . the infant child."

I paused again.

"His name? Tell us his name, boy?"

"Jesus of Nazareth."

A profound silence existed over the group. No spoons clinked against bowls, no one spoke for the space of ten heartbeats, and then pandemonium broke loose.

"You mean the Healer," Raheb said.

"The Teacher? The Prophet?" Hosea added.

"The one we are going to seek?" Raheb continued. "You've known this all along and never spoke of it until now?"

"I . . . the rabbi sent me to find him too," I said. "But I wasn't sure if I should speak of it or not. Rabbi Kagba had heard that old Herod killed the boy babies of Bethlehem, trying to murder a challenger to his throne. The rabbi says Herod even killed his own sons."

Hosea nodded in agreement.

"That's why Jesus grew up in secret," I said. "But for three years my teacher has been hearing of the miracles and the wisdom of this Jesus." I waited again for the babbling to cease. "My teacher sent me to learn if the stories are true. To see for myself if Messiah has come."

"It is a question written very much on all of our hearts," Hosea acknowledged. "By the Feast of Dedication, we will know."

Chapter 20

*O*ur caravan camped beside a creek flowing down from Mount Hermon. Even though it would still take two more weeks to reach Jerusalem, I felt great excitement on this Sabbath. On the day after tomorrow we would enter the northern reaches of the Promised Land.

I was especially eager to set foot in Eretz-Israel. Soon I would see my grandparents and my brothers.

"From Dan to Beersheba, our land stretches," Hosea said when he announced our location. "Of course, King David ruled much farther north than this. And his son, Solomon, farther still. Now the country is all broken into little patches for this Herod or that Herod . . . but the land is still the land. It will all come right when Messiah comes to rule as King."

The *Havdalah* service had already concluded. Now a mixed group of northbound and southbound travelers swapped gossip by firelight. While the men talked politics, I visited with a pair of ten-year-old twin boys named Jachin and Sorek, who sometimes completed each other's sentences.

"We're going to Damascus," Jachin said.

Sorek concluded, "To see our uncle."

Hugging the pack containing the cup, I asked, "And you come from Jerusalem?"

"Near there," Jachin said. "Bethlehem."

"The place where the Temple lambs are raised," his brother explained.

Hearing the name of the village brought Rabbi Kagba's tale to my mind. "Isn't that where the prophet named Jesus was born?"

"Him? Naw, he's from . . ."

"Nazareth."

"But we saw him once," Jachin added. "Last year, at Tabernacles, I think."

"And you heard him speak?" I persisted.

"Sure," Jachin said. "But we didn't understand what he meant."

Sorek offered, "He said if anyone was thirsty they should come to him and drink. But he didn't have any water with him, not even a cup."

"And what did the grown-ups say to that?" I asked.

"Some of them think he's crazy," Jachin said.

"Some people say he's a prophet, and some say he's King Messiah," Sorek added.

Then Jachin concluded, "But the Pharisees and the priests don't think that. Not at all."

The air was very still that night as I slept . . .

The fronds of the date palms lining the road hung limp in the flickering firelight. The sky revolved overhead.

Eventually the easily recognized form of the Lion of Judah spun into view directly above me, accompanied by one of the seven lights. Awakened by no cause I could identify, I studied the stars. I thought the extra spark of light was Shabbatai but wasn't entirely certain. If the wandering star was in fact the Lord of the Sabbath, there was a close conversation going on between it and the star in the lion's paw called Regulus, the Little King.

"It was on just such a night that David studied the stars," a familiar voice commented. "Like tonight, Shabbatai was in the form of the Lion in those days too. But David's thoughts were on other things."

Even without asking the identity of the speaker, I said, "Hello, Joseph. So you have a story for me about King David?"

"You're already in it," the Dreamer corrected. "Look."

It was true. Without any noise or sense of motion, the caravan camp had vanished. The night sky was identical, including the presence of the Lord of the Sabbath, but now I lay on a hillside in front of a cave. The hilltop was fortified by a stone wall. Looming over the very crown of the knoll was a massive terebinth tree. In the distance the lights of a small village twinkled.

"Where are we?"

"This place is called Adullam," Joseph said. "Over there, those lights you see are Bethlehem."

"But why are we here?"

Joseph gestured for silence and pointed to a ledge a dozen feet away beside the tree trunk. Four men stood there, conversing by the light of a single torch. They were dressed as warriors, with swords by their sides and round shields slung across their backs. Three of the men wore conical metal helmets. The fourth was bareheaded and his hair, like his beard, was red.

The red-haired man spoke. "That's my home there," he said to the other men as he gestured toward the twinkling lights of Bethlehem. "I tended my father's sheep from the time I was eight or nine years old."

A fellow shepherd! I felt an instant connection to the speaker. A shepherd boy, grown into a warrior-king.

"I sometimes led the flock to pasture below this very spot," David continued. "Up here is a good place to watch over them. In those days there were lions in these hills. Bears too sometimes."

The description of the danger caused me to shiver and look over my shoulder. I wished Beni was nearby. I could always rely on the dog for warning.

"Back then, when I was kept many nights away from home," David said, "I looked at the lights, just as now, and dreamed of being back in Bethlehem. Do you know what I missed then? A drink of water from the well by the gate. It still seems to me that no water quenches my thirst like that water does." David shrugged. "The Philistines garrisoned there are worse than any lions or bears. Not only can they not be driven away as easily, but their presence in my home town feels evil to me."

The shepherd king's tired face showed longing, I thought.

David added, "I wish someone would get me a drink from that well!" Then he turned his back on the sight and entered the mouth of the cave.

David's three comrades exchanged looks and nods, but their captain did not witness the sign of agreement. From a stack of weapons beneath the terebinth, each of the three men selected a stout, oak-handled spear mounted with a forged, dagger-shaped blade.

One of the men raised his head and scanned the night, causing me to do the same. "Four hours till dawn," he said.

"Time enough," another agreed, and the three set off down the slope at a jogging pace. "Quiet and speed, yes?"

"Grab hold of my cloak," Joseph instructed me. "Unless you want to try running to keep up with them."

What followed this instruction happened with a rush. With no sense of fear, I found myself soaring over the Judean hills like a hawk on an updraft. Joseph and I spiraled toward the outline of the Lion of Judah, then downward again toward Bethlehem's glow.

"Watch!" Joseph urged.

Though very little time seemed to have passed, David's warrior companions were already on the outskirts of the City of David. Hidden in a creek bed, they waited until a pair of Philistine guards had passed, then burst out of concealment. As quickly as the sentries turned, they were stunned by blows from the spear shafts.

The three Jewish soldiers moved as a single shadow under the eaves of a cottage. Waiting until another sentry moved away, the three flitted across the intervening space toward a gated opening at the far side of the city wall.

I marveled at their bravery. By the light of a single watch fire I counted ten sleeping Philistines. Then I ticked off twenty similar watch fires before losing count. Two hundred of the enemy against three!

"There is the well," Joseph said.

A wooden frame held a leather waterskin balanced above a stone-encircled shaft. The well was near the city gate, but the area around was completely void of shelter or concealment.

Standing beside them in the darkness, I heard David's men converse. They were at the last building before the naked expanse of the village square. There were no guards in sight.

"I'll get the water," the leader of the three instructed, "while you keep watch."

When the loop of rope holding one end of the lever was released, the goatskin bag plunged into the well with a muffled splash. The trio of Jewish warriors froze for an instant at the sound. When no alarm followed, the leader hoisted the bulging container aloft.

Grasping the sack with one hand, he slashed the supporting rope with his sword. "That'll give them a surprise come morning," he said.

The men were halfway back across the open space toward where I stood when warning shouts rang out. "Captain! Two sentries down! Spies in the camp! Sound the alarm!"

A guard in a watchtower over the gate heard the cry and hammered on a shield with his sword. The clanging ripped apart the quiet of the night. Soon the alarm was raised in every corner of Bethlehem.

At the city gate the Jewish captain paused with the water-skin in hand. "Go on," one of his friends urged. "We'll make it hard for them to follow. Just don't spill it!"

Within moments a score of Philistines converged on the gate. The first rank was skewered on Jewish spears, making the others hesitate. Side by side, the pair of David's soldiers fought within the narrow confines of the gate where they could not be outflanked.

Swords rang against shields, and men cried out with pain. A heap of fallen Philistines clogged the portal and had to be dragged aside before fresh troops could continue the battle.

The Jewish soldiers agreed it was time to leave. I also urged them to go, but they could not hear me. "Let's go before they send a company around the outside of the wall behind us."

With final thrusts and slashes, the pair melted into the darkness and sprinted into the brush. Within seconds, it seemed to me, they overtook their leader toting the water bag.

"Back to the cave," Joseph warned. "Hang on."

After a swooping flight that would have done credit to a bat, we were back beneath the terebinth. David's men were already there. David stood beside them, examining the blood oozing from a dozen superficial wounds and calling for them to be attended and their injuries bandaged.

"Where is your cup, lord?" the leader of the trio requested.

Darting into the cave, David's servant emerged with a silver chalice.

"Yours?" I asked.

"And yours, cupbearer," Joseph confirmed.

Holding the cup at arm's length, David allowed his men to raise the waterskin and fill the gleaming container until it overflowed. Drips of water from David's well splashed my feet.

The shepherd king regarded the brimming chalice for a long time. At last he shook his head. Having the men step back a pace, David lifted the cup toward the now-graying sky. "To you, O Lord, I lift this cup." Then, as he poured it out on the ground at the base of the terebinth, he said, "Be it far from me, O Lord, to drink this. Is it not the same as the blood of these men, who went at risk of their very lives? May I ever be worthy of how you have blessed me with friends of such courage, loyalty, and sacrifice."

"See," Joseph instructed me, "where the water pools on the ground and mingles with the blood of David's warriors? Remember: even a cup of water may be a valuable offering. Remember: obtaining a drink of living water may be free and still be costly at the same time. Now wake up, Nehemiah."

"Wake up? I'm not asleep," I protested.

But it was Raheb who shook my arm and repeated the command. A yellow sun hung over the eastern hills. "Are you going to sleep all day?" my protector teased. "Let's get going. Only one more Sabbath till Jerusalem."

My first view of Jerusalem was exactly as my mother had described it to me in countless bedtime stories: "When you see it from afar, you think it's a snow-covered mountain, set with gold. Closer up, you'll see that people from everywhere in the world gather to see the Temple of the Almighty."

Then she added, "We have a reputation. No other people have a God so near and so attentive to their needs.

"If the wind is calm, the smoke of the sacrifices is a thick, black column, propping up the sky. And when the breeze carries it toward you, your mouth will water from the smell of roasting meat and spices. And oh, the music and the babble of voices. You could carry me all over the world, blindfolded, and put me down in Jerusalem, and I would know my home without looking!"

The sights and the sounds and the aroma: it was all true.

I also recalled how Mother frowned sometimes and admitted, "It isn't all wonderful there, Nehi. It is crowded. Some parts are very dirty, and you must be watchful for pickpockets and thieves." Brightening, she concluded, "But it's wonderful to be there, just the same. The Temple, the Temple! There is no other like it in all the world. And your grandparents will be so proud when they meet you. So very proud!"

Now that the moment of meeting was fast approaching, I hoped her words remained true. I was nervous about the news I carried but intensely eager to see them and my brothers.

It was late afternoon on the first day of Hanukkah when I parted from the caravan at the Damascus Gate. Hosea's charges had arrived at an inn outside the northern wall of the city. Raheb and his family were going to accompany me to the Street of the Weavers before saying good-bye.

However, just inside the battlements, patrolled by Roman sentries, we met a crowd of people flowing toward the Temple Mount. "Hold on, friend," Raheb said, accosting a passerby. "Is it time for the evening sacrifice? Is that why everyone is rushing?"

Squinting at the winter sun obscured by clouds, the man shook his head. "It's the rabbi from Nazareth," he explained. "He's teaching and healing up there on the mount. Everyone is going to watch and listen. Some say he may be arrested . . . or will flee. This may be our last chance to see him." Pulling free, the man dashed away with the multitude.

Gathering in a doorway out of the press of the throng, Raheb said, "You hear? He's there now—Jesus! Tobit, your eyes! We should go at once so we don't miss him." To me, he added, "Nehemiah? You'll come with us. Yes? You want to see Jesus too? We'll take you to the shop afterward."

I wanted to see Jesus . . . but I wanted my own family more.

"Just go," I offered. "I know my way from here. Mama taught me. It's this way," I said, pointing. "Two turns and the Street of the Weavers is right there. I can't miss it."

Raheb looked doubtful. "I don't think . . ."

"Please," I insisted. "I want you to. And I will see you again, I promise." Looking pointedly at the scarf wound around Tobit's head, shielding his damaged eyes, I concluded, "You must not miss Jesus."

After that, our good-byes were brief. Michael hugged me, said he'd never forget me. Raheb and his sons told me I had been a great blessing to them on the trail. Raheb renewed his vow that even after paying my debt to the caravan, he still owed me far more than he could repay for rescuing his granddaughter.

All the time their eyes returned to the Temple Mount. The air rang with the clatter of sandals going to see the Healer.

"Go on!" I said again.

And they were gone.

I made my way up the crowded Street of the Weavers. Every caravansary and inn and private house was bursting with travelers who had come for the holiday. I was lucky. I knew I had a place to stay. I imagined knocking on the door of my grandparents' shop and meeting them for the first time. What a celebration there would be!

A sudden breeze coursed through the narrow lane like icy water in a river. Snowflakes swirled like downy feathers around me.

The faces of travelers turned up in wonder as they trudged through the unusual weather. Hands extended, palm up, to catch the flakes. Children tasted frozen water for the first time. It was a sort of miraculous sign to many who believed that any unusual storm or event in nature was sent by God as a message from heaven. What was the Lord saying on this snowy afternoon in Jerusalem? To religious Jews, pure white covering Jerusalem was the Lord's promise that Israel's sins, though as scarlet, would soon be made as white as snow. What else could it mean?

Not all considered the weather a blessing, however. Few beggars were in sight; the storm had driven them underground. I spotted Herodian and Roman soldiers scattered among Jewish travelers. Many had come to the Street of the Weavers to shop for heavy winter cloaks. My fleece boots and sheepskin coat protected me from the chill. I was dressed as the son of a shepherd would dress in winter. It was fortunate that when I had fled I was clothed in the proper gear of a cold mountain autumn. Even so, my nose and ears were cold.

I pitied the ragged street urchins in tattered clothes who made their living as torch bearers and who lived in the quarries beneath the Temple Mount. A half-dozen boys about my age clustered around a feeble scrap wood fire burning on the street in a metal pot. The boys were known as link boys or Jerusalem Sparrows, a poor and too plentiful flock. As pilgrims passed the boys called out, offering to serve as city guides. It was not yet dark enough for travelers to need torches, so business was bad for them. The Sparrows kept one another warm by huddling close.

I thought about the Messiah I had come to find, the king named Jesus whom Rabbi Kagba had knelt before. Was Jesus in Jerusalem too? Did he raise his face to the sky and smile as snowflakes clung to his beard? Rabbi Kagba had seen him as a baby during this same season when snow had fallen on Bethlehem and the Hanukkah lights had blazed in the Temple. I knew every detail of the story, including the horrific slaughter of Bethlehem's babies by Herod.

Thirty-three years had passed since the birthday of the Son of David. Not much had changed. The Romans were still here. The Herodian guard patrolled the crowds of Jerusalem. Where was this man called Jesus who would drink from Joseph's cup and lead our people to freedom? Rabbi Kagba had taught me that when Jesus was crowned, there would be no more suffering or poverty.

I searched faces, but no one looked kingly to me. The poor were everywhere. Clearly King Jesus was not yet on his throne.

Snow crunched beneath my feet. I tucked my chin deeper into my coat as my anticipation grew. I felt as if I knew this lane well. My mother's stories of her home had prepared me for the noise and the bustle of Hanukkah pilgrim crowds. Merchants

179

were removing woolen cloth, heavy wool cloaks, and finished prayer shawls from the fronts of shops. I knew from my mother that I would find my grandparents' business was the best and the busiest, always crowded and prosperous. I imagined her here as a little girl, and my longing for her became almost unbearable. I refused to let myself cry. I was too big for that. I had been through too much to give in now. Only a few minutes more and my grandmother would wrap her arms around me. *Did she look like Mama?* I wondered.

Mama had mentioned the smells of the city. But today the white blanket of snow hid the sheep dung and garbage littering the pavement and filled cracks and crevasses until rough-hewn stones were smooth. Along with the scent of damp wool cloaks, the fresh, familiar tang of snowfall reminded me of winter in my mountain home.

In the midst of the holiday crowds, the pristine meadows and pine trees of my homeland seemed another world away. I wondered about my mother and father. For the first time I considered how I would tell my brothers and my grandparents about the bandit attack and my adventures as I traveled to Jerusalem. I would not be able to report as to the fate of my mother and father. Would my brothers think I was a coward for running away? Would they believe me if I told them about Joseph's cup, the Great White Hart, and my thousand-mile trek to find the Messiah? I hoped they would not be angry that I had not returned to the camp to find out if my parents were alive.

Even so, I was energized by the excitement of seeing my brothers again and meeting my grandparents for the first time.

"Fourth shop from the high end of the Weavers," I recited, navigating the final steps carefully so as not to slip on paving stones.

The light in the sky grew dim. I looked to the top of the street and counted down. "One . . . two . . . three . . . four!"

I gasped and halted in my tracks. The little shop of Boaz the Weaver was gutted from fire. A white carpet of new-fallen snow in front of the charred door had no footprints.

I had traveled one thousand miles! It could not be that I had come so far for nothing!

I counted doors from the head of the street again. "One, two, three!" Tears brimmed over. I wiped them away with the back of my hand.

Plucking at the sleeve of a heavily cloaked woman, I cried, "I am looking for the shop of Boaz the Weaver! Do you know—"

"Burned down." She jerked her thumb toward the shell. "'Twas the finest weaver on the street. Some say 'twas no accident."

"But . . . are they all dead?"

She mumbled on. "Murder, if it was set deliberate. One perished in the disaster."

"One dead! Who?"

Her tone was matter-of-fact. Old news. Grief over and done with. "It was a visiting grandson what died. Roof fell in on him."

One of my brothers, dead! I stared in horror at the fallen beams and scorched stone. "Which? What was his name?"

"Lord above, I couldn't say. Big family it was. So many of them."

"Where are the others?"

The woman stared at me with sudden interest. "And who are you?"

"When did it happen?" I had imagined the reunion with such joy.

"Autumn. Around Tabernacles. But . . . who are you that it matters?"

181

Tears streaked my cheeks. No holding them back. "I'm Nehemiah. Youngest son of Lamsa and of Sarah, who used to weave here in her father's shop. I'm grandson of Boaz the Weaver whose shop this was. My three brothers were here . . . It was . . . You speak of my brother and the fire! Dead in the fire! But which brother? Do you know the name?" Images of my older brothers at our parting so long ago flooded my memory. Who could imagine that we would never see one another again?

She considered me in stunned silence. "You! Here? Son of Sarah! And herself married a herdsman from Babylon. Herself gone so long and so far away. Don't know which grandson it was that died. There are more than a few grandsons. You know that well enough. It's a big clan. Where is your mother, boy?"

I could not take my eyes from the rubble. "I . . . I don't know," I whispered. "My grandfather Boaz. My grandmother . . . Mama lived here. I know the stories. Fourth door from the top of the Street of Weavers. I came to find them. My family. My brothers. Please! Can you help me?"

"They've gone away, I heard, to live near your mother's sister."

"But where?"

She clucked her tongue. "You poor child. Where's your mother? Your father? I imagine they aren't far from you, eh? Well, it'll be hard news for them."

"My mother has many sisters. Where are my grandparents? My grandfather? Boaz the Weaver? Please tell me if you know."

"Sorry. Can't say. Don't know. Not sure. Gone to the seashore, I heard. Lost everything. Some reason for the bad fortune, no doubt. Punishment doesn't come without a reason. So. You never know."

Anger against her welled up in me. How could she say such a thing? Accuse so unjustly? What had my father and mother done wrong to deserve an attack by bandits? What had I done wrong to lose my family and my pleasant life? "You are wrong! And it's wrong to say such a thing!"

She raised her head indignantly and sniffed the wind. "I see you are an insolent, prideful boy. Pride. Reason enough for the House of Boaz to burn down over his head. Tell your mother and father when they come. Go to the elders at the Temple. Your grandfather's prayer shawls . . . famous, as you know. Your family was very proud of that, I am sure." She sniffed. "Someone among the priests will no doubt have the details of where they've gone. Where to find them." She brushed her hands on her skirt, indicating our conversation was over. "You should learn to respect your elders, or worse than this will come upon you. Even so . . . I am sorry for your bad fortune, boy." She scurried off, leaving me alone in the middle of the darkening street.

Chapter 21

The gloom of twilight settled over the Street of the Weavers. I sank onto a cold, blackly charred beam in the ruins of my grandfather's shop and wept. Months of longing and hope for reunion with my family were turned to ashes beneath my feet. I felt the presence of death in this place where my brother died. Which brother? Who among the three was no longer living? In my imagination I lived the deaths of each. I tried to picture my world without them.

I touched Joseph's cup, wrapped in the bag beneath my cloak. Oh, the suffering of all who had drunk from this cup! I closed my eyes a long moment. When I opened them again, I saw the city in a new way. The world around me had a sharpness of detail I had never seen before. Death had brought a new clarity to life. Beyond the shattered walls of my grandfather's shop, crowds thinned and businesses were shuttered.

As it darkened, Hanukkah candles appeared in the windows of homes and businesses. The warm glow and companionship of the orphan Sparrows' fire beckoned me. Several boys lit their torches and hailed travelers, leading them away from the Street of the Weavers. I climbed out of the destruction of my life and made my way down the steps to the watch fire.

Four Sparrows remained, warming hands and backsides

when I approached the blaze. Their torches were yet unlit, propped against a wall. Potential customers seemed fewer than ever. I hesitated just beyond the ring of light. Surly young faces lifted. Eyes narrowed with suspicion. They stared at me, hating me for the warmth of my fleece coat and mountain boots.

The leader, a gaunt boy of about eleven, considered me. "You want a torch, or what?"

A red-haired boy about my age rubbed his hands together. "He don't want a torch. He's been up the street there, visiting ghosts."

Two dark-haired boys, whom I guessed to be brothers, exchanged a glance. "Ghosts?"

Their red-haired companion nodded. "He's been up in the ruins of the weaver Boaz. Ain't you, kid?"

I nodded.

The leader tilted his head and took a step toward me. "You're not from around here. Not with such a coat and warm boots. Where are you from?"

I answered, "From the land where Eden used to be. Paradise . . . north of Babylon. The great mountains beyond the two rivers."

"I am Timothy," said the leader. "That is Red. On account of his hair. And these brothers are Obed and Jesse. Their father was a religious sort before the Romans killed him."

"I am called Nehi. Nehemiah. But Nehi to all who know me."

"Why are you here?" the brothers asked in unison.

"My family." The words caught in my throat.

Red asked, "What was you doing in the ruins of the weaver's shop?"

I could barely speak. "My mother grew up there. It belonged to my grandfather and his father on back for generations."

185

Timothy raised his chin. "So, are you related to Boaz?"

Red echoed the question. "Your mother? She the daughter of old Boaz and his wife?"

I nodded. "Boaz. My grandfather. I came all this way to find them."

Red snorted. "Well, you come here for nothing. They've been gone awhile. I seen the fire. Never seen anything burn so hot or fast. There was a young man died in it too. Burned up. Horrible thing. Screaming for help. No help for it. A grandson. What relation of yours?"

"Please. Do you know the name of the boy who was killed?"

The four Sparrows exchanged looks, but none had an answer. "Sorry."

"I had three brothers," I replied hoarsely. "Now I have two. But I don't know which one died."

This revelation brought silence to us all. I held my palm over the fire, then drew it back quickly. Too close to the heat. I imagined . . .

The leader cleared his throat. "Your grandparents were good to us boys, always. She, the lady, brought us fresh bread sometimes. Not crumbs or scraps, but real hot, steamy, fresh bread."

"She was good to us," the brothers agreed.

Red added, "I suppose we should return the favor. What are your plans, Nehi?"

"I don't have any plans now." I glanced toward the ruins. "There is what is left of my plans."

The leader puckered his brow. "Nice coat and boots. You'll be warm enough."

"I am grateful to the Eternal. Grateful for . . ." Though I was grateful for my warm clothes, the grief I felt made gratitude for anything else difficult.

Red asked, "Where will you sleep tonight?"

I shrugged. "Don't know."

Timothy instructed, "Stay with us, then. We are going to the Temple Courts tonight. They'll be lighting the giant Menorah and giving out bread to everyone after the service."

"We share what we get, see?" Red said. "If I get a crust, but you get a whole loaf, we share equal. Get it?"

One of the brothers spoke. "And you can sleep with us Sparrows in the quarry afterward. It's the least we can do, seeing how your grandmother fed us. We have charcoal fires there to warm us, and we divide the bread among ourselves."

Red put his arm around my shoulder. "Come on, then. You've come to the right place."

I could not speak to thank them. The lump in my throat made it hard to swallow. I had gone from being alone and friendless to being taken in and cared for by the orphan boys whom my grandmother had cared for.

It was because of free bread that I missed meeting Jesus of Nazareth that very night. The brothers, unlit torches in hand, wanted to immediately find fares to guide.

Red and Timothy argued against it: "If you come too late, the loaves will be all gone. Every beggar in Jerusalem will be on the steps below the Royal Porch."

As the brothers scampered away in the gathering gloom, Jesse retorted over his shoulder, "We heard there's a band of pilgrims coming in from Bethany tonight. We'll earn enough pennies to buy our own bread!"

When I questioned Red about it, he replied there was no reason not to have both bread and pennies, so he and Tim and

I set out. At the far south end of the Temple Mount, a group of Pharisees distributed barley loaves. It was a *mitzvah* to provide for the needy, and the Pharisees made a great show of it. An assembly of the ultra-pious fraternity, in sumptuous robes and broad phylacteries, gathered on the steps between two passageways. They looked on from some distance away as their servants tended wicker baskets of round, hard bread. When each container was emptied, a trumpet blew to signal that another full vessel had been uncovered.

As we waited in a line of beggars, Tim remarked in a low voice, "The bread doesn't taste worse because they blow their trumpets over it."

"The Pharisees always salt their gifts that way," Red added with a grin.

I was warm enough in my cloak and boots, but my friends stomped their feet and clapped their hands as we waited in the cold. The file of waiting supplicants snaked back and forth across the steps. It moved forward very slowly.

As we neared the front of the line, someone hurriedly approached the largest Pharisee. The man's sandals clattered on the steps in his haste. "He's there now," I heard the man say. "Solomon's Colonnade."

Three of the Pharisees gathered in conference. It was then I overheard them mention the name Jesus.

"Jesus of Nazareth?" I repeated.

"Has to be," Tim said. "Look at how agitated the fat Pharisee is."

"Jesus is here? Now?"

"Other side of the mount," my friend said. "You want to see him?"

I nodded eagerly.

"Come on, then." Darting around the three people ahead of us in the queue, Red snatched up two loaves of bread and shouted a thank-you while Tim secured one more.

"This way," Red urged. "In here."

There were two tunnels in the south face of the Temple Mount, called the Huldah Gate in honor of the prophetess. These passages led beneath the Royal Porch. Sloping steeply upward, they opened onto the Temple plaza at the south end of the Court of the Gentiles.

We emerged from corridors choked with the smoke and soot of flickering torches to be blasted by cold air. Snow had begun to sweep across the expansive courtyard. The plaza was brightly lit by four towering menorahs. Shining in the lamp-light, swirling showers of snow formed lazy spirals. Leaning back, I looked up. The descending pillars of icy crystals reached into the sky like ghostly fluted columns.

"But where is he?" I said with frustration.

"This way," Tim urged, and we sprinted on. We hugged our loaves of bread as we ran. I kept one hand on Joseph's cup.

From a distance I heard the Levite choirs singing hymns of praise and thanksgiving. I saw a crowd of people jammed between the shuttered booths of the moneychangers and the columned portico lining the eastern rim of the court.

"There." Red pointed. "He'll be in the middle of that mob."

"Wait," Tim warned, laying his hand on my arm to stop my headlong charge. "Temple guards."

A dozen green-uniformed and helmeted sentries marched with purpose toward the assembly. Reaching the back of the throng, they roughly thrust the onlookers aside.

"What? What's happening?" I demanded, tugging against Tim's restraint.

"You know the high priest doesn't like this Jesus," Tim said.

"Looks like they're going to arrest him for sure," Red added.

"Arrest the Messiah? Why?"

Yanking me around in front of him, Tim demanded, "What do you know about it? You said you just got here."

"Yes, but I . . . I have to see him."

I was too late.

Fearful of the scowling guards, the crowd dispersed.

Red gestured to the pair of brother Sparrows who edged toward them. "What's happened?" he asked as they drew near.

"Jesus, the rabbi from Galilee," one brother said. "He was with the folks from Bethany. They hired us to link for them."

"The priests was going to arrest him," the other sibling explained.

"Or kill him. Said he was a blasphemer. We was standing near him."

"That's how we helped. We saw the guards and snuffed out our torches . . . and Jesus slipped away."

"Away," I repeated in distress. I could not locate my family, and now I had let my mission slip away as well. "Where's he gone?"

"Why does it matter?" Red asked. "He's escaped."

I started to explain, then stopped as I spotted the embroidered hem of a prayer shawl flapping in the breeze. That bright blue band with the scalloped rim embroidered with white letters of the *Shema* was my mother's workmanship. There could not be two shawls that much alike.

Pulling free of Tim's hand, I approached the young man wearing the shawl and tugged at his arm. "Sir," I said, "that tallith. Did you get it at the shop of Boaz?"

The tall, aristocratic-looking man smiled. "In fact I did. Why do you ask?"

"Because I am their grandson. I am Nehemiah. Called Nehi. I just came here from beyond the two rivers to find them." It was too difficult to explain, and I waved my hand in frustration.

"By your accent I knew you are from the East," the man said.

"My mother, Sarah, is their daughter. I didn't know their shop had burned. Do you know . . . can you tell me . . . where my family has gone?"

Again the smile. "It so happens, I can. My shawl . . . your mother's work, yes? Her skill sought after and well known. I ordered it a year and a half ago and received delivery only weeks before the fire. So, Joppa. On the seacoast. Staying near relatives. Does that help?"

"Yes. My aunt, Mother's older sister, lives there. Her husband, Adonijah, is an exporter of woolen cloth."

"I know Adonijah, the fabric exporter. Your aunt and uncle live near the custom house at the quay."

"One more thing, sir. They say one of my brothers . . . perished in the fire. Do you know . . . I mean, I don't even know which . . ."

Sorrow clouded the cheerful face. "I heard someone had been lost, but no, I'm sorry. I don't know his name." He gazed at me intently. "Nehemiah, do you have a place to stay, boy?"

Looking back at the row of raggedly dressed Sparrows, an elbow peeking out of a rent in a cloak here and a knee showing through a hole there, I knew I could not desert them. "Yes," I said. "I am with friends."

"Very well, then. Should you need me, my name is Joseph of Arimathea . . . the Younger. The Sparrows are clever. They can find my home if you need me. And since it's too cold for many fares tonight, boys, here." Joseph shook a leather bag of coins over each upturned palm, dispensing pennies, then met my eyes again. "Joppa," he said again. "You'll find them."

He turned to go. The snow was falling harder now, obscuring the flames of the menorahs.

"One more thing, please," I pleaded. "Rabbi Jesus. Do you know where he's gone?"

"After tonight," Joseph said, casting an angry glance toward a knot of priests pushing beggars out of the way in their haste to escape the cold, "I believe he would be wise to leave Jerusalem. What his destination might be . . ." He sighed and we parted.

Timothy rubbed his cheek as he considered the departing merchant. The prayer shawl billowed in the breeze like the lifted wings of a soaring bird. "So, Joseph of Arimathea knows your family. I'm impressed. He is a rich man. You are well connected. Why would you choose to stay with us rather than in his mansion?"

I shrugged. "You said you would share the bread with me. I've been looking forward to it all night."

"Well then. Come on." Red clapped me on the back. "Bread and pennies, see? And a nice warm cavern to go home to."

I felt safe in the company of the link boys. Their torches lit the way for us as we made our way down the slick paths to the caverns beneath the Temple Mount.

Red locked arms with mine. We held one another steady. He explained the working of the Sparrows' charity as we descended into the vast shelter. Solomon's quarry was reserved for the orphan sons of Jerusalem.

By decree of the ruling seventy of the Sanhedrin, Solomon's former stone quarry was a shelter for torch-bearing Sparrows from the ages of about five to twelve. In recent years, after bullying and abuse had increased among the population, married couples who were servants of righteous families took turns living in the cavern as custodians. These were called shepherds. The shepherds' tent was erected inside at the center of the quarry. Outside the tent flap a fire blazed in a rock-lined pit like the hub of a wheel. From the center, smaller camp fires spread like spokes. The number of Sparrows varied. This month Red told me there were just under two hundred boys. These were organized and grouped by age. The youngest and most vulnerable children slept nearest the main fire and the overseers' tent. *They were like the lambs in my father's lambing caves*, I thought, as we neared the entrance of the shelter.

We approached a row of latrines outside and stopped to use them.

Timothy explained, "It's not so bad. We all contribute our wages. Work crews of boys haul water and wash clothing. The older boys cook and help distribute bread. Torches are donated by the Temple charity. That fellow you met, Joseph of Arimathea, is a big contributor."

I involuntarily touched Joseph's cup tied at my waist. I pondered the fact that, just like Joseph of old and his coat of many colors, I had met a man named Joseph who now wore my mother's finest prayer shawl. *Did it mean something?* I wondered.

"Our fares are set by law," Red continued. "Nobody dares cheat us these days. We get paid when we carry our torches. Whoever don't pay gets hauled up before the judges and whipped."

Timothy coughed into his hand. "It's better now than when I first came. In the spring, when the days get longer, we don't have so much business. The farmers come, and lots of boys get hired to work outside the city. Lucky ones get apprenticed in trades."

Red pantomimed a hammer blow. "I'd like to be a blacksmith. Work by a forge. Never be cold again. That's what I'd like. But . . . it's not so bad."

Timothy plucked my sleeve. "Except we have no one . . . not like a family. Not like somebody like you. A shepherd's son. What a coat. And such boots."

Red agreed. "If you was on your own, going to Joppa, there's some in the pass who would kill you for such a coat and boots. But not here. They can't hurt you here."

Again my thoughts went to the danger of travel and the offer of Joseph of Arimathea to help me. Perhaps I should speak with him again.

The Sparrows' cavern was dimly lit by the fires. Smoke curled lazily upward and drifted like mist against the blackened stone ceiling. Groups of Sparrows made their nests in fresh straw.

I followed my new friends to the shepherds' tent, where we placed our bread into heaping baskets for distribution.

Timothy said over his shoulder, "You know what I heard about Jesus? The one you're so keen to meet? He fed five thousand people with five loaves of bread and two fish."

Red shook his head in disbelief. "We sure could use someone like him here in Jerusalem."

"Aye," Timothy agreed. "But no wonder the priests hate him so. If even half the rumors are true about Jesus, he makes them and all their fine charity look small, don't he?"

Red argued, "Don't know why he doesn't just call down fire from heaven, if he's the Messiah like they say. He healed a blind beggar named Peniel, who begged his whole life at Nicanor

Gate. If he can give Peniel eyes, why can't he make bread grow from trees?"

I asked, "Why don't you follow him and see for yourself?"

The boys exchanged an uneasy look. Timothy explained, "You know what would happen if we left our place to follow Jesus?"

Red blurted, "They'd throw us out, just like they did to poor Peniel after he could see. The elders chased him out of Jerusalem. Told him to never come back to synagogue! Threatened his parents. He was disowned. If us Sparrows went out the gates even one time to meet Jesus? When we came back, our places would be gone. There'd be some other boy carrying my torch."

"It ain't worth it."

"No. Ain't worth it," Red echoed. Dozens of fellow link boys hailed my friends as we passed. This was a sort of family. They were brothers, united by suffering and loneliness. They were bonded, just as the shepherds' families who watched my father's flocks were bonded to one another. I realized this was the one haven of safety for orphans in the vast and dangerous city. For a Sparrow to lose his place beside the fires of Solomon's quarry was to lose everything.

We washed in a common trough and then made our way to the circle of twenty-five boys, where Timothy and Red introduced me all around. Then we heaped up clean straw to make our beds.

My stomach growled. "How much longer?"

Red raised a finger. "The last of the brothers will be returning soon. We count them all. Timothy is captain of our circle. He will count and report. We don't eat until we're all in the roost, so to speak. Not one is left out."

Minutes ticked past, and stragglers arrived at the cave one

by one. They snuffed out their torches and picked their way through their companions settling into their home group.

It was late, and baskets of bread had yet to be divided and distributed. I was exhausted from grief and disappointment. Hunger gnawed at my belly and kept me awake. I fixed my gaze on the shepherds' tent, waiting for an adult to emerge and take charge.

"When?" I asked again.

Timothy shrugged, counted the boys in our circle, then stood. "Wait here," he instructed. He made his way toward the bread baskets outside the overseers' tent. Waiting in a line of other captains, he seemed confident and undisturbed by hunger pains. At last an elderly couple emerged. The white-haired man raised his hands and blessed the meal, then took charge of distributing a half loaf for each Sparrow to our captains.

Red said, "If all your family is dead, maybe you can come here. Come live with us all. Become a Sparrow."

I gave a half smile and thanked him for the invitation.

From here and there in the cave I heard the sound of coughing. It was hard to imagine being sick without my mother to tend me. I tried to imagine living the lonely life of a boy in Solomon's quarry. A hush of anticipation fell over the cavern.

My eyes stung with tears as I took my bread from Timothy. What if all my family was dead? Or what if I couldn't find them? I remembered my mother's cooking in the sheep camp. Meat roasting over the fire. Sometimes trout. Fresh bread slathered with butter. Vegetables. Nuts and dried fruit. Rich cheese.

I held the crust of bread in my hands and tried to be thankful. How I longed for Mama's gentle voice and sweet prayers for me as she lit the *Shabbat* candles.

Timothy sat down cross-legged beside me. "What are you

staring at? This isn't bread Jesus conjured up. Looking at it won't make it grow bigger." He tore at his morsel. "Eat!"

I nodded and raised the scrap of supper to my mouth. It was tasteless and stale. The generosity of the Temple charity was somehow tarnished by the lack of quality of the bread. But when a boy was starving, he would not complain.

I studied Red as he picked off small mouthfuls and seemed to savor each bite. Behind, in the ring of younger boys, someone began to cough with the force of a barking dog.

Timothy paused but did not raise his eyes. After a while he replied, "It's the season when so many boys get sick. The sickness carries many away." Then he leaned close to me. "Nehi, get away from here. Quickly. Tomorrow. Go see the man who wears your mother's prayer shawl. Beg a favor of him. An escort to Joppa. Find your family if you can. Leave this place."

Chapter 22

*T*he day was cold, the air clear and biting. Blackened snow, fouled with soot and grit and churned into slush underfoot, was heaped in corners and alleyways. Only the parapets surrounding the roofs and the tops of walls enclosing terraces and gardens still boasted coats of pure white.

Red, Timothy, and I stood outside the gates of the manor belonging to Joseph of Arimathea, the Younger. It was set just inside the wall of the Holy City, on a hill atop Jerusalem's far southwestern border. The home was modest in comparison to the palace of High Priest Caiaphas, or that of another Pharisee named Nicodemus, both of whose dwellings we had passed in coming from the caverns. Yet those grand homes were near enough to be called neighbors. The finely fitted amber sandstone of this wall and the ornate scrollwork of this gate proclaimed the wealth of the family within.

I was at my destination, but now I hesitated. My fingers touched the knob of a bell pull that hung beside the gate. I flinched away from the chilly brass and stopped.

"Go on," Timothy urged. Guessing at the cause of my reluctance, he added, "He said you could call on him for help."

I offered a crooked grin. "That was kind of him." Sweeping

one hand across my shepherd's garb, I continued, "But this is daylight. Do I look like I belong inside these walls?"

"So he gives us each another penny and tells us to go away," Red said pragmatically. "Go on, ring it. If you don't, I will."

Plucking up my courage, I gave the rope a tug. We heard no corresponding signal from within.

"Harder!" Timothy ordered.

This time a melodious jangling sounded inside the enclosed courtyard, followed immediately by the rhythm of swiftly tapping feet. We heard the sliding swish of a bolt being withdrawn. The portal was opened by a pleasant-faced woman older than my mother, but of the same size and build, and about the age I guessed my grandmother to be.

"Bless me," she said, running her eyes over the three of us, then fixing her gaze on me. "However did you get here so soon? And where have you left Abel?"

"Ma'am?" I said. "Is this the home of Joseph the Younger?"

"Of Arimathea the Younger," Timothy corrected.

"Aren't you the link boys I sent Abel to summon?"

I was baffled and then grateful when Timothy responded as our leader. With a bow he indicated Red and himself. "We have the honor to be Jerusalem Sparrows. At your service. But we don't know of any summons, nor were we sent here by anyone named Abel."

"Then why have you come?" she asked, bending forward. Her brow furrowed, but it displayed the same good-natured lines as her smiling mouth. Suddenly her expression cleared, and she put her knuckles on her hips. "Wait! What did you say your names were?"

"I'm Timothy, this is Red, and the one we guided here . . .

the one who is seeking admittance . . . is Nehemiah of Amadiya."

She laughed then, a peal of laughter that rivaled the chimes of the bell pull.

The youthful form of Joseph of Arimathea, again wearing my mother's unique handiwork, emerged from the home's entry across the courtyard. "Hadassah? Have they come? I want to send for—" As his eyes lighted on me, he stopped.

Grasping my shoulders, Hadassah pulled me in front of her, facing the young master. "I believe you wanted to locate Nehemiah, grandson of Boaz the Weaver?" she said.

The housekeeper ushered us into the receiving room of the home, where I encountered still more surprises: Raheb and his son Tobit, from the caravan, were also there!

"So now our party is complete, I think," Joseph said. "But perhaps explanations are called for."

The mystery was soon unraveled. Joseph said, "I did not realize you had traveled with my friends. Otherwise I would have insisted that you come home with me. You see, my father is partners in business with Raheb here, and the two of them with Lazarus of Bethany."

I was listening to the explanation, but I could not stop staring at Tobit's face. There were no bandages, and his eyes were not watering or red or puffy.

"They were in the group from Bethany I met on the Temple Mount," Joseph continued. "And they have been staying in the Bethany home where Jesus of Nazareth has also been residing. I think Tobit may want to add something."

Both Tobit and his father wore wide grins.

"Healed me!" Tobit responded. "I knelt beside Jesus. He

dabbed my eyes with mud, then told me to go and wash. Now I can see perfectly!"

"And Dinah, my boy Yacov's wife," Raheb added cheerfully, "says she believes she will be barren no longer. Says when she touched the fringe of the rabbi's tallith she felt something change, knows it."

I had missed my own encounter with Jesus of Nazareth. "That is truly amazing, wonderful news," I said. Then I asked Joseph, "But you sent for me, sir?"

He smiled. "I thought about it all the way home from the service. It is not an easy or a safe road for a boy to travel to Joppa alone. I have a load of exports I'm taking to a ship waiting there. You can go with me. Two more days, and then on your way."

Two days, and Jesus no farther away than a home in Bethany? "You are very kind. Thank you." I could see Jesus, complete my mission, and then locate my family in Joppa. I said as much to the group.

Raheb shook his head. "They've gone. The teacher and his band of students."

"Gone where? Gone far?"

"Far enough, I suppose," Raheb explained. "The other end of the country. Up to Perea, they said. Complete wrong direction from Joppa altogether."

Once more I found myself part of a caravan, but it was a far cry from tramping through the brush, herding goats. Joseph of Arimathea rode a fine, prancing sorrel horse at the head of a file of ten camels loaded with trade goods. This was a wealthy commercial venture, carrying the wines of Bethany for shipment abroad. Wicker baskets strapped to the flanks of the camels each contained amphorae of the latest vintage.

There were no straggling drovers coaxing lame animals, nor any lost children to be accounted for. The journey from Jerusalem to the sea coast would be completed in two days, rather than the weeks I had spent on the trail from Zakho. Instead of walking, I was mounted on a cooperative red-haired donkey named Esau. The bindings securing the fleece pad on which I rode were silk. Though still dressed in my thick coat and shepherd's boots, I felt like a prince.

We were accompanied by Terah, Joseph's steward. All the camel drovers were armed with short swords. Counting myself, we made a party of thirteen. As one of the main highways in Judea, the road from Jerusalem to Joppa was patrolled by Roman legionaries, a party of whom overtook us in quick march. The Roman officer, a centurion on a black horse, saluted Joseph as he rode by.

After we passed a village identified for me by Joseph as Emmaus, we entered a narrow, rock-walled canyon. The track descended rapidly from the heights of Jerusalem.

"This is the same route Joshua followed when he routed the Amorites," Joseph observed. "And the same course Judah Maccabee came up when he launched the great battle near Emmaus and freed our land from the Greeks."

I was surprised when, a mile later, the road climbed back out of the gorge, crossing the summit of a row of hills to its south.

Once atop the ridge, we paused to let the animals rest. Joseph handed me a bottle of water flavored with lemon juice and a sesame seed cake dripping with honey and scented with cinnamon.

We rested beside a shining bronze plaque affixed to a stone

pylon. Even though I had never been on this road before, I did not need to see the newly placed mile marker to know we were on a recently completed Roman road. The perfectly smooth, level, cobblestone surface, bordered on both sides by curbing, attested to the efforts of the Empire.

"Say what you like about the Romans," Joseph confided in me, "but they are superior engineers. The two greatest needs of this land are aqueducts for water and better roads. The Romans surveyed this." He swept his hand over the ravine from which we had emerged. "For a thousand years and more, the road to Jerusalem has gone up that canyon, following every bend of the stream bed. This new route saves three miles of the journey and is much more pleasant."

The wind out of the west had a surprising saltiness about it. A distant line of dark blue, bisecting the world from north to south, confirmed that I really did scent the ocean.

We camped for the night eighteen miles from Jerusalem. The hill on which we stopped was the last elevation above the coastal lowlands. The Plain of Sharon spread out before us—a tattered blanket sporting patches of brown earth, yellow stubbled fields, and gray rock outcroppings.

The sun was still high in the west. Joseph saw my questioning look and answered my unspoken query. "There is good water here—and some grazing. Better than we would find on the lower slopes. Tomorrow will be an easy half day's journey."

Within moments a pavilion was set up for Joseph, which he invited me to share. A fire was kindled, and a haunch of mutton soon roasted on a spit. South of our chosen camping place was a solitary knoll crowned with the tumbled stones of a ruined fortress.

"Gezer," Joseph said. "Built by the Canaanites long ages ago, then captured by the Philistines and the Egyptians in turn. Later it was fortified by King Solomon."

"But no one lives there now?" I asked.

"Owls and badgers and foxes. Why?"

"I thought I saw someone moving among the boulders at its summit."

Shading his eyes against the sunset, Joseph studied the remains of Gezer. "A wild goat, perhaps?" He shrugged. "Tell me again the story your rabbi told you, the one about seeking the infant Jesus."

Even Rabbi Kagba seldom drilled me as did Joseph of Arimathea on that occasion. He wanted to know every detail, making me rack my brain for barely remembered bits of the tale. Between bites of roast meat and chunks of fresh bread, I tried to keep pace with Joseph's insatiable appetite for more about Jesus of Nazareth.

"All within the Sign of the Two Fish: Jupiter, the Righteous King, and Saturn, the Lord of the Sabbath . . . coming together and moving apart and coming together again, three times in a year and a half." I waved my dinner knife toward the horizon. Jupiter, together with Mars and the moon, danced between the signs of the Bull and the Twin Brothers.

"The Sign of the Two Fish means our nation," Joseph said eagerly. Lifting his chin into the breeze, he murmured wistfully, "Could it be true? Could Messiah come in our lifetime? Could the cup of prophecy be filled and ready to be drained?"

At his words I touched again Joseph's cup at my waist and remembered more of what my teacher had said. "'And a sword will pierce your heart too,'" I quoted from memory.

"Eh? What's that?"

I recounted what Rabbi Kagba had told me about the prophecy over Jesus' mother at his dedication in the Temple. "The rabbi did not like the sound of those words."

Joseph shook his head slowly. "Neither do I. There is much I do not understand. In one place Holy Scripture says Messiah will 'proclaim freedom for the captives and release from darkness for the prisoners.'[1] Like releasing us from the grip of Rome," he added in an aside to me. "But in another place doesn't it say, 'He was pierced for our transgressions, he was crushed for our iniquities'?[2] How can they both be true? I've heard Jesus teach. I've seen his miracles. I want to believe in him, but something holds me back."

The discussion was interrupted by a shout from the shadowed highway: "*Shalom* to the camp."

Drawing a short sword, Joseph's steward leapt to his feet and took a stance between his master and the unknown intruder. The ten guards drew their weapons and formed a protective circle about the camp.

"Easy," said a hooded, cloaked figure, advancing to the edge of the firelight. "I'm alone. No threat to you."

Terah and the guards relaxed slightly at those words, but I did not. I remembered how Zimri's band of outlaws had sought shelter at my father's camp before attacking us.

"Can I come to the warmth?" the stranger inquired.

This man was bulkier than Zimri's sinewy form, and his voice was gruffer. I let the tension leave my shoulders.

"Come in and welcome," Joseph invited.

The newcomer squatted between Joseph and me, extending broad, calloused palms toward its warmth. His face bristled with a coarse, wiry beard. The heavy ridges of his eyebrows made his eyes into deep holes above a crooked, flattened nose.

"Is it safe to travel alone so late, even on this highway?" Terah asked.

The lone man shrugged. "Perhaps not." With those words he stretched, lifting his left hand high above his head.

It was the same signal Zimri had given to launch the bandit attack on my father's camp! "Joseph!" I said with alarm, but too late.

The robber's right hand darted into the fold of his robe. A knife flashed in the firelight before he seized me with one arm. He yanked me to my feet and pressed the blade to my throat.

Joseph's guards sprang forward. The bandit barked at them, "Get back or he dies! I am bar Abba, and you know I mean what I say."

Bar Abba! The notorious murderer who slaughtered and stole while pretending to be a freedom fighter. This was the assassin Zimri had said he was going to Judea to join.

"Hold!" Joseph shouted to his men. Then to my attacker: "What do you want?"

A ring of cloaked men appeared from the darkness at bar Abba's sign. There were as many of them as Joseph's entourage.

"Want?" Bar Abba smirked. "I want your men to throw down their weapons. And then I want your camels and your shipment."

As the tip of his dagger jabbed my neck, Joseph ordered his men to drop their swords, and they complied.

I recognized Zimri even before he spoke. "Didn't I tell you this would work?" he said to bar Abba as he strode forward. "For some reason they value the life of this shepherd's cur." Approaching me, he threatened, "You are so much trouble. I will enjoy slitting your throat."

"No, you won't," bar Abba corrected. "He makes a valuable hostage. Remember who is chief here. All right, quickly now."

Struggling in bar Abba's grasp, I shouted at Zimri, "What about my mother? What about my father?"

Zimri sneered and shook his head, drawing his thumb across his neck.

A dull, hollow ache swelled up in my chest, threatening to choke me. I no longer cared whether I lived or died. I let my hands be tied behind my back. A rope leash around my throat was handed to Zimri.

I watched without seeing while Joseph and Terah were stripped of their fine clothes and valuables. After being forced to repack the camels, Joseph's attendants were trussed up like chickens in the marketplace and piled in a heap.

It was when all but three of bar Abba's men had sheathed their weapons and grasped the lead ropes of the camels that I heard the shout from the black hillside: "Now!"

Suddenly, beside each of the robbers appeared a pair of Roman soldiers, their javelins prepared to skewer all of bar Abba's men. The legionaries looked to a muscled, russet-haired centurion for their orders.

A tug on the rope jerked me off my feet, and the tip of Zimri's knife dug into my ear.

"Call off your men or he dies!" Zimri snarled.

The centurion shrugged. "Go ahead. He's nothing to me. The only difference to you is, if you kill him, I will kill you here and now . . . crucify you where you stand. But if you don't, you might actually live to have a trial. Doesn't matter to me. Your choice."

The pressure of the knife in my ear increased for a moment. My heart beat wildly.

Then Zimri tossed down his blade. A pair of Roman soldiers pinioned his arms to his sides.

Desperate to escape, bar Abba flung himself at the centurion. His upraised sword swept toward the officer, who parried it with his own. Their blades rang together. Bar Abba jabbed at the Roman with a knife in his other hand.

The assassin was larger and stronger, bull-like in his fighting. The centurion was cool and quicker in his movements.

Lowering his shoulder, bar Abba attempted to butt the centurion out of the way and did succeed in knocking the Roman down. As the bandit chief tried to flee, the officer caught him by the ankle and brought him sprawling to the ground.

Immediately the officer planted one knee against bar Abba's back, but the bandit whipped around, slashing with his dagger. The knife edge skittered off a metal bracelet on the Roman's wrist.

Then the Roman drove his clenched fist into bar Abba's chin, following through on the blow by letting the point of his elbow crash against the robber's cheekbone.

Bar Abba sagged, and the fight was over.

Once order was restored, Joseph of Arimathea confronted the Roman. "Marcus Longinus. How could you risk the life of this boy like that?"

"Would it have been better to let that scum carry him away to be killed later or sold as a slave? No, I know his kind, cowards who will do anything to save their own hides. You'll see. Bar Abba and Zimri will race to see which one can sell the other out faster." Then to me he said, "But I am sorry, son. I would not want you harmed for anything."

Resuming his discussion with Joseph, the centurion explained, "I've been after bar Abba for three years. We received word that his band was hiding in the ruins of Gezer. When we saw your camp, we expected they would attack you."

"So you staked us out like a goat to draw in a lion!" Joseph protested.

"A little gratitude, if you please," Marcus Longinus corrected. "It is bar Abba's practice to leave no living witnesses to his robberies. What would have happened if we had not been here at all?"

To that question, Joseph had no response.

As the sun rose, the troop of Roman soldiers and their prisoners set out toward Jerusalem while we returned to our trek to Joppa. All I could think was that I was alive . . . but now I knew my parents to be dead.

Chapter 23

*A*s we approached Joppa, the highway skirted olive groves and stands of pomegranate trees. Still lower on the downward slope were vineyards, their gnarled trunks standing in the wintry chill like upright walking sticks. Savagely pruned until only a single pair of branches was left upon each vine, the barren rows looked the way I felt inside.

Joppa was built on a promontory extending out into the sea. Waves crashed around the western base of its hundred-foot-tall summit, dotted with houses. I was fascinated by my first view of the Great Sea. I had heard of it, but nothing in Rabbi Kagba's teaching or my parents' descriptions prepared me for how vast it seemed. Nor was its appearance comforting. It appeared to me a trackless wilderness where drowning could be expected at any moment.

Approaching Joppa as we did from the southeast, the morning light shone directly on the city, but its appearance was not improved by it. The town was built entirely of gray rock. I saw no color, nor even any whitewash, to relieve the dullness. Flat-roofed boxes were what passed for homes. They varied in size alone but not in shape.

Perhaps it was the weariness in my own soul that drained any interest in Joppa from me. I wanted my mother and father. I wanted my home. I wanted things to be as they had been before this ordeal began, only now never could be again.

Joseph of Arimathea tried to engage me in conversation by recounting bits of Joppa's history. "This is where King Hiram of Tyre landed the cedar beams from Lebanon used to build our Temple. And you remember it was from Joppa that the prophet Jonah tried to flee from the Almighty." He gazed into my staring, uncaring eyes and abruptly began prattling. "Jonah," he repeated awkwardly. "No harbor, though. Rowed out to the ships. Out there." Vaguely, he gestured toward a row of vessels bobbing at anchor, then shut his mouth and kept it closed.

My grandparents, I learned, lodged with a man called Simon the Tanner. While tanning was a despised, smelly trade, it was also lucrative. Simon's home was among the largest dwellings in Joppa. Simon was kin to Nicodemus the Pharisee and well known to Joseph.

These and other such random thoughts bobbed in my head like the vessels on the waves. I had never met my mother's parents before. I wondered if they would be pleased to see me, or hate me because I was alive and my mother was not. I was certain my brothers would blame me. How could they not, when I halfway blamed myself?

When Joseph's caravan arrived in the street outside Simon's home, he asked me to wait with Terah while he entered to alert the household. It was, he said, so we would not catch them by surprise, because we were arriving earlier than expected.

His small deception was meant to be an act of kindness, but it did not fool me. I knew he wanted to deliver the news about the death of their daughter before he introduced me to my grandparents.

Moments passed. An older couple emerged from the gate. The woman was short and plump. The man, not much taller, but slimmer. Both had pale, drawn faces. The woman tottered slightly, clutching the man's arm for support.

"Boaz, Rebekah," Joseph said, "this is your grandson, Nehemiah. Nehi, here are your—"

Dropping to her knees, my grandmother extended her arms toward me. In her face she looked so much like my mother!

Bursting away from Terah's hand on my shoulder, I ran to her and fell into her arms. She pressed me to her, letting me bury my face in her neck, both of us weeping. We rocked back and forth, she and I, clinging to each other for comfort.

She was perfumed with the aromas of baking: flour and spices. But there was also a faint hint of jasmine and lavender and rose . . . just like my mother.

My grandfather stood awkwardly beside us both, stiffly patting first one head and then the other. "Come in, come in," he kept urging, as if grief would be less if hidden from daylight.

My grandmother and I shuddered as one, and we both sniffed. Drawing back slightly, she held me at arm's length and peered into my eyes. "Dear, sweet child. I see your mother. I see my Sarah."

Once inside the house we sat on a bench with me between my grandparents. Each of them held one of my hands. My grandmother patted my hand over and over again.

"Where are my brothers?" I said. "When can I see them?"

"They've gone . . . left for Amadiya . . . before word came that you were in Jerusalem."

"But how can I . . . ? I've got to see them," I said with desperation. "I have to tell them . . . you know."

Gently, my grandfather said, "I've already sent a messenger

after them. He's well mounted and riding fast. He will catch them and turn them around. Don't worry."

"And which . . . who . . . ?" I asked and stopped, fearing to bring more sorrow into this grief-stricken gathering.

"What is it, my boy?" Grandfather asked.

Joseph came to my aid. "We heard that one of your grand-sons—one of Nehi's brothers—was killed in the fire. But we did not learn the name."

"Oh," Grandmother said abruptly.

I saw the hurt of the recollection hit her like a slap to the face, and my own heart was pierced again. "I'm sorry. I'm so sorry," I said, uncaring whether I made sense or not.

"Terrible! Terrible!" Grandmother murmured. "It was the drunken brother of a cloth merchant. A guest. He started the fire. Not one of my grandchildren. But a horrible end for anyone."

How could I feel crushed and lifted both at the same time? Not one of my brothers, but both of my parents? Good news, bad news. Relief and groans coming heartbeats apart?

"We are rebuilding the shop," my grandfather confirmed. "It will be complete by Passover. But what with the crowds and all . . . well, we won't try to move back until after the holiday."

For a long time we did not notice Joseph, standing self-consciously beside the door. "I should go," he said. "I am going with my cargo as far as Alexandria. If tide and wind cooperate, I will return in two Sabbaths. With your permission, I will look in on Nehemiah again then."

For a time, immediately after his departure, I barely noticed that Joseph of Arimathea had gone. I was so grateful to be with my grandparents . . . to feel their love and know the security of being in their home . . . that I wanted no more adventures! For so long I had been on the run, or in hiding, or facing bandits, or living by my wits, that I was ready to be a child again, though I would not have admitted it if asked.

My grandmother's embrace and the gruff kindliness of my grandfather kept my days free of sorrow or fear. When I woke in the room next to my grandparents, it took me a moment to recognize where I was, and then I took comfort in my grandfather's snores. By the sound of his rasping breath, I received proof that I was physically safe.

With that reassurance, I next prayed earnestly to return to sleep as quickly as possible, before my thoughts overwhelmed me. My brothers had still not returned, and the deep-rooted guilt I felt at having fled from Zimri remained unresolved.

And then there was the matter of my mission and the Cup of Joseph. Opinion was divided, it seemed, about Jesus of Nazareth. Was he a healer, a miracle worker, a prophet sent by the Almighty—or a charlatan, a deceiver, a traitor, or a collaborator?

How was it possible for the Messiah, the Anointed One, the long-awaited prophet promised through Moses and all the others, to be unrecognized as who he truly was? Was it Jesus who was flawed . . . or men who were blind?

Perhaps we could have resolved these questions by going to Jerusalem, but my grandparents refused to take me.

Shortly after my arrival in Joppa, word came that a plague was strangling the Holy City.

"The choking sickness," Grandfather called it. "All who can afford to are fleeing the city. Thanks be to the Almighty that we came away before it struck. The fire, you see, was a blessing in disguise."

"But the poor beggars," Grandmother lamented. "Things

like these always hit the homeless the hardest. Those who cannot escape—who have no money for warm clothing and good food—are the first to die."

I thought of my friends: Red, Timothy, and the others, and wondered how they were. The caves beneath the city might remain above freezing, but they could not be called either truly warm or entirely dry. I myself had seen how the Sparrows struggled to obtain enough to eat.

"Can't we go help them?" I asked. "Do something for them? They helped me."

Grandfather would not even consider it.

Grandmother said, "It's good that you want to help, Nehi, but your grandfather is right. We cannot risk returning there. Not now."

There soon came a day when my nighttime worries and frets crept into the daylight hours. The comforting *thump* and *swish* of shuttle and frame as my grandmother worked her loom no longer reassured me. Instead, the sight of her laboring over the skeins of blue and white thread reminded me how very much I missed my mother and my home in Amadiya.

Grandmother noticed when I leaned against the door frame, gnawing on my lower lip and frowning. When my grandfather emerged from his makeshift counting office, I heard her whispering to him but could not make out what was said.

"Nehemiah," Grandfather said, clapping his hand on my shoulder, "let's go down to the waterfront. There's a shipping agent there I want to visit. Besides, there are some famous sights in Joppa that visitors come especially to see. You might like it."

I was grateful for the diversion.

"Even without a proper harbor," Grandfather explained, "Joppa is a famous seaport. Greeks and Persians and our people all come here to visit."

I had not seen anything especially noteworthy in Joppa, so I was curious what would draw attention from many different races.

A series of rocky ledges that formed one bit of Joppa's shoreline marched in ranks out into the salt water until disappearing beneath it. Some distance offshore they reemerged as dangerous reefs, barely breaking the surface, poised to tear the bellies out of unsuspecting ships.

Only one rock reared much higher than the waves. From the place I stood it appeared about the size and shape of the oak cabinet in my mother's workshop in Amadiya—the one in which she kept the finest thread for the most elaborate, custom-ordered prayer shawls.

I remarked on this to Grandfather, but he assured me it was really much larger. "About the size of the shed where we keep the chickens."

This did not sound much more impressive to me. I must have appeared skeptical that anyone cared about so insignificant a chunk of rock.

"Doesn't look like much," Grandfather agreed, "but that's Andromeda's Rock. It's the place where she was chained; later she was rescued by Perseus."

Now I recognized the tale, as repeated to me by Rabbi Kagba. "I know about this," I said. "My teacher showed me the star patterns from the story."

According to ancient legend, Andromeda's mother had angered the Greek gods by her prideful boasting. They sent a sea monster to destroy their cities. The attacks would only stop if she sacrificed her daughter, Andromeda, to the monster. The legend had a happy ending when a hero named Perseus, riding Pegasus, the flying horse, killed the monster and rescued Andromeda.

I nodded. "She, her mother, Perseus, the horse, and even the monster are all named in the heavens, at least by the Greeks. And the other people who live in our country—the Parthians who used to be Persians—say their race was founded by Perseus and Andromeda."

Grandfather looked unhappy. "You know this story very well already."

"But I like seeing the place where they say it happened. Is it true?"

Grandfather brightened at my expression of interest. He inclined his head and offered with a grin, "Perhaps an enterprising Greek merchant opened an inn here and needed to attract travelers."

"Didn't the prophet Jonah leave from here when he tried to flee from the Almighty?" I inquired. "Joseph told me that."

"And in Jonah's story the Almighty made a great fish swallow Jonah, not to kill him, but to save him," Grandfather mused. "That's kind of like a sea monster, isn't it?"

Now my thoughts were racing. "Who lived here before the Greeks or us Jews?"

"The Philistines. They worshipped a god named Dagon. He was supposed to be half man and half fish."

"Now that'd be a monster," I said, picturing the image. "What about the people Jonah was supposed to preach to? What did they worship?"

"The wicked old city of Nineveh?" Grandfather pondered aloud. "I think they worshipped Dagon too."

"So when Jonah came alive out of the great fish and preached, they saw how much greater our God was than theirs. Even sea monsters obey the Almighty."

Grandfather wiped his forehead. "Have you thought about training to become a rabbi, Nehemiah?"

"Rabbi Kagba says I could be a scholar, like him," I reported honestly.

"He may be right there," Grandfather agreed. "I wonder what your mentor would think about what Jesus of Nazareth said about Jonah."

"Jesus? He talked about Jonah?"

Grandfather shrugged. "So says a Pharisee customer of mine. He doubts Jesus is really the Messiah, so he asked the man from Galilee to give him a sign. 'What sign will you perform, so I might believe in you?' he says he asked."

After all I had heard about lame men being made to walk and blind men to see and even dead children raised to life, it seemed to me like a very rude question. However, I inquired, "And what did Jesus say?"

Stroking his full, white beard, Grandfather stared at Andromeda's Rock and returned, "Supposedly all he said was, 'No sign will be given to it except the sign of the prophet Jonah.'"[1]

"The sign of Jonah? What does that mean?"

Grandfather spread his hands wide. "I have no idea. Neither did the Pharisee, though he likes to be thought very learned. 'A runaway prophet?' the Pharisee said. 'A disobedient man?'" Grandfather chuckled at remembering the exasperated Pharisee, and when he chuckled, he wheezed and then coughed. "I said, 'Doesn't this Jesus preach repentance, just like Jonah?' And he said, 'But that's not a sign! All prophets do that!'"

"What about being swallowed by the great fish?" I ventured, wide-eyed at the thought.

Grandfather was seized with a paroxysm of laughter and coughing. "That's just what the Pharisee said! Said he'd like to see Jesus manage that one!"

"Three days in the fish," I pondered aloud. "Buried at the bottom of the sea. Like being dead and then coming back to life. That truly would be a sign."

"Eh? What's that you say?"

"Nothing, Grandfather. Just thinking aloud."

Chapter 24

*T*he news from Jerusalem did not improve. True to my grandparents' premonitions, the plague of the choking sickness fell hardest on the beggars of the Holy City. Word had come to Joppa from Grandfather's business acquaintances that nearly all the Sparrows were stricken with the illness and many had died.

No one but God kept account of Sparrows, it seemed. No one knew any of the names, living or dead. Had my friends survived?

The Pharisee who brought the news said it was a sign of God's judgment on sin. "Just like cripples and those who contract leprosy," he said. "This disease is proof that God strikes evildoers and lawbreakers. No one among the truly pious is in jeopardy."

I felt myself staring at the man. He was speaking of my friends as if they deserved this affliction! But I knew those the Pharisee thought pious, by which he meant the wealthy, had fled from disease or locked themselves behind high walls and barred gates until the plague snuffed itself out, together with the life of the last victim.

"I have heard," my grandfather said, "that Lazarus of Bethany, widely regarded as a righteous man, has taken on himself the role of caregiver to the beggars, especially the link-bearer children."

The Pharisee sniffed. "I'm sure he means well—a charitable act. But he's misguided. Those orphan beggars? Pickpockets and thieves, every one. No doubt they deserve this punishment."

I struggled with anger at his fat, pompous, arrogant face! The Pharisee must have seen the burning hostility in my eyes because when he glanced at me, he swiftly turned away.

My grandmother had also noticed my distress. She came and stood beside me. A calming spirit, like that I had always known from my mother, enveloped me.

My grandfather, his eyes narrowed and his voice polite but cold, explained, "My daughter and her husband—this grandson's parents—were attacked by bandits and are likely dead. You should be more careful in what you say about orphans."

I clung to my grandmother and sobbed as the weight of Grandfather's words fell across me. So he, too, believed my mother and father were dead!

"Didn't mean . . . ," the Pharisee fumbled. "Your family aren't beggars," he finished awkwardly. Lifting the weight of several chins, the Pharisee nodded curtly to a waiting servant, who had stood silent with downcast eyes. The Pharisee completed his transaction for a dozen expensive prayer shawls and left.

"Listen, Nehemiah," my grandfather said, "I'm sorry you had to endure that preening Pharisee. I didn't mean to upset you. We will not lose hope. Not you or me or your grandmother. The plague in Jerusalem is a terrible thing. Even your rabbi Jesus seems to have fled from it."

A single clay lamp burned in the hall outside my bedroom. Flickering light tossed fragments of shadows against the walls. The tiny flame labored to push back the darkness. It exhaled a ribbon of sooty smoke that streaked the plaster and pooled overhead like an upside-down puddle of oily water.

Every night my grandmother lit the lamp—to comfort me, she said.

Every morning she scrubbed at the wall and climbed on a chair to clean the ceiling.

I sat cross-legged on the floor, my back to the entry. The meager illumination fell over my shoulder onto Joseph's cup. The lambskin wrapping lay across my lap.

Idly, I scratched the blackened surface of the cup but could not raise an answering gleam. There was not even so much shine as what reflected from my fingernails. Unlike the wall and the ceiling soiled with smoke, the tarnished surface of the cup refused to be cleaned.

The obstinate stain matched my own gloomy outlook.

Did everyone I loved die? Were my parents dead? And Rabbi Kagba? Were my friends in Jerusalem all gone? Was I a curse and a danger to my grandparents?

What if this unattractive object was not really Joseph's cup at all? What if everything I had experienced had been for nothing? What if everything I had believed had proven untrue—worse than false, treacherous?

Yet, as I reviewed what Rabbi Kagba had taught me, I could not extinguish the remaining glimmer of hope. He had spoken confidence into my life. Like the diminutive glow of the oil lamp, part of me still worked at pushing back bleak despair. I had dreamed of Joseph the Dreamer. Together we had witnessed Father Abraham and the king-priest Melchizedek, and King David and his mighty men.

Dreams, I argued with myself. *Only dreams and no substance in which to place any trust.*

And Adam's Hart? There was the something I could not explain away. I had ridden the White Hart.

Together with the cup I held in my hands—tarnished and unlovely but real and significant—the memory of the hart confirmed everything my mentor had prophesied over me: I would see Messiah. I would be cupbearer to the King.

"Your thoughts can be hopeful and gloomy by turns," remarked a familiar voice.

"I was just thinking about you," I replied to Joseph the Dreamer, who stood in the corner of my room. "And yes, you're right. But the path is so uncertain. The weight of grief and suffering seems all out of proportion to the fragment of hope."

Joseph nodded. His expression was sympathetic and not at all disapproving or disappointed in me. He said, "When I was in the pit, pleading with my brothers for my life, do you think I was cheerful?"

I shook my head. Though Joseph was used by the Almighty for great purposes, his life was no less difficult because he believed in his destiny.

"When I was in prison, for something I did not do," he offered, "I dreamed of home. I dreamed of my father, of my brother, Benjamin, of my mother, Rachel, who had died long years before. I missed her a lot."

This was painful for me to hear. Even knowing that in *olam haba*, the world to come, all was put right, I was still sorry on Joseph's behalf.

"And when I awoke amid happy thoughts of home and being loved, only to find myself on the wet, stinking floor of the prison in Egypt, do you think I did not grieve for what I had lost?"

I shook my head. "It must have been a torment."

"Every day!" Joseph confirmed. "And each day I had to

draw on the tiny bit of hope given me by the faith of my father and grandfather." Joseph flicked his fingers toward the lamp outside my door. Pinprick sparks shimmered upward, as when my mother tossed spice into the Sabbath flames for a sweet savor.

"Hope," Joseph said earnestly, "is no less real because it seems small amid the darkness. Faith is no less yours to claim because you struggle against doubt."

Below me my grandparents had a dinner celebration with a few close friends, but none were my age. I heard their banter, but no one present was interested in talking with me.

As soon as I was excused from supper, I came to the rooftop. The location carried my thoughts back to an earlier year—that Purim when Rabbi Kagba opened the skies and showed me the heavenly cup and the celestial hart. Bundled again in my shepherd's coat and boots, I peered into a cloudy sky for some glimpse of my old starry friends. Misty banners, torn from the fabric of the storm, carried news of the tempest toward Jerusalem but did not linger in Joppa.

Waves crashed against Andromeda's Rock. Long swells swept in from the northwest, to land with hollow, jarring thuds on Joppa's promontory. I wondered if they came from Cyprus, or perhaps as far away as the Pillars of Hercules.

The wind howled in my ears, screeching pipes to the drumbeat of the breakers. These were lonely, disquieting sounds on a lonely, unpeaceful night.

Still no word of my brothers. No news about my teacher either.

I was safe, I was loved, I was cared for, yet I was restless.

Several houses up the street I glimpsed a man striding purposefully along as he passed beneath a blazing torch. He was alone and completely wrapped in a long cloak, with a hood over his head. The wind threatened to turn his robes into sails and spin him off east, like the clouds.

Like a ship quartering into the gale to avoid being flung on the rocks, he had to lean into the blast. *Why would anyone be out on such a bitter night?* I wondered. I rubbed wind-plucked tears from my eyes and watched.

Two houses away he stopped. Peering back the way he had come, he counted entries, as if uncertain of his destination. When his tabulation ceased, he was pointing at Grandfather's gate!

Beneath my gaze he pulled the bell rope, but no one answered. Between the tumult of the storm and the merrymaking, I doubted if anyone would. "They can't hear you," I shouted. "Are you seeking Boaz the Weaver?"

A familiar face lifted toward me. Joseph of Arimathea corrected, "Yes, I am, Nehemiah. But I'm also seeking you!"

"Wait! I'll be right down!"

Moments later Joseph warmed himself in front of the fire amid a crowd of attentive onlookers. He answered my grandmother's question about why he was out on such a fearful night. "And well you might ask. I barely got off my ship from Alexandria before the storm hit. They were so anxious to sail off toward a safer harbor that they almost threw me overboard. Just like Jonah, eh?" He smiled. "My steward was expecting me and met me. Just in from Jerusalem, he has received some startling news. My business partner, Lazarus of Bethany . . . ?"

"Friend of Jesus of Nazareth," Grandfather remarked. "Yes?"

"Caring for the Jerusalem Sparrows, he took sick with the strangling sickness."

"And Jesus healed him?" Grandmother asked.

"No . . . he died," Joseph corrected.

I was stunned and shocked. My heart sank.

A rotund spice merchant laughed mockingly. "That's a prophet from Galilee for you. Couldn't even save his own friend!"

"No," Joseph continued slowly. "But Jesus brought Lazarus back from the dead."

After a stunned silence, a tumult of queries equal in volume and confusion to the storm outside barraged Joseph.

"What d'ya mean?"

"Then he wasn't really dead!"

"But he's real, I tell you!"

"Four days in the tomb," Joseph said. "Really and truly dead, and Jesus called him out of the grave . . . so they say."

"That'll light a fire under High Priest Caiaphas. The whole country will want to see Jesus and Lazarus both!"

Joseph ignored the mocking banter and addressed my grandfather. "Has any word come directly regarding Nehemiah's parents?"

Grandfather shook his head. "We've still had no *real* word about them . . . good or bad," he emphasized with a look at me. "Only what the bandit Zimri implied." He paused. "Then again, he is a bandit and not to be trusted and cruel by choice."

A spark of hope, like the pinprick sparks that had shimmered upward when Joseph gestured toward the lamp, ignited in my heart. Could the bandit have lied? Might my parents still be alive somewhere? And searching for me?

"Then," Joseph said, "here is a request: I would like to take Nehemiah on as an apprentice in my export business, if he agrees. I want him to accompany me to the Holy City when

I leave tomorrow. Of course, his parents may not give their consent when they return, but until then, you can approve his employment, if you will."

Turning, Grandfather put his hands on his hips. With raised eyebrows he looked a question at me.

I nodded eagerly. "Yes, please!" I confirmed.

And so it was settled.

Chapter 25

Our journey to the home of David ben Lazarus in Bethany was briefly interrupted outside the Holy City. Joseph reined his horse and dismounted near a stone wall outside Jerusalem.

Two men stacked carefully hewn limestone blocks to form a waist-high barricade. The wall surrounded a newly planted garden. Inside the enclosure was a border of fragrant juniper shrubs. The place was busy with workmen. Boys about my age mixed mortar. Older boys worked as hod carriers, assisting the masons.

At the sight of Joseph, I noticed heads lean together and anxious whispers pass between the laborers. Whatever this building site was, Joseph clearly had authority over it. He pushed aside a wooden gate as I slid from my donkey and hesitated.

"Come on, then," he instructed. I tied our mounts to the limb of a tree.

The gate opened onto a winding gravel path that was a beehive of activity. Another boy, wielding a branch of a juniper as a broom, swept the curving track clear of dust. A man wearing the apron of a stone mason edged the path with more stacked stone. Joseph greeted the mason, then asked, "Where is Hyram?"

The stone-setter indicated a grass-covered knoll at the back of the property. Between the fence and the small hill were beds of lavender. When the weather warmed, the lavender would perfume the air with rich sweetness.

The trail skirted a pair of ancient olive trees, so gnarled and massive at their bases that the garden must have been constructed around them. The path ended against a rocky knoll. The flank of the hillside in front of me was faced with flat stones. At the center of the wall's base was a square hole, slightly shorter than me, leading inward.

A man emerged from the opening. He wore his mason's apron with one corner turned up, designating him the overseer of the work. "*Shalom,* Master Joseph," he said.

"*Shalom,* Master Hyram," Joseph returned. "You've made good progress."

"I think you'll be pleased with the tomb." Hyram tugged his forelock.

"I think my father will be pleased too. I am eager to have it done before the Passover holiday."

I felt a pang of renewed guilt. According to our beliefs, it was a very necessary mark of respect for children to see their parents honorably interred. Joseph was paying great homage to his father with this gift.

I, on the other hand, had run away. My father and mother, if dead as I feared, may have remained unburied except for the kindness of strangers. I squinted with the pain of regret.

Though I did not speak, Joseph noticed my distress and somehow understood its cause. "We will not give up hope, boy," he whispered to me. Then, to divert me, he asked, "Would you like to see inside? I have no torch, but I think there's enough light."

I nodded.

A massive stone disk, taller than me, stood on edge in a

channel cut for the purpose. It rested against the outer wall of the tomb and was wedged there by a block beneath it.

I eyed it suspiciously. "Safe?"

Joseph nodded. "But once the wedge is removed, the covering rolls into place, sealing the entry."

The master mason explained proudly, "When shut, it will take at least four men to roll it back up the slope. Sir, would you like to inspect the work?"

Joseph nodded, then motioned for me to go first. "Go ahead. Go in."

The opening was so small that even I had to duck to enter. Joseph followed me. The mason remained outside.

Inside, the floor was lower than the entry, so I stood upright. I was surrounded by hewn stone walls bearing the fresh marks of hammers and chisels.

There was no carving or other adornment in the tomb, but the corners were all perfectly square. Every angle was completely uniform. The floor, walls, and ceiling were smooth and level. It had cost a lot of labor and expense.

On three sides of the chamber were low benches cut out of the very rock. Each was the length of a man lying down and about twice his width. Because the tomb was brand-new, there were no bone boxes or niches cut in the walls, as would be true when multiple generations of Joseph's family had been buried there. It was a rich man's tomb, different from the primitive burial caves of my homeland.

"It's almost like a little house, you know? When no one's in it." I paused. "I mean, nobody dead."

Joseph touched the cool wall. "Yes. I suppose. I like to think of this place as where my family will gather to await the resurrection at the last day. We are not Sadducees, who expect no resurrection. No, my father and I expect to be reunited, even if parted for a time. Of course," he added thoughtfully, "if what Jesus did for Lazarus is true, then perhaps all of what we know about death will change."

There seemed nothing left to see or say, especially since my mother and father were again strongly, forcefully in my mind.

The mason lowered his face and smiled in at us. "Is it to your liking, sir?"

Joseph gave a short laugh. "I am in no hurry to move in, but I am sure it will be a comfortable place to wait for the resurrection."

The mason stepped aside as we emerged. "I was hoping you would be pleased with our progress."

Joseph touched his money belt. "A bonus if you're finished before Passover. I'll return before *Shabbat* to pay the workers for their labor up to now."

I squared my shoulders and attempted to match the stride of Joseph as we returned up the gravel path to our mounts. I felt the eyes of the boys take me in furtively, then look away. Perhaps they imagined I was the son of the wealthy merchant.

"Come along." Joseph untied the reins and gave me a boost onto my donkey. "The day is passing, and I want to reach Bethany before sunset."

It was dusk when we passed the Mount of Olives and reached the hamlet of Bethany, a couple miles east of Jerusalem. The villa of Lazarus was set below a hill crowned with a fig orchard, in the midst of a vineyard.

I shuddered at the thought of all that had taken place here over the last weeks. I hoped I would have a chance to meet and speak to a real, live dead man. I wondered what he would look like and imagined it all somewhat fearfully, but with excitement.

The vines had been thoroughly pruned. Twisted stalks, crusted with gray bark, looked like roots protruding out of the red earth. But even amid winter's desolation, rebirth was apparent. Beginning where each branch grew nearest the trunk of the parent vine, pairs of tiny, dark green leaves fluttered.

"Banners of returning life," Joseph said to himself. Then he turned and spoke to me over his shoulder as we rode. "What do you know about vineyards?"

I shrugged. "My folks are shepherds. Papa drinks wine, which comes from vineyards. That's it."

Joseph gave a laugh. "The wines of Lazarus are drunk by emperors and kings as far away as Brittania. It comes from here. As hard as it is to believe right now, in six months these hillsides will be completely shadowed by lush growth. The branches will be bent with the weight of the clusters. And the laborers of David ben Lazarus will harvest them so he can work his magic. From dead sticks to the taste of new wine in three quarters of a year."

"So kings drink it. Lazarus makes good wine, then?" I said.

"The best! He says it takes the vines nine months to give birth, but the children of his vineyard will travel far and wide."

"I bet my papa said *Kiddush* on *Shabbat*. Your friend's wine poured into cups in Amadiya," I said, thinking of home and Joseph's cup at the same time.

Joseph nodded vigorously. "Shared in Rome and Alexandria." Then in a more thoughtful tone he added, "It's strange. Every year before this the wine is what I wanted to talk about—how many barrels, how much to charge, where it would be shipped. My family is proud to be his partner. But this year? I want to hear from him his own story about what happened. Was he really dead? What was it like? Who is this Jesus?"

These were the very questions in my head.

From the vineyard a cheerful voice joined our conversation. "Yes, Master Lazarus was truly dead. I can vouch for that. But still, those are all very good questions! Very good, indeed."

A young man, perhaps as old as twenty but thin-bearded, fresh-faced, and smiling, emerged from the shadows beside the fence enclosing the vineyard. "*Shalom,* sir. The master and his sisters are not at home. They've all gone off to follow Jesus. Leaving the vineyard in the care of Samson, the steward. But who knows when they'll be back? The Herodians would like Lazarus dead permanently."

Joseph stopped his horse and pivoted the animal to face the stranger. "I can understand that. But . . . who are you, and how do you know so much?"

"My name is Peniel. I've seen you here before, sir. I am also one blessed with the vision of Jesus." He touched his eyes. "I serve as a messenger from Lazarus to his servants."

I knew the name of Peniel. He was one of those whom Jesus had miraculously healed of blindness.

Joseph nodded. "Ah. Yes, I remember now. Peniel, the beggar of Nicanor Gate. The man born blind, they say."

I blurted out, "The one Jesus gave eyes. I heard about you from one of the Sparrows."

He bowed elaborately. "That's me. They'd love to put my eyes out again, I fear. So I stick to the back roads and mind my own business. One thing you learn as a beggar, silence is a virtue. You learn more if you act dumb or invisible." Grinning still more widely, Peniel stroked the nose of Joseph's horse. "Now I'm learning to be a scribe. I love a good story. So, you are here seeking Lazarus?" He snapped his fingers in recollection. "Master Joseph . . ."

"Joseph of Arimathea, the Younger . . ."

As we dismounted and entered the Lazarus home, Peniel explained, "The Temple rulers—high priest and others—they want to kill Jesus . . . Lazarus too. They already tried. So the master and our band have gone away from Jerusalem."

"Gone?" My voice and Joseph's chimed as two octaves of the same note.

"Don't worry," Peniel reassured us. "I was sent back to meet those Lazarus said might be coming. I can guide you to them. That's my job . . . that and learning your stories." Then, addressing me, Peniel asked, "And you are a servant to Joseph?"

"Apprentice," Joseph corrected, giving a lift to my pride. "Nehemiah bar Lamsa. From Amadiya near Gan Eden."

"You have an unusual accent." Peniel eyed me with pleased curiosity. "We won't travel until tomorrow. There's a fire and a kettle of stew and fresh bread. What do you say? Will you stay up late and tell me your tale? I'll tell you stories of Jesus if you will tell me how you happened to come from Paradise to Jerusalem. If I can share a ride on your donkey, we can reach the village where Jesus is within a day."

Part Three

Jesus told them, "You are going to have the light
   just a little while longer.
Walk while you have the light, before darkness
   overtakes you.
Whoever walks in the dark does not know
   where they are going.
Believe in the light while you have the light,
   so that you may become children of light."

JOHN 12:35–36[1]

Chapter 26

$\mathcal{T}$t was after dark when we arrived at the village where Jesus and his followers were staying. Campfires of pilgrims dotted the hillside outside the walls.

Peniel, whose eyesight was keen even in the darkness, led the way toward the gate of the inn. "Jerusalem is only a day's walk from here. But somehow the people know. They've heard Jesus is here, so they camp here. Build their fires by the road in hopes he'll show himself."

Joseph replied quietly, "And my friend Lazarus?"

Peniel answered, "Yes. Yes. They all want to see Lazarus. To speak with him about where he was. What he saw, you know? Yes. Everyone wants to see Lazarus."

Joseph was silent for a few paces, and I guessed that, like everyone else, he was anxious to see his old business partner and learn the truth. "Lazarus. Good man. The Herodians want Lazarus dead . . ."

Peniel lifted a brow. "Dead again, you mean."

"Dead is dead. And as much as they want to kill Jesus, they want Lazarus dead . . . permanently. Jesus and his disciples mustn't come to Jerusalem for Passover."

In the distance the lights of Jerusalem gleamed through the haze of smoke like a new constellation in the mist.

Peniel raised his fist to knock on the gate of the inn. "Master Joseph, is that why you've traveled so far to find the Lord? To warn him of danger? Why you've come by night? You could have given me the message. I would have delivered it to him. So, what's your story, if you don't mind my asking? I do love a good story."

I could hear a smile in Peniel's voice.

Joseph cleared his throat. "I am no different from everyone else."

"Except you're very rich." Peniel laughed and banged on the gate. "Not that money means anything to Jesus. But money will open these gates. Just watch."

The watchman growled, "Gates are closed for the night. Go beg a place beside a pilgrim's fire."

Peniel replied confidently as he held silver coins up to the peephole, "It's Peniel. A friend of the master. Go ask the big fisherman."

"They're all gathered 'round in there," the gruff voice answered. "Your master is teaching. Mustn't be disturbed, Peter says."

"A denarius for the one who opens the gate. Two more for the innkeeper who provides a place to sleep and bread."

"How many of you?" hissed the sentry.

"Two men. One boy. Go on. Peter the fisherman will tell you. Say to him, Peniel is waiting outside the gate."

The port slammed shut. Minutes passed before the bolt of the gate slid back and the hinges groaned.

"Hurry," instructed the gatekeeper. "There's a mob would like to break in here. Beggars and sick among them."

When Joseph and Peniel had walked through the entrance, the gatekeeper tugged me by my coat, as if I weren't moving fast enough for his liking. Then he slammed and locked the gate behind us. His hand whipped out to snap up the coin in Peniel's fingers before scuttling away into the shadows.

Peniel shook his head, then set off through the dark courtyard of the caravansary. "I guarantee he wouldn't have bothered to fetch Peter if there hadn't been a coin in it for him."

Joseph remarked quietly, "How much would it take for the sentry to open the gates to the Temple Guards?"

We moved to the watch fire and warmed ourselves. A large, bearded man stepped from the portico. I spotted a dagger tucked into his belt.

"It's Peter," Peniel mumbled. "Not happy."

Peter gripped the weapon with one hand as he challenged, "Peniel. So, you're back at last. With news from Jerusalem, I hope. And who are your friends?"

"*Shalom*, Peter," Peniel greeted him. "This is Joseph of Arimathea. The younger Joseph. A merchant and friend of Master Lazarus. He was on a journey when all unfolded with Lazarus . . . Missed it all."

"And? Why sneak in here by cover of night? Business couldn't wait?" Peter was clearly irritated.

Joseph extended his hand. "I am a friend of Master Lazarus, as your companion explained. A partner in wine exporting. If you speak with Lazarus, he will vouch for me. I am here to warn your master—"

Peter's chin rose in defiance. "You think he doesn't know? That we don't know? This could have waited till morning, Peniel." He shifted his gaze to Joseph. "Look, money will buy people like you a lot of things, but Jesus doesn't care if you're rich or poor, see? He treats everyone the same. Money won't buy an audience with the Lord. He's teaching. Pharisees sitting there among us. He's giving it to them straight, and they don't much like it." He turned his surly gaze on me. "And what are you here for, boy?"

I stammered. "I . . . I am . . . My name is Nehemiah. Cupbearer."

Peter waved his hand dismissively. "So what?"

Fumbling for the precious cup at my waist, I held it up. "I . . . you see, sir . . . I brought this . . . a gift for . . ."

Peter squinted at the ancient vessel, then snorted with disdain. "If Joseph of Arimathea's silver won't buy you an audience to see Jesus, why do you think this dirty old cup will open the door?"

"But . . . I came so far! It's Joseph's cup," I pleaded.

Peter shook his shaggy head. "Peniel! Are you crazy? What were you thinking? You want me to interrupt the Lord for this?" Lifting his chin, he scoffed, "So, Joseph of Arimathea, some of us can't be bribed. Your journey is for nothing. Now we are all warned: Caiaphas wants to kill Jesus. And kill Lazarus. Big surprise. You can go now." Then, "Let your friends out the way they came, Peniel." Peter spun on his heel and reentered the building.

I thought that except for Roman soldiers or bandits, Peter was one of the rudest fellows I had ever met. We stood together, silently staring after him. My heart sank. Though Peter ridiculed the gift, surely Jesus would recognize the Cup of Joseph the Great when he saw it. Silently vowing I would never again show the cup to any man but Jesus, I replaced it in its bag.

Peniel's good humor was undiminished. "Sorry. Sorry. He's not a bad sort, really. Just unpleasant when he doesn't get his sleep. He's been standing watch with his sword drawn . . . just in case. I should have known, eh?"

"Perhaps Lazarus?" Joseph asked. "He will be glad to see me."

Peniel held up a finger to his temple and laughed. "Without fear! Lazarus slept like a dead man, but now that he is awake, he is always happy to see old friends."

Peniel hurried into the inn, leaving Joseph and me stretching our hands to the fire. Only a few minutes passed before our guide came out on the portico and, with a wave of his hand, called us to enter. As we approached, he put his finger to his lips and nodded. I followed Joseph and Peniel into the inn's large dining room, where travelers were fed. The space was packed with people. Rich and poor sat together on the floor in front of Jesus. Some listened with wondrous expressions on their upturned faces. Others among the crowd glared at him with resentment. Firelight flickered behind the teacher as he taught them. All were hushed as the clear, pleasant voice of the one I had been searching for filled the room.

"There was a rich man, who used to wear purple and fine linen, and every day he ate and drank and spent his wealth extravagantly for his own pleasure. And there was a poor man named Lazarus, who was laid down at that rich man's door . . ."

All eyes then turned to a fellow sitting near Jesus.

Joseph whispered, "That is Lazarus. There."

Excitement tickled my stomach like a feather. It was like the first time I met the Great White Hart in the forest or heard a new story from Rabbi Kagba. I would have laughed for the joy of being so close to Jesus. Perhaps he heard my happy thoughts.

Jesus locked his kind brown eyes on my face and met my smile with a nod. He had gained everyone's attention by speaking of the man he had raised from the dead.

Jesus continued his story. "Poor Lazarus lay there at the rich man's door. He was afflicted with boils. He longed to fill his stomach with crumbs that fell from the rich man's tray. Dogs came and licked the poor man's boils."

I saw those who were wealthy stir uneasily. Jesus was a wonderful storyteller. I was fascinated instantly.

"Now it happened that the poor man died, and the angels carried him into Abraham's bosom. Then the rich man died and was buried. And while the rich man was tormented in Sheol, he lifted up his eyes from a distance and saw Abraham, with Lazarus in his welcoming embrace. And the rich man called in a loud voice . . ." Jesus cupped his hands and shouted, "'O my father! Abraham! Have mercy on me and send Lazarus to dip his finger in water and wet my tongue, for I am tormented in this flame!'"

I shuddered at the vision of it.

"Abraham said to him, 'My son, remember you received your pleasures when you were living, and Lazarus his hardships. And look—now he is comfortable and happy here, and you are suffering. Besides all these things, a great gulf is fixed between us and you. So those who wish to cross over from here to you cannot, neither from there cross over to us.'"

I studied the rich men in the hall. Their faces were not happy. Here and there among the best dressed I spotted fear in their eyes.

"The tormented man cried to Abraham, 'If that is so, O my Father, I beseech you! Send Lazarus to my father's house, for I have five brothers! Let Lazarus go and testify to them, so they may not also come to this place of torment!'"

There was a hush in the room. Everyone knew that the real Lazarus had indeed returned from death to testify.

But Jesus continued with the story. "Abraham said to the tormented man, 'They have Moses and the Prophets. Let your brothers hear them!' But the rich man called out to Abraham, 'No! My father Abraham! But only if a man from the dead goes to them, they will repent!' Abraham replied, 'If they will not hear Moses and the prophets, neither will they believe, even if a man should return from the dead!' "[1]

Silence descended upon the room as Jesus finished the lesson. The rich men were mostly Pharisees who had come from Jerusalem to challenge Jesus and see Lazarus with their own eyes. Now they stared at Lazarus and contemplated the purpose of Jesus' story.

The death and resurrection of Lazarus was proof of the absolute truth of Jesus' story. Even though a man had returned from death to bear witness of eternal life, the leaders of Israel refused to believe the five books of Moses and they rejected Lazarus, the living, breathing evidence of Jesus' identity!

I considered the combined years of the elders of Israel who sat in the room. Surely their ages, if added together, would equal the years since Moses had parted the Red Sea. Yet they rejected the prophecies of the five books of Moses and were searching for reasons to reject Jesus. I was only a boy, and I believed that Jesus was our Messiah! Hadn't my own rabbi told me his name and the prophecies of his coming? So why was Jesus so feared and hated? I remembered also that Joseph of old, dreamer of dreams, had been hated by his brothers and yet had saved them all. Hatred of a righteous one was not rational. Surely what men intended for evil, God meant for good.

I slipped my hand into the pouch and touched the cold silver of Joseph's cup. I was sure that Jesus of Nazareth was the long-awaited Messiah, Son of David, the King of Israel! The books of Moses, all the prophets, and now Lazarus returned from the dead, all bore witness.

I glanced up at Joseph of Arimathea for his response to the teaching. He was, after all, a very rich man. His lips were tight, his face pale. A ripple of outrage swept through the wealthy in the congregation. Poor men grinned smugly, suddenly proud of their poverty. The crowd between us and Jesus was densely packed with knots of men arguing the point of the message. I saw Jesus slip out, surrounded by his disciples. Peter glowered over his shoulder.

Joseph clasped my hand and stepped back in the shadows into a small anteroom stacked with dishes, lest he be recognized by his friends from Jerusalem. Peniel followed us. Through the parted curtain I watched as some began to leave. They cast menacing glances at Lazarus as he followed Jesus.

Peniel inclined his head and said in a matter-of-fact tone to Joseph, "So. That's Jesus. He has a way of tossing the cat among the pigeons, as the saying goes. He's offended every rich man in the room, eh? And you. You're richer than most of them put together. What do you think?"

"My friend Lazarus of Bethany is also a wealthy man. He was rich when he died. Rich when Jesus called him from the grave. This parable is flawed, I fear. So, what do you think?" he asked Peniel. "Will wealth cast a man into hell?"

Peniel laughed. "I was a poor, blind man who begged at the Nicanor Gate. I can close my eyes and recognize the bitter voices of many in this room. I tell you, after I was healed, they hated me and cast me out because I was blind and now I see. Jesus gave me eyes to see. But a dark heart is much harder to heal. My heart recognized the Lord before I ever saw light." He put his hand on my shoulder. "Nehemiah? What do you think, boy?"

I hesitated and tried to imagine what Rabbi Kagba would say. "I think . . . the parable isn't flawed. What he said here tonight is true."

Peniel nodded as a great man in luxurious purple robes swept past. I opened the curtain just wide enough for him to see me. His lip was curled in disdain. He looked down his nose at me and chuffed away.

Joseph frowned. "What's Jesus want? That we give away our wealth? Live like paupers?"

"Not the point. You missed the point," Peniel replied calmly. "Lazarus was wealthy, yet he gave of his wealth and ultimately risked his life to help the poor children of Jerusalem. Lazarus lived among the beggars—became one of them— while these . . . others . . . slammed their gates and stayed comfortably in their warm houses. They did not raise a finger to help. These fellows worship wealth and success. They have the prophecies about Jesus and reject them. Now even when they have proof that Jesus is the one we have waited for, they reject the prophecies and reject the testimony of Lazarus, a man who has returned from the dead. Nothing will convince them. That's the point of the story. Not about going to hell because you have money. No. It's about rejecting truth. Jesus is truth. My restored vision will not convince them. Look at their backs as they go. These are not men who will be embraced by our Father Abraham."

That night all the wealth and position of my master were unable to purchase a room in the crowded caravansary. One night's lodging cost as much as a week's would have cost. Friends and enemies of Jesus all slept in bedchambers beneath the same roof.

There was not one bed remaining in the establishment. Jesus and his disciples took up an entire wing.

Joseph again asked Peniel, "I have traveled a long way to

meet Jesus, and so has the lad. Please, go tell my friend Lazarus I'm here."

Peniel hurried to the sleeping quarters of Jesus and his band. When he returned, he shrugged cheerfully. "Peter is on guard duty tonight. If it was James or John . . . maybe. But the followers of Jesus are not men to be trifled with. As the Lord sleeps, they draw their swords and post themselves as guards across every entrance lest an assassin creep in and . . ." He drew his finger slowly across his throat. "These are dangerous times. Your friend Lazarus paid for tonight's lodging for all of us. Most everyone's asleep now. Sorry." He yawned. "As for me, my quarters are in the stable with the rest of the boys. Sorry. You'll have to wait till morning."

My master slept on a cot in a tent, hastily pitched on the roof of the inn. I saw the glint of moonlight on the blade of his sword as he unsheathed it. I was given a thick fleece on the floor as my bedroll. Lying down just inside the tent flap, I could see the stars. I longed for my mother and father and our mountain home. The story in the constellations was the same no matter where I lay my head.

I wondered what Rabbi Kagba must have felt the night before he learned of old Herod's plots and warned the parents of the newborn King of Israel to flee from Bethlehem to Egypt. More than three decades after that time, constellations still shone brightly in heaven, telling the story of the Messiah and the great battle for mankind's redemption. On earth, the son of Herod the Butcher King had taken his father's place and still sought to destroy the Redeemer.

I studied the starry cup of salvation, which hung between the Virgin and the Lion of Judah. The Atonement star, the one Rabbi Kagba referred to as the Heart of the Virgin, was poised directly above the outline of the cup. Keeping pace with their passage across the heavens was the distinctive outline of the Lion of Judah.

My fingers closed around the cup, and I quietly whispered the portion of Jeremiah that had been read on the day of my circumcision.

> "The word of the LORD came to me saying,
>   'Before I formed you in the womb
>   I knew you, before you were born I set you apart!'
>   'Ah, Sovereign LORD,' I said, 'I am only a child!'
> But the LORD said to me, 'Do not say, "I am only a child." You must go to everyone I send you to and say whatever I command you. Do not be afraid of them, for I am with you and will rescue you!'"[2]

I was unafraid as I fixed my gaze upon heaven's goblet. I was certain that my journey and my role as cupbearer had been preordained like the path of the stars, long before my life on earth had begun. I did not fear the assassins of Herod Antipas, who were surely lurking very near. I was unafraid of the Pharisees, who envied the love of the people for Jesus, or the Romans, who feared his power and plotted his destruction. God's plan was written in the books of Moses and inscribed above me in the stars. My name, Nehemiah, cupbearer to the King of kings, and Joseph's name were woven into the story too.

An owl hooted from a tree in the courtyard. Pilgrim fires beyond the walls of the inn burned to embers. The whole world was waiting for the dawn when the rightful owner of Joseph's cup would be crowned as Israel's true King!

I closed my eyes at last. "I am not afraid, heavenly Father,"

I prayed as I drifted toward sleep. "I know that my King Jesus rests beneath this very roof. Nothing can turn back your purpose. What men intend for evil, you intend for good . . . to save the lives of many. And I am nearly at the end of my journey."

All the world was asleep. A cool breeze stirred the fabric of the tent. Even in my slumber the sounds were familiar. I dreamed of my father's sheep lying in the moonlight of our high mountain pastures. The smoke of pine and wood from the pilgrim fires blended with the familiar song of a nightingale on the rooftop. Was I in a village in Eretz-Israel? Or in my distant homeland? I could not tell. I felt comforted with the sense that my mother was asleep near me. She sighed and turned over on her bed. In the distance I saw the strong silhouette of my father standing watch over his flocks.

The wind carried his voice across the miles. "Nehi?"

"Here I am, Papa," I whispered.

"Where are you?"

"Here. On the rooftop of an inn near Jerusalem, Papa. Apprenticed to a rich merchant." My answer confused me. Was I not at home? "I'm dreaming," I said aloud.

"You are Nehemiah," noted a voice that was not my father's.

"Cupbearer to the King," I replied. I touched the ancient cup and opened my eyes.

The dream dissolved, and every detail of my journey flooded into my consciousness.

Someone was walking on the rooftop pavilion. My master did not awaken. Parting the flap, I saw a man standing on the parapet. With stars above him and watch fires below, he seemed almost suspended between heaven and earth. He looked out across the hills and valleys toward Jerusalem. In an instant I recognized him.

"It's him. It's Jesus," I whispered, clasping the cup and crawling out from the warmth of my nest.

He turned his head slightly as I emerged. I knew he heard me. It was cold, and my feet were bare. Shoeless feet seemed proper, somehow. I remembered the instruction of God to Moses when he approached the burning bush: "Take off your sandals, for the place where you are standing is holy ground."[3]

I approached slowly, holding the cup in both hands as an offering. I halted an arm's length from his back. The moonlight cast his shadow over me. There were no clouds in the sky, yet the breeze carried the fresh scent of rain.

"Sir?"

"Nehemiah." There was a pleasant smile in his voice when he said my name. I was not surprised that he knew me. I thought he probably knew everything. "You are a long way from home."

"Yes, sir. From the mountains of Gan Eden, I came to find you. To bring you this . . . this gift."

My reply seemed to satisfy him. "Well then, Nehemiah. Just where you are meant to be." He turned then and smiled down at me with my outstretched hands and upturned face. His eyes seemed sad as he studied the gift for a long moment: the cup, Joseph's cup, tarnished and neglected, waiting to be filled. "And how is my old friend, your teacher, Rabbi Kagba?"

"Alive when last I saw him. He wanted to come to you himself but sent me with this instead."

He nodded, pressed his lips together, and touched the rim with his index finger. "In his place you will bear the cup into Jerusalem as I enter the city, Nehemiah."

"Please, Lord. Will you take it from me now? It's been a

terrible burden. I almost lost it once. I dropped it in the woods with the Great Hart. And you see, I didn't polish it. No one knows what it is. Who it belonged to. I was afraid of thieves, so I left it as we found it. Not even a thief wants an old tarnished cup. They couldn't recognize it as it is."

"But you, Nehemiah, you know what it means."

"Yes, sir. The rabbi told me. And Joseph, son of Jacob, the Prince of Egypt himself, appeared to me in dreams. He told me it means something that your earthly father's name is also Joseph, son of Jacob. And that you are called Son of Joseph."

Jesus smiled. "Everything means something."

I blurted, "Now I'm so close and I'm afraid I'll lose it. Afraid I'll fail you."

"No chance of that." He placed his hand upon my head. "You'll have to carry the cup for me until it's time for me to drink from it. You'll travel with us now. A boy among the other boys, Nehi."

I felt relieved. The burden was lifted. I had found Jesus. Or rather, I had searched and searched until at last Jesus had found me on the rooftop. I knew I would be safe with him. Joseph's cup would be safe beneath his protection. "I am your servant, Lord."

"There's work to be done before Passover. It's the duty of the cupbearer to polish the cup. I'll need it shined up, inside and out, for our Passover supper together in Jerusalem. Hidden beneath the tarnish of the ages, you'll find the pattern of the cup is quite beautiful."

I was suddenly very tired. I drew the cup against my heart. "I was dreaming of my mother and father. Of my home."

Jesus bent down until his eyes looked deeply into my eyes. "They are well, Nehemiah. You will see them when the time is right."

I inhaled and exhaled deeply as the grief of months vanished with his assurance. Peace flooded my heart. I had no doubt then that I'd see them again . . . somehow, somewhere. If Jesus could heal the suffering Tobit and the blind Peniel and bring the dead Lazarus back to life, surely he could accomplish the goal of reuniting me with my parents. My memory of the throat-slashing motion of Zimri that had announced to me their death now faded in the light of the clear truth in Jesus' simple words. "Thank you, Lord."

"Now, go to sleep. And tell no one about our conversation. Tomorrow you will join the boys who follow our camp."

"How will I know when to give you the cup?"

"You'll know. Very soon."

He kissed my brow, and I returned to the warmth of my fleece bedroll. My head barely touched the pillow, and I was fast asleep.

Chapter 27

Morning came late and gloomy. A bank of dark thunderheads, low on the eastern horizon, blocked the sunrise.

I opened my eyes as someone quietly recited morning prayers inside the tent. I recognized my mother's weaving in the prayer shawl wrapped around the man, but the voice was not familiar to me.

"Blessed is he who spoke and the universe came into being. Blessed is he who keeps the whole world going."

Was I home in the shepherd camp of Amadiya? On the road? In Joppa? Jerusalem?

I sat up slowly, and my hand fell upon the cup. I remembered then. The inn. Jesus. Lazarus. Peter. Peniel, the cheerful scribe.

"Blessed is he who does what he says. Blessed is he who decrees and finishes." It was not my father but Joseph of Arimathea who recited the blessing upon the day. "Blessed is he who has mercy upon the earth. Blessed is he who has mercy upon creation. Blessed is he who gives a good reward to those who fear him."

My conversation with Jesus on the rooftop last night returned to my memory in a flash, as a dream returns to mind when one is fully awake. I stared at the cup and wondered if I had truly met Jesus here, or if the meeting was only a dream.

"Blessed is he who lives and endures forever. Blessed is he who rescues and redeems us. Blessed is his name!"

Rubbing my eyes, I stared at Joseph. He was a good man, searching for the truth like everyone else.

"Blessed are you, Lord our God, King of the universe and our merciful heavenly Father, who is praised by your people and glorified by the tongues of your pious servants. We praise you through the songs of David, your servant, O Lord our God, with praises and songs. We glorify you and declare your Name and your rule, O God; your great Name glorified forever and ever. Blessed are you, Lord, the King who is to be praised."

I offered my small "Amen" at the end of my benefactor's prayers.

"*Shalom*, Nehemiah." Joseph removed his prayer shawl.

"Good morning." I stood and yawned. I smelled baking bread, and my stomach growled.

"You're hungry." Joseph folded the prayer shawl I had watched my mother fashion so very long ago. "Throw on your cloak. Let's go."

I washed, dressed, and laced my sandals, then followed Joseph down the steep outside steps. As my foot touched the pavement, I heard the loud bang of the barn door and the angry shouts of a dozen boys. A brawl tumbled out of the stable into the courtyard. Like a pack of puppies, the tribe seemed divided into two factions.

Two boys about my age grappled and fell, then rolled on the ground. Punches punctuated the cheers and jeers.

"Get him, Avel!"

"Slaughter him, Davin!"

"Don't let him get away with that!"

"Shut his lying mouth!"

"In the gut. Hit him in the belly!"

"That's it. That's it!"

Pious heads popped out of windows to observe. Pharisees, prayer shawls billowing like the wings of gulls, swooped into the melee.

Then I spotted Jesus, framed in a doorway. He observed the battle for only an instant, then waded into it. Grasping both combatants by the backs of their tunics, he separated them. Still they swung. Jesus held them out of reach of one another as they flailed, then finally gave up. They scowled at one another across the gulf of his arm's reach.

The crowd grew thick—Pharisees, servants of Pharisees, and the men and women of Jesus' band. They looked on in silence.

"Avel." Jesus looked at the bloody face of the fair-haired boy in his right hand. "What's this?"

Avel wiped his nose with the back of his sleeve. "This . . . this cur—"

Jesus shook Avel a little. Avel fell silent. Jesus addressed the boy in his left hand. "All right, then. What's your name?"

A gruff, ragged servant of one of the Pharisees replied defiantly, "He's my boy. Davin is his name. We are in service to Hamid, a Pharisee of Jerusalem and a member of the council."

Davin spat, "And your boy Avel swung first."

Avel shouted, "He was calling you names, Master! Said you are a fraud. Said it was all tricks what you do!"

Davin wriggled and kicked at Avel. "It's true. My father and my master say you're nothing but a troublemaker! Say you're nothing. Nothing! Going to turn the world upside down and get everybody crucified!"

Davin's father raised his chin and stepped forward. "All true. Now I'll thank you to put my boy down."

Jesus effortlessly swung the boy into his father's reach. Then he set Avel to the side. "Go on, Avel. That's enough."

The father placed his son behind him and drew himself up to challenge Jesus. His hands clenched and unclenched. For a moment I thought he would strike Jesus.

Peter rushed between them and faced off with the father. "Get back! You . . . you and that devil's spawn of yours! You're nothing but scum! Pawns of Israel's oppressors."

I spotted Avel's bloody face scowling out from among Jesus' disciples. A woman took his arm, guided him to the side, and dabbed his nose. The crowd of onlookers became a divided mob.

The opposition shouted and cursed Jesus as a pretender and a blasphemer.

Jesus' followers defended their teacher vehemently.

"Jesus can fight for himself, all right!"

"Lord, call down hell fire on them! Burn them up—like Elijah!"

Jesus' eyes flashed angrily, and I thought for a moment he might summon bolts of lightning and brimstone from the sky. Instead, he raised his hand and addressed his people. "That's enough! Be still. You don't know what you are saying!"

Instantly both factions fell silent. Jesus searched the faces of the opposition, fixing his gaze on one opulently dressed Pharisee.

Joseph muttered, "That's Hamid."

Jesus summoned the ruler. "Come here, Hamid. Take your servant and your servant's son. The place to settle this debate is not here. Not now."

The ruler snapped his finger and called his servants as if they were dogs. He warned Jesus, "The time is coming. You are right about that. It will be settled."

The confrontation broke up. Those who had come to discredit Jesus grumbled as they returned to the business of saying morning prayers and preparing to travel to Jerusalem.

Joseph and I hung back as Jesus stooped in front of Avel and the woman tending his nose.

"Well, Avel. You'll have two black eyes, I think." Jesus looked up at the woman. "A cold compress, eh, Mother?"

I knew her name from the stories Rabbi Kagba had told me. Mary. She was beautiful. Her brown eyes with flecks of gold had smile lines at the corners. Hair and eye color was so much like her son.

Mary nodded. "Not broken. Not this time, eh, Avel?"

"No. I'm sorry." The boy cast his blue eyes downward, then hung his head. "I . . . I just couldn't help it. He was so . . . so . . ."

I was surprised that Jesus did not reach out and staunch the flow of blood or heal the bruised eyes. Jesus said quietly, "Pray for the boy you think is your enemy, Avel. Perhaps he will one day learn the truth for himself and become your brother."

"I could have shut his mouth."

Mary murmured, "Poor boy. Yes, Avel, pray for him. He doesn't speak his own words, but only repeats what he has been taught."

Jesus patted Avel on the back. "No more of this, Avel. It solved nothing, as you see."

Avel's friends circled around him. Jesus' disciples joined them.

Jesus said, "Things that cause people to sin are sure to come, but woe to the person from whom they come. It would be better for him to be thrown into the sea with a millstone around his neck than to cause one of these little ones to sin."[1]

Peter growled, "I'll pray for them. Pray them right into

hell where they belong. I look forward to the day when we bury these . . . hypocrites! I'll never forgive them for such arrogant disrespect for you, Lord. Who knows what other sins they hide?"

Jesus did not acknowledge Peter but continued speaking as if he had not heard his words. "Watch yourselves. If your brother sins, rebuke him and if he repents, forgive him. If he sins against you seven times in a day and seven times comes back to you and says, 'I repent,' forgive him."[2]

The apostles said to the Lord, "Increase our faith!"

Jesus held up his thumb and forefinger, demonstrating how a small fragment of faith could accomplish mighty deeds . . . such as forgiveness. "If you have faith as small as a mustard seed, you can say to this mulberry tree, 'Be uprooted and planted in the sea,' and it will obey you."[3]

At that instant, Joseph placed his hand on my shoulder. "There's Lazarus." He inclined his head toward the man I had seen near Jesus the night before. He stood behind Jesus' mother and spoke to Avel over her shoulder. In the morning light Lazarus looked to be about the same age as Jesus. He glanced up at Joseph, then came to where we stood at the foot of the stairs.

"My old friend." Lazarus clapped my master on his back. "I'm glad you've come."

"I returned to Joppa and heard all the news," Joseph said, making the same gesture of companionship. "I came straight away to find you . . . to see. The news was all . . . about you. Is it true?"

Lazarus replied with a single nod. "Yes. If it had not been for Jesus, you would have returned home and found my place at the table empty and my cup poured out."

For a moment Joseph's eyes brimmed with emotion. He did

not remove his hand from Lazarus's shoulder. "Well. Well then. We have both been on far journeys, it seems. One for business and the other for . . . for . . . ," he stammered.

"For the business of the Kingdom of God." Lazarus lifted his chin slightly. His brow furrowed. "It is more beautiful than we could ever have imagined . . ."

"The parable that Jesus told last night . . . It seems this is a far land in which every man will want to dwell. I must speak with him. I have a question that only he will be able to answer. If it is possible."

"Yes. Yes. I know he'll want to speak with you. Tonight is *Shabbat*. Then after that?"

Joseph cleared his throat. "I've got to return to Jerusalem before *Shabbat*. Some business to take care of. But then I'll come back." He added, "My apprentice, Nehemiah, I'd like him to stay here among Jesus' followers until I return."

Lazarus agreed with a laugh. "Nehemiah. Well then, you can stay among our boys. There are a dozen or so who travel with us. They all have duties in the camp. You may have noticed Avel, whose desire is to be a bodyguard." He laughed. "We will put you to work."

And so it was that Joseph delayed his conversation with Jesus. He would return first to Jerusalem to inspect the completion of the family tomb, since Passover was rapidly approaching. If the work was done, he would pay the wages of the men who labored there.

"Please, Master Joseph," I asked, "while you're there, can you go by my grandparents' shop? I'd like to know if it's really getting rebuilt."

Joseph agreed to check on the work in the Street of the Weavers, then left me in the care of his friend Lazarus.

So it was that I took my place among Avel and his two brothers, Ha-or Tov and Emet. Ha-or Tov was twelve, had curly, red hair and pale skin, and was the eldest of the three. Avel was ten and a cheerful boy. Emet was six, fair-haired like Avel, and had somber brown eyes. A wild sparrow perched on his shoulder, flitted to his head, and then to his hand. He fed the bird bread crumbs and called him *Yediyd*, which means "friend."

It was the bird and his endearing actions that made me laugh for almost the first time since the night my father's camp was attacked. There was a story in the bird—a tiny sparrow crushed by the hands of evil, but then healed by Yeshua and now a gift of great joy to a poor boy, Avel said, nodding at his little brother.

The brothers had once been counted among the orphan boys of Jerusalem, living in the caverns beneath the city as Sparrows until they were adopted by an old shepherd of Bethlehem named Zadok.

Zadok had the look of a man who had been mauled by a lion. I had grown up with men who were scarred and battered in the battle to protect the flocks from wild beasts. He was missing one eye, wore a patch over the socket, and his face was creased with an old wound.

That morning he fed the livestock, which were a part of Jesus' band of followers. Mary, the mother of Jesus, spoke to the old man cheerfully as he passed. She and a number of other women served the disciples breakfast. It seemed to me that perhaps Mary was related to Zadok in some way. There was a familiar family bond between them.

The children of the camp ate separately from the adults. I was seated between Avel and Emet. Between bites of bread and eggs, the brothers poured out the story of Zadok.

Avel wore his black eyes like badges of honor. He shrugged.

"Look at my old father there. That patch. A spear hit him in the face, and that's where he lost his eye. Jesus could give him two eyes, but he don't want it. He says his face is a reminder of what the Herods did to his sons, and he is proud of his wounds."

Emet added, "Zadok's a fighter too. So I guess it's right we're his sons."

The old man had spent his life watching over the flocks at Bethlehem. He had a wife and three small sons when Jesus was born in a lambing cave. He had seen angels appear in the sky and had been among the first to hold the infant King of Israel. Mary, Joseph, and the baby had stayed in Zadok's house. When the Magi arrived to pay homage, it was at the home of Zadok where they found Jesus.

I had heard some of the story from Rabbi Kagba. The foreigners had warned Mary and Joseph to flee from Herod. Then the soldiers had come. I was familiar with that much of the tale.

Avel filled in the rest. "Zadok fought the Herodian guards like they were wolves. But he was struck down, and his boys were slaughtered by the soldiers of Herod the Great. So Zadok lost his sons and his eye in the fight. He carried a deep scar across his face and in his heart until Jesus returned to Bethlehem many years later."

Ha-or Tov added, "We three were lost sheep, see? Homeless. No family. Then Jesus healed us—my eyes."

"My broken heart," Avel added.

"My ears, my mouth," Emet said.

Ha-or Tov picked up the story. "And then Jesus brought us to the house of Zadok in Bethlehem and entreated Zadok to accept us as true sons."

So it was that Avel, Emet, and Ha-or Tov had filled the places and hearts of the family that had been lost.

Now old Zadok and his boys were among the circle of about
a hundred close followers who had left every worldly possession
to be with Jesus.

Breakfast nearly finished, Emet rested his chin in his hand
and tilted his head slightly like a puppy waiting to be fed. "All
right, then. Now you know everything about us. We know
nothing about you. Except that you talk funny. You're not from
around here, for sure. What's your story?"

I thought of the hart. The cup. My great journey. The purpose of my life and the meaning of my name. Surely they would
not believe me. I summed up everything: "I am also the son
of a shepherd. His name is Lamsa. And my mother, Sarah, is a
weaver of prayer shawls in the land where Eden once was on
earth. Very far from here."

The little bird flitted from Emet's shoulder to Avel's right
index finger when he pointed at me. "There's got to be more
to it than that."

I stuck out my finger, and the sparrow hopped onto my hand.
I laughed and then spoke the horrible words as if they were nothing. "I was separated from my family when bandits attacked our
camp. My grandparents are in Joppa, and I am an apprentice to
Joseph of Arimathea."

"A very rich fellow." Ha-or Tov narrowed his eyes. "So why
did he leave you here?"

The question was so straightforward I could not think of any
answer but the truth. I passed the sparrow back to Avel, who
kissed it on the beak, then handed it to Emet.

"My true master—Joseph of great reputation—has given
me a task. I'm to polish his family's old *Kiddush* cup for Passover.
I'll bring it to Jerusalem."

Emet asked, "That's it?"

I replied, "That's it."

Avel's head bobbed thoughtfully. "Have you got it? The cup, I mean?"

I reached into the pouch and produced the tarnished vessel. Holding it out to my new friends, I said, "That's it. Clean it. That's my task."

The three were unimpressed. Avel shrugged. "Joseph is so rich he could buy all the *Kiddush* cups in Jerusalem. Brand-new. Gold, even. But he's got to have this old thing, eh?"

"It goes way back." I rubbed it with the fabric of my tunic. "Tradition."

Avel agreed. "Well then. Good luck, Nehemiah. That's all I have to say. Fellows like your master think tradition is everything. If Joseph wants an old beat-up cup for Passover, I guess you're stuck with it. It'll take you all the way till Passover to get it shined, I think."

Ha-or Tov stuck out his lower lip. "Suppose it's just all that color. Black. You scrub and scrub and . . . nothing."

I turned the thing over in my hand, hoping for even a glimmer of light, but the tarnish of ages was thick and unforgiving of my task. From across the courtyard I heard Mary laughing with two other women and a small girl. I remembered what my rabbi had taught me: for his safety, the birth of the King of Israel, Messiah, Redeemer, was hidden from all the world in a stable. But above the earth the stars of the heavens proclaimed his coming.

"One day, in God's timing, the curtain will be pulled back and the glory of the Holy of Holies will shine forth."

I frowned at the dark cup in my hand and knew that the dark layer would somehow be stripped away to reveal its secret.

Chapter 28

M ary and other women labored in preparation for the *Shabbat* celebration, which would begin at sunset. Only a handful of Pharisees remained at the inn. The rest had returned to Jerusalem. The gates of the caravansary were closed and locked, preventing crowds from mobbing the place where Jesus stayed.

Within the earshot of everyone Jesus took his place in the portico and told stories no one had ever heard before.

In the courtyard of the inn was a large mulberry tree. Climbing up, cup in hand, I shared a thick lower branch with the sparrow, Yediyd. As I drank in Jesus' tales, I rubbed at the blackened silver with a soft scrap of fleece. I worked until my fingers ached. My efforts to polish Joseph's cup seemed hopeless. Only a slight gleam of silver shone through at the rim and on a raised, rounded shape on the side. Perhaps a cluster of grapes? I wondered. I wished now I had begun to shine it long before.

Others in the camp labored so they could rest with the Master during *Shabbat*. I would not complete my task before *Shabbat* began at sunset, when I would be forced to lay it aside. And when I resumed? Perhaps I would not even have it cleaned before Passover!

Could I have come so far and suffered so much, only to

end my journey in abject failure? The cup was so unworthy of presenting to anyone, let alone the Messiah. Hopping up to a smaller branch near my head, Yediyd bobbed and flicked his tail, sensing my anxiety.

Jesus unfolded a lesson that seemed directed at me. "Suppose one of you had a servant plowing, or looking after the sheep."

My head rose at the mention of shepherd's work. I was familiar with the nature of a herdsman's labor. There was never a day of rest for a shepherd. The task of caring for the flock was endless.

Jesus continued, "Would you say to the servant when you came in from the field, 'Come along now and sit down to eat?' Would you not rather say, 'Prepare my supper, get yourself ready, and wait on me while I eat and drink. After that, you may eat and drink'? Would you thank the servant because he did what he was told to do?"

How many times had my family eaten a *Shabbat* meal prepared by hireling shepherds around the watch fire? And when my father and brothers had finished their *Shabbat* meals, they took their turn watching the flocks. Only then did the hireling shepherds eat.

I scrubbed at the stubborn tarnish and pictured the scene Jesus described. It seemed to me he glanced at me in the tree. Yediyd bowed and preened. "So you also, when you have done everything you were told to do, should say, 'We are unworthy servants; we have only done our duty.'"

Jesus' words confirmed I had not done my duty until my assignment was complete. Only I did not know how to accomplish the task given me.

A barrage of questions erupted from the disciples as I clambered down from the mulberry tree. Bypassing them, I hastened over to where Mary laid out and smoothed the wrinkles from prayer shawls that had recently been cleaned.

Some of the knotted corners were tangled and messy. Unhurriedly, Mary prized out the snarls so the fringes hung properly. She was chatting pleasantly with Martha, the sister of Lazarus.

Noticing me looking on, Martha observed, "Mary is the best at untying knots there is. No one else has the patience or the skill."

I held the cup out to Jesus' mother, confident she did not know what it was, but that perhaps she could tell me how to make it bright and suitable to present.

"Nehemiah?" A smile lit the crinkled lines of her face. She turned her brown-gold eyes on me. Stepping around the corner of the building, she wiped the flour from her hands on a blue-and-white apron. "So you are here at last, cupbearer."

Suddenly my words were not my own. "Hail, Mary . . . highly favored of the Most High. Favored among all women!"

She answered, "Blessed be the one who sent you. I have been looking for you. Not at all as I expected."

I thought she was speaking of my rabbi. "My teacher, Rabbi Kagba, whom you knew from early days, sends his greetings to the mother of the Lord. He told me you are a gracious and righteous woman, and that you would help me."

She smiled again. "Ah. The student of Rabbi Kagba, among the Magi from beyond the two rivers."

"He sent me in his place. Told me to bring your son this final gift from distant kings who knelt to him and recognized him first among all men, except for us shepherds."

She took the cup from me and peered into the dark well of it. Her pleasant eyes grew sad, and I thought for a moment she must have seen something terrible and tragic in it.

Mary whispered, "Your burden is a very old one, Nehemiah. To know something wonderful . . . that what men intend for evil, God intends for good. Yes. A sword to pierce a mother's heart. To know and yet never to speak of it."

"Joseph's cup. The ancient son of Jacob, who saved all his people after his brothers meant him evil."

"Only a few would recognize the glory of this cup."

"Unless I clean it, it won't be worthy." I showed her my chapped fingers.

Once again I became just a boy, and she became a woman of practical household knowledge.

She instructed, "You'll never get it clean only by scrubbing. The tarnish is too deep."

"Then how?"

"Come with me."

First, Mary immersed the cup in a pot of boiling water and left it there. She led me to a stack of baggage that traveled with the camp. Rummaging through wooden boxes, she produced a plain container crusted with white powder. "Natron," she said. "From the shore of the Dead Sea."

I knew it well. Natron was a common substance carried for trade among the caravans that crossed my father's lands. It was a form of salt, a preservative. First found at the springs of Wadi al Natron in Egypt, the ancients used the mineral to embalm royalty. It was a chief ingredient in the preservation of fresh fish. Mixed with olive oil, it made a fine soap.

With a long metal spoon, Mary fished out the vessel and wrapped it in a towel. The cup seemed unchanged to me, yet she assured me the boiling water had loosened the grime. Then she measured out a small amount of the pale mineral and mixed it with olive oil and lemon juice. Placing the substance in a wooden bowl, she instructed, "Rub this on when the metal cools a bit. With time and effort the cup will reveal what lies beneath the crust of ages."

Jesus, Lazarus, and the other disciples left the caravansary in the afternoon to teach and to heal among the multitude of pilgrims who gathered outside the gates. My new friends, Peniel the scribe, Ha-or Tov, Avel, Emet, and the old shepherd, Zadok, accompanied them. Even the little sparrow, Yediyd, chirped once, ruffled his feathers, then flitted away and swooped over the wall of the inn to pursue them.

Only the women remained behind to prepare for our *Shabbat* supper. I wanted to fly away with all my heart. But the morning lessons of Jesus about a servant sticking to his task kept me rooted beside the mulberry tree.

Mary examined my progress on the cup and frowned. "Perhaps it's more than tarnish. It seems . . . yes . . . as though it may have been in a fire. Scorched. Smoke." She presented me with a second batch of cleanser. "You'll conquer it. You wouldn't have been given the task if it was impossible."

With the second application the black crust began to transfer from the cup to the fleece cloth. I held it up to the light. The faint image of a cluster of grapes and leaves on a vine had begun to emerge. I shared the joy of my progress with Mary. She held the object tenderly, in both hands, as if it were a bird with a broken wing. With a tone of awe she remarked, "Look here. Scorch marks. Yes. You can see the scar. The silver passed through the fire. *Tish b'Av* . . . It must have been."

"*Tish b'Av?*"

She traced the outline of the vines as though she had seen them before. "You know of it, Nehemiah. The day the Babylonians destroyed Solomon's Temple." She kissed the chalice. "Joseph's cup had a place of honor in Solomon's Temple. And then, when Jerusalem burned, the cup and all the other treasures disappeared."

I answered, knowing the story well. "Our people were exiled and made slaves. And when the captivity ended, many Jews returned with Nehemiah. But my father's family never returned to Eretz-Israel."

Mary touched my forehead. "Until now, this moment. Until you returned, bringing it with you, Nehemiah, cupbearer to the King. Blessed be God forever." She pressed it into my hands and returned to her preparation.

The caravansary was filled with the delicious aromas of cooking food. Fresh bread. Lamb roasting in a deep pit. Everything was ready when Jesus and the company returned.

But still the cup was not finished as the sun sank lower to the horizon. My friends gushed about the events and miracles of the day.

Avel grimaced. "There were ten of them. Lepers!"

Emet pantomimed missing limbs and shuffling gaits.

Ha-or Tov held his nose and said, "We smelled them coming!"

Yediyd the sparrow riding his shoulder, Avel exclaimed, "And then . . . all ten! Jesus says to them, 'Go show yourselves to the priests.' Ten of them at once. And they left and all were healed as they went! But only one bothered to come back and say thank you."[1]

Peniel inquired of me, "So, how was your day?"

I replaced the cup in its pouch. "Quiet."

The boys were still yammering as they went to wash.

Mary sought me out and asked to examine the result of my labor.

"Half done," I mumbled, trying not to think of all I had missed in that glorious day.

"Come with me." She brought me to a clay pot in the stable. "Water and new wine," she said, removing the lid and dropping the paste-covered cup into the liquid. "This will be our last work until *Shabbat* ends. Now we rest and let God finish what he began."

"If you say so." I felt like a failure.

She stooped until her face was inches from mine. "Truly, Nehemiah. It is *Shabbat*. You have not failed. Only . . . rest and rejoice now. Great things await us as you bring the Cup of Joseph back to Jerusalem, and it is revealed at last."

Our *Shabbat* supper was served in the open courtyard of the inn. Low tables were spread with heaping platters for our feast and crowned with wildflowers gathered from green velvet hills.

The departing sun, shimmering like molten silver, set the sky on fire as it dropped into the western horizon. Even in my homeland I had never seen such colors in a sundown. Clouds like the orange and red banners of an angelic army unfurled above our heads. I thought of the two angels I was taught accompany every Jew to Sabbath supper.

Jesus wrapped himself in his prayer shawl and sang *"Shalom Aleichem,"* welcoming the Sabbath. "Peace upon you, O ministering angels, angels of the Exalted One—from the King who reigns over kings, the Holy One, blessed is he." His voice was a clear, bright baritone, rivaling that of the finest cantor, and seemed to color the air around us. "May your coming be for peace, O angels of peace, angels of the Exalted One—from the King who reigns over kings, the Holy One, blessed is he."

I wondered if Jesus had commanded the beauty of this evening into existence just for the joy of those whom he loved. I had not seen such glory before. Nor have I seen any sunset like it since.

"Bless me for peace, O angels of peace, angels of the Exalted One—from the King who reigns over kings."

We sang the next lines with him. "The Holy One, blessed is he. May your departure be to peace, O angels of peace, angels of the Exalted One, from the King who reigns over kings, the Holy One, blessed is he."

The voices of men, women, and children were charged with expectation as we sang, "May your departure be to peace, O angels of peace. He will charge his angels for you, to protect you in all your ways . . . your going and returning, from this time and forever more."[2]

Natural light faded to lavender and bright pink; then Mary lit the candles at the table of her son and his favored disciples. She stood above where he was seated. As she gazed down at him, her eyes contained the same deep sorrow I had seen when she looked into Joseph's cup for the first time. She briefly patted his shoulder. It was a gesture of pride and encouragement. But there was something else. I heard a whisper in my heart and knew that this was the last ordinary *Shabbat* mother and son would share together. I think that good woman sensed the end of all things familiar as well.

Jesus placed his hand over Mary's finger, raised his face to her, and sang *"Lecha Dodi"*:

"Wake up, wake up, for your light has come!
Rise up and shine; awaken, awaken, utter a song.
The glory of the Lord is revealed on you.
Why are you downcast? Why are you disconsolate?

In you will my peoples afflicted find shelter
as the city is built upon its hilltop."

We all joined in the song as holiness descended and filled
the place.

"O Sanctuary of the King, royal City—
arise and depart from the unheaval.
Too long have you dwelt in the valley of weeping.
He will have compassion upon you."

The voices of Jesus and Mary blended in perfect harmony as
they must have over a lifetime of Sabbaths.

"Shake off the dust—arise!
Don your splendid clothes, my people.
Through the son of Jesse, the Bethlehemite,
draw near to my soul, redeem it!"

Lazarus sat at his right hand, John at his left. Others, including
Peter and Zadok, shared the head table. A handful of Pharisees
was among the guests, but mostly it was a family gathering.

Martha and the other Mary, the two sisters of Lazarus, sang
the blessing at my table. But I missed my mother. I longed to
see my father's face. I remembered the wonderful discussions of
Torah that seasoned every morsel of my family's *Shabbat* meals.

And then stars winked on above our heads. The music and
prayers turned to questions.

A Pharisee seated opposite Peter lifted his hand and asked
Jesus, "Rabbi! Rabbi? When will the Kingdom of God come?
We all look for it, as the song says."

Jesus answered, "The Kingdom of God does not come with observation, nor will they say, 'Here it is,' or 'There it is.' Because the Kingdom of God is within you."[3]

Everyone understood the question, and I think there was a little disappointment at the answer. Everyone, including me, longed for the moment when the King, the Son of David, would accept the crown of David, son of Jesse. When would he take his rightful place in Jerusalem and establish the kingdom of righteousness on earth forever?

Jesus did not expand on his answer until the meal was ended and the last song was sung. The strangers and doubters among us drank their last cup of wine, recited their prayers with perfect memorization, and toddled off to bed.

The embers of the fire burned low, and one by one the candles burned out. The other boys went to sleep in the stable. Though I was tired, I took my place behind the mulberry tree and listened as Jesus spoke to a few disciples who remained.

"The time is coming when you will long to see one of the days you have spent with the Son of Man, but you will not see it. People will tell you, 'There he is!' or, 'Here he is!' Do not go running off after them. For the Son of Man in his day will be like the lightning, which flashes and lights up the sky from one end to the other.

"But first I must suffer many things and be rejected by this generation. Just as it was in the days of Noah, so also it will be in the days of the Son of Man." He swept his hand over the remains of our feast. "People were eating and drinking, marrying and being given in marriage, up to the day Noah entered the ark. Then the Flood came and destroyed them all.

"It was the same in the days of Lot. People were eating and drinking, buying and selling, planting and building. But the day Lot left Sodom, fire and sulfur rained down from heaven and destroyed them all.

"It will be just like this on the day the Son of Man is revealed. On that day no one who is on the housetop, with possessions inside, should go down to get them. Likewise, no one in the field should go back for anything. Remember Lot's wife! Whoever tries to keep their life will lose it, and whoever loses their life will preserve it. I tell you, on that night two people will be in one bed; one will be taken and the other left. Two women will be grinding grain together; one will be taken and the other left."

"Where, Lord?" Peter asked.

I heard Jesus reply, "Where *tzion* is, there the eagles will gather together."[4]

I was the son of a shepherd, and I had learned the meaning of Jesus' parable from experience. Was it not the psalm my mother prayed over me every night of my life?

"He who dwells in the shelter of the Most High will rest in the shadow of the Almighty. Surely he will save you from the fowler's snare . . . He will cover you with his feathers, and under his wings you will find refuge."[5]

I had always loved the eagles of my high mountain home. Eagles mated for life and tenderly fed, protected, and raised their young together. The behavior of eagles marked the seasons for us shepherds. In the spring, Mama and I had observed as eagles spread their wings over giant nests and protected their vulnerable chicks. In the summer they taught the fledglings to fly by carrying them on their wings. In the autumn, sensing the onset of fierce winter storms, the great eagles gathered and circled in the heavens before they took their young and flew away to a safe haven. Those of us who were shepherds on earth knew the significance of eagles gathering in the heavens. When we saw this sign, it was time to move the flock to safety.

Some may say that night they heard Jesus use the Hebrew word *ah-tzam*, which means "body."

"Where the body is, the eagles will be gathered."

But my ears, long accustomed to the ancient Hebrew pronunciation still used in my mountains, heard him utter the word *tzion*.

On that *Shabbat* night beneath the stars, Jesus told us that, when the time was right, we would recognize the signs, and he would gather his flock from Zion into a refuge where they would be safe from storms that were coming upon the earth.

These were my thoughts when I finally could not hold my eyes open. *Shabbat* rest overcame my ability to take in even one more word. I fell asleep with my back against the trunk of the mulberry tree.

Chapter 29

*A*ll day I sensed the profound holiness of this Sabbath and did not want it to end.

Outside, the clouds broke briefly. Three stars hung in the sky as the *Havdalah* service began, separating Sabbath holiness from the six ordinary days of the week. It was the end of the seventh day. I had marked my journey across the vast wilderness by counting Sabbath rests.

Havdalah means "separation." That evening we could not have known that Jesus would soon be separate from us. Jesus' friend, Lazarus, was given the honor of leading us in the ritual.

Everyone knew that Lazarus, the owner of sacred vineyards, had died and been called back to life by Jesus. Lazarus had experienced separation from this world and knew from experience that after death comes life. He poured *Havdalah* wine made from grapes of his own vineyard.

Lazarus lifted the cup to recite the first blessing of the *Havdalah.* "*Baruch atah Adonai.* Blessed are you, Lord, our God, King of the universe, who creates the fruit of the vine."

I answered with the guests, "Amen."

Every Jew could recite by heart this blessing. These very words had been spoken by Melchizedek to Abraham.

Isaac, Jacob, Joseph, and Moses had recited the ancient

blessing from the beginning of our nation. King David had blessed the waters of Bethlehem as he offered the cup to the Lord. "Blessed are you, who made all things exist by your word. By whose will all things come to be."

On this night, seeing Lazarus and Jesus together, *Havdalah* took on new meaning.

Jesus, by his word, had turned water into wine. He had called forth from the grave a man who had been dead four days. I was only a child, yet as I watched, I understood. Lazarus spoke, and I knew that Jesus was the fulfillment of everything proclaimed in the first blessing and those blessings yet to come.

The second *Havdalah* blessing was recited over the fragrant spices. It was Mary, the beautiful sister of Lazarus, who came forward to present the spice box to Jesus.

Rabbi Kagba had taught me that the spices represent a compensation for mankind's loss of the *Shekinah* spirit. My rabbi, along with other wise men from the East, had offered *Havdalah* spices to the infant King of Israel.

Shekinah had departed from the Temple, but Jesus was the embodiment of all *Shekinah*'s glory and peace.

Jesus thanked Mary for her gift, then opened the spice box. Intense fragrance swirled into the room. He breathed it in, then passed the box, first to his mother.

Lazarus proclaimed, "Blessed are you, Lord, our God, King of the universe, who creates . . ."

Jesus' mother inhaled deeply of the scent. Perhaps the memory of the first box of spices given to her baby boy made her smile. She passed the spice box on to Lazarus. He closed his eyes, breathed in, and nodded. His brow furrowed. I wondered if he recalled the smell of the burial spices that had covered his body when he came out of his tomb?

The reality of seeing Lazarus alive filled me with awe. I considered, for the first time, that perhaps Jesus would raise my parents from death. I would ask him when I presented him with Joseph's cup. All things would be made new now that the King was coming to Jerusalem!

The third blessing was recited over a candle with three wicks. Jesus lit the candle from a few remaining embers. It was unlawful to kindle a fire during Sabbath, so this ritual marked the end of the day of rest.

I was not mistaken. Lazarus looked directly at Jesus when he proclaimed these words: "Blessed are you, Lord, our God, sovereign of the universe, who creates the light."

Three wicks, but one flame—impossible to distinguish one from another. The candle was passed from hand to hand, finally coming to me. I was the last to hold the light.

With a nod, Lazarus signaled me to bring the candle forward to the head table. Lazarus took it from me, and I resumed my seat.

We raised our cups and sipped the last wine of Sabbath, leaving a few drops in the bottom.

Then Jesus, the Light of the World, poured blood-red wine from his cup onto a plate. Jesus' face and the light of the three-wick candle were reflected in the wine.

He took the light from Lazarus and held it high as we all spoke the final blessing together. "*Baruch atah Adonai, Eloheinu, melekh ha'olam* . . . Blessed are you, who separates sacred from secular; between light and darkness; between Israel and the nations; between the seventh day and the six days of labor."

Then Jesus slowly lowered the flame toward the wine he had poured out. He hesitated and then, with a sigh, dipped the wicks into the wine and extinguished the flame. In that instant his reflection vanished, along with the light. "Amen," he said quietly, dipping his finger and touching wine to eyelids, mouth, heart, and the back of his neck.

In my heart I heard the word *separation*. I sensed the end of something . . . and the beginning of something. But what? I imitated the actions of Jesus. Dipping my finger into the drops of wine that remained, I anointed myself. Though my family had not followed this custom of anointing with wine, I felt somehow that everything Jesus did meant something.

Surely Jesus would be crowned during Passover. He would establish his kingdom and take over the palace in Jerusalem. Perhaps, when Jesus drank the last drops of wine from Joseph's cup, there would be no more simple Sabbath meals shared with us common folk.

We sang a psalm at the end of the service, then all began to laugh with joy.

Everyone laughed except Jesus. What was the sorrow I glimpsed in his eyes?

Zadok called to me along with his sons. He clapped me on the back and presented us each with a toy wooden sword he had made. The blades were engraved with the Hebrew word *Chazak*, which means "courage."

As the grown men talked, the women cleared the tables. I crossed swords with Avel, Emet, and Ha-or Tov. My thoughts, however, were on Joseph's cup, which had been soaking for days. I could hardly restrain myself from running to Mary and asking her to fetch it for me. But I played like a boy with my companions and pretended to be thinking of nothing else.

At last Yediyd flew from its perch and settled on Emet's shoulder. Emet found crumbs to feed it, and I hurried to find the Lord's mother. She cleared dishes from the table with the other women.

"Do you think it's finished?" I asked, tucking my sword in my belt.

She knew instantly what I meant. "The cup! It has begun, at least. While we rested, the new wine was at work. And you've been thinking about it today. Waiting for the day to end? Come on, then. Let's have a look."

I followed her to the wine jar containing the precious chalice. Using a long spoon, she fished it out of the concoction. The paste had nearly dissolved. Wine dripped from the metal.

Mary examined it. "Ahhh, a stubborn case. But this will give you a start." At first it seemed unchanged; then Mary picked at the rim with her finger and a dark strip peeled off, revealing bright silver beneath. Finely engraved grape leaves shone beneath. Mary wrapped the cup in a towel and gave it to me. "It is worthy. Yes. Beneath centuries of neglect, tarnish, and soot there is something so beautiful . . . Look! Nehemiah, you'll have to be diligent. For his Passover supper in Jerusalem. The tarnish will yield to you, if you don't give up."

Sabbath officially ended, but Jesus continued teaching into the night. I held the cup in my hands and rubbed and rubbed as Jesus spoke. Layers of grime began to wear away under my patient labor. The beauty of the silver slowly shone through.

It was late when Joseph of Arimathea arrived at our lodging. He had left Jerusalem the moment Sabbath ended, in the company of several Pharisees who were his friends. They had ridden hard through the rain to reach the village where we stayed. Joseph and the others were soaking wet but did not stop to change. I spotted Joseph when he slipped into the dining hall.

Joseph stood, dripping, at Lazarus's back while his two companions moved to sit beside the once-dead man.

Avel frowned at the cup and complimented my labor. "Well, it's something, isn't it?"

"Maybe by Passover." I scrubbed harder.

Avel leaned in closer and whispered, "That's Rabbi Gamaliel, who came in with your master. A member of the council of seventy. And Nicodemus, his nephew, with him. Must be important if they rode all this way through the storm. Gamaliel and Nicodemus are good friends of Lazarus. They come often to hear the Lord teach. Zadok says they're good men."

In the distance thunder boomed and rain sluiced off the eaves. The storm drummed on the rooftop.

By candlelight, Jesus told us one last story.

"Two men went up to the temple to pray, one a Pharisee and the other a tax collector. The Pharisee stood by himself and prayed, 'God, I thank you that I am not like the rest of men, extortioners, grafters, adulterers, or even like this tax collector. I fast twice a week; I give tithes on everything I earn!'"

I saw the shadows on Joseph's face. His eyes narrowed as he pictured the scene. His expression was set like flint as he listened. I did not know why he lingered in the back while his friends had taken their places with Lazarus.

"But the tax collector, standing afar off, would not so much as raise his eyes to heaven but beat his chest, saying, 'Oh God, be merciful to me, a sinner!'"

Jesus looked across the heads of the crowd and seemed to speak directly to Joseph. "I say to you that this man returned to his house more righteous than the Pharisee. For everyone who exalts himself will be humbled, and everyone who humbles himself will be exalted."[1]

There was a stirring among the rich exalted men in the crowd that night. I heard them muttering as they made their way to their bedchambers. Only Joseph, Gamaliel, and Nicodemus remained behind with Lazarus, Zadok, Peniel, and the twelve of Jesus' closest disciples.

A few of us boys stayed in the room. I tucked the cup into its pouch and moved forward with my friends, wanting to show Jesus my progress.

Peter and James rebuked us. "Go on to the stable with you! The master is tired."

But Jesus heard them and called us to him. He placed his hands on our heads and blessed us.

I will never forget what happened after that. Jesus put his hand on my shoulder and said, "The Kingdom of heaven is for those who are like these boys. I say to you, he who will not receive the Kingdom of God like a little boy will never enter into it."[2]

I tried to think what he meant by that. What set boys apart from the men who towered over us? Yediyd perched on Emet's head. He reached up to scratch Yediyd's feathery belly. Avel drew himself erect and grinned at a sour-faced disciple. Ha-or Tov, who clasped a wooden sword, raised it high, saluted, and bowed. And I reached into the pouch and held the half-clean cup up to show its renewed gleam to the rightful owner.

"By Passover," I promised.

Jesus smiled. "Boys. The happy stewards of God's Kingdom."

Then Joseph cleared his throat and asked Jesus, "Good Teacher, what must I do to inherit everlasting life?"

Jesus leveled his eyes on Joseph's face and smiled. "Why do you call me good? There is no one good, except One, that is God. You know the commandments: 'Do not commit adultery,'

'Do not murder,' 'Do not steal,' 'Do not bear false witness,' 'Honor your father and your mother.'"

Joseph's face seemed so eager as he answered, "All these things I have done from my boyhood." He looked at me, and I knew by his reply that he was trying to tell Jesus that he was indeed trusting God like a little child.

Jesus lowered his chin and moved his hand from my shoulder to that of Joseph. "You lack one thing."

"What is it, Lord?"

"Go. Sell everything you have and give it to the poor and you will have treasure in heaven. Then come, follow me."

The light in Joseph's face dissolved into sorrow because, as everyone knew, Joseph was very rich.

When Jesus saw his sorrow, he said quietly, "How difficult it is for those who have wealth to enter into the Kingdom of God! It is easier for a rope . . . *khav-la* . . . to go through the eye of a needle than for a rich man to enter the Kingdom of God."

Thunder clapped and those in the room muttered, "Who then can be saved?"

Avel, who stood apart from us a few paces, told me later he thought he heard Jesus say it was easier for a camel . . . *gam-la* . . . to go through the eye of a needle than for a rich man to enter the kingdom.

That would have meant it was impossible for any rich man to be saved! How could a camel pass through the eye of a needle?

But I was there at Jesus' right hand and I heard him speak the Aramaic word *khav-la*, "rope," distinctly. Though rope and camel sound alike, I understood, by the unchanged language of my homeland, exactly what Jesus said. As a son born to a weaver, I knew well enough that to thread a rope through the eye of a needle meant that only a single strand could fit. In my earliest childhood I sat at the feet of my mother and watched her weave a bell rope—*khav-la*—to hang around the neck of a ram. The rope began with one single thread between her fingers.

Strip away all the extra fiber and what remains is one thread. The core of a rope is a single strand. In the end, only that core thread will fit through the eye of a needle.

Jesus spoke the truth. A man is born in this life with nothing and will take nothing with him when he leaves. Rich or poor, it is only that thread of faith in God at the core of a human soul that will pass through the gates of eternity.

Jesus answered, "Those things which are impossible with men are possible to God."

The metaphor made perfect sense to me.

Simon Peter shook his shaggy head and waved a brawny hand to encompass threadbare clothing and worn sandals. "Look! We have left everything and followed you!"

Jesus answered, "Truly I say to you that there is no man who leaves houses or parents, or brothers or sisters, or wife, or children for the sake of the Kingdom of God, who will not receive many times more at this time, and in the world to come, life everlasting."[3]

These words seemed to please the disciples. Visions of wealth and government positions made them smile. I saw their expressions light up, and I knew why, even though I was a boy.

It was after this that Joseph, Gamaliel, and Nicodemus drew Lazarus and Jesus and his closest followers aside and explained why they had come that very night through the rain.

"You must not go to Jerusalem," Nicodemus said. "There is a plot that reaches from the palace of Herod into the heart of the Sanhedrin. Herod and the high priest are now the best of friends. It is the common hatred of you that has given them common cause."

Jesus thanked them for coming and wished them good night. I remained by the fire, polishing the cup. Did he not see me there?

Lightning flashed through the windows. Thunder shook the house.

When the room was empty, Jesus said to his twelve closest friends, "We are going up to Jerusalem, and everything that is written by the prophets about the Son of Man will be fulfilled. I will be delivered over to the Gentiles. They will mock me and spit in my face. They will scourge me and curse me and kill me. On the third day I will rise again."[4]

I found a quiet place to be alone in the stable. Removing the cup from its covering, I admired the pattern that had begun to emerge. It had been so black and dingy—seemingly disreputable—so how could it be so valuable? How could something so shabby be the heir to so much history and prophecy? Why wasn't it shined up and in a palace somewhere before we found it? How could it be that so much meaning was contained within something so obscure?

Thunder boomed and echoed hollowly, rolling around the hills outside.

I thought I fully understood the vessel's significance. In Abraham's case, it was a symbol of worship and reverence for the Almighty. With Joseph the Dreamer, the cup represented how God's plan may permit suffering, but never suffering without purpose. For David, it was an emblem of kingship and divine appointment and recognizing that loyalty and faithfulness might bring danger and sacrifice.

But if nothing was left to be revealed, why had the cup been so tarnished? Why couldn't I polish it before now? It had possessed no form or comeliness to make it desirable. In its former state it was a very poor gift for anyone, let alone for Messiah.

While still puzzling over the chalice, I returned to our bed of straw and fell asleep . . .

✿

"*Shalom,* Nehemiah."

"*Shalom,* Joseph. I was expecting you," I replied to the Dreamer.

"You have been thinking about the cup, yes? Here is a psalm for you: 'For in the hand of the LORD there is a cup of his wrath . . . and all the wicked of the earth drink it down to its dregs.'"[5]

I shivered. "I don't like the sound of that."

Cupping my face in his hands, Joseph said, "Have no fear, Nehemiah. Would you like to meet someone?"

"Where are we going this time?"

"We're already there. See?"

In a tiny room, no larger than the pantry in my home in Amadiya, sat an elderly man with a furrowed brow. His flowing hair and equally long beard were both snow white, like the hart's hide. *A prophet, surely,* I thought. At first I did not recognize the repeated scratching noise I heard. By the smoking light of a single oil lamp I saw a pen in the prophet's hand. He was intently inscribing line after line on a roll of parchment.

"Who is it?" I asked.

"Look over his shoulder," Joseph encouraged. "See if you can read what he's written there."

I read, "'Behold, I have taken from your hand the cup of . . . my wrath.'"[6]

"This is Isaiah," I said. "He writes of the time when God's judgment against Judah will be complete and the exiles will return to the land."

"Very good!" Joseph applauded. "The rabbi has taught you well. And answer me this: Why was the nation judged?"

"Because we were stubborn and rebellious and arrogant. Because we did not listen to the prophets who warned us not to worship other gods."

"Again, well said. And is such a judgment only leveled against nations? What does the Almighty expect of each man?"

"The same?"

"Now, Nehemiah, answer me this: How is the cup of wrath emptied? Can it just be poured out? Or must someone drink it?"

"This is a riddle and not a lesson," I objected.

Joseph smiled. "A fair objection. Look to see what Isaiah has now written."

"'He has no form or comeliness . . . that we should desire him.'[7] That's what I said about the cup," I noted. "But I still don't understand."

In response Joseph pointed at the parchment, urging me to bend closer to the scratching pen.

The prophet read aloud what his pen had recorded. "'But he was wounded for our transgressions, He was bruised for our iniquities.'"[8] Laying aside the quill Isaiah raised his face and his hands to the ceiling and groaned aloud. "Ah, but no, Lord," he said. Then, as if weights pressed on his arms, his shoulders sagged. The pen was inexorably reapplied to the scroll. The writing resumed.

A peal of thunder rattled the shutters of the prophet's chamber.

I'm sure I wore an expression of horror to match Isaiah's.

"No wonder Isaiah looks so miserable," I said. "He is writing this about the Messiah? About our coming king? But how can it be?"

Joseph's index finger remained outstretched, forcing my eyes back to the inscription.

" 'The LORD has laid on Him the iniquity of us all. . . . You make His soul an offering for sin.' "[9]

"Like a drink offering," Joseph commented.

Isaiah wrote, "Because He poured out His soul unto death . . . He bore the sin of many, and made intercession for the transgressors."[10]

"Please, no more," I pleaded. "Messiah is going to die? Why? How can it be?"

Joseph spoke gently to me. "For the cup of God's wrath to be removed once and for all, it is necessary for someone to drink it. Every last drop. Every consequence of sin and rebellion from our Father Adam to the last man on earth—every debt, yours and mine—must be paid. Either we must drink it, or someone who is both willing and able to drain the cup must do it for us. Do you see?"

Thunder grumbled and muttered outside as it drifted off to the east.

"No," I protested, "I don't see and I don't want to. Please take me home. This is a bad dream. I want to wake up."

The lip of the cup had pressed a groove into my cheek. The outside of the bowl was damp with my tears.

❧

It was not yet light. The boys of the camp slept in fresh straw. We were sprawled this way and that, like a pile of puppies. Our wooden swords were planted in the soft ground of the stable. The tiny sparrow perched on a hilt, its head beneath its wing.

Avel's arm lay across my face. Emet's feet were too close to my head. Ha-or Tov was mostly buried in our bedding. Peniel had long ago climbed into the loft and snored contentedly apart from our disheveled sleeping quarters.

Dawn was only beginning to creep up the eastern rim of the sky when Joseph came to the barn door. My eyes opened at the groaning of hinges.

"Nehemiah!" he called in a loud whisper.

I was already awake but exhausted. Long hours I had wrestled with what Jesus said about being killed and rising again. I did not know what he meant, did not like it, but was afraid to ask him to explain further. In all that I was not alone. Whispered conversations, some angry, some fearful, had circled round the disciples the way the stars pivoted overhead in a single night.

"Here I am," I replied.

"Get up, Nehemiah," Joseph urged. "Dress quickly. I've had a message. We must set out for Jerusalem at once."

Slipping out from the blanket atop the straw, I tugged my robe over my tunic. After donning my sandals, I secured the cup around my waist.

Stepping outside, I glanced at the sky. The thunderstorm had passed, leaving chilly, sparkling air in its wake. Clearly visible in the south, the constellation of the Snake Handler prepared to crush the head of the serpent. And the serpent was still poised to strike the hero's heel.

Beside the entry was a half barrel set in the ground as a watering trough. Plunging my head into the chilly water did little to make me more alert.

"Trouble?" I asked.

"Matters I must attend to," he replied. "But also, there is something waiting for you in the Holy City."

"For me?" I said doubtfully, plucking a bit of straw from my hair.

Joseph did not explain but turned to greet Lazarus as he strode across the courtyard.

No one slept well after Jesus made his strange, ominous prophecy. Lazarus bore a pained expression.

"Nehi?" I heard Avel's voice call from inside the stable.

"Make your good-byes," Joseph instructed. "We're leaving right away."

"You're leaving?" Ha-or Tov asked.

I shielded my eyes as sunlight beamed over the rooftop. "Master Joseph says something is waiting for me."

My trio of friends gathered around me.

Peniel joined us.

"It must be something good," Peniel observed.

We stood in sleepy silence, hugging ourselves awake. We were not trying, yet could not help overhearing the conversation between Joseph and his friend Lazarus.

"I have many sources," Joseph said. "In both palaces—Herod's and Lord Caiaphas's. I even know a few of the servants in the governor's household. Whatever they are plotting, I'll find it out. I'll be able to warn you before you come to Jerusalem."

"We will come," Lazarus responded. "You don't know him as I do. He'll not draw back. His face is set like flint on Jerusalem. This is why he came. And as for me, I'll never be afraid of death again."

Birds in the mulberry tree awakened, and the air resounded with chatter. There was a hint of sage and lavender on a gentle breeze.

Behind us Jesus called out, "*Shalom*, Joseph. Lazarus . . . and my boys."

I stepped into view so Joseph would know I was ready to leave and also because I wanted to speak to Jesus before we departed.

"Rabbi," Joseph said, "I have something I want to give you." Summoning me to his side, Joseph sent me to get the dark blue cloth pouch embroidered with David's harp and the Lion of Judah.

When I retrieved it from Joseph's saddlebag and presented it to him, he looked at me with a question in his eyes.

I nodded my approval.

Opening it, Joseph withdrew the specially ordered prayer shawl my mother had made. "I want you to have this," Joseph said, presenting it to Jesus. "It was woven by Nehemiah's mother for me. But the boy agrees . . . we want you to have it."

Jesus accepted the prayer shawl. "In time for morning prayers. Also in time for Passover." He seemed pleased. Putting it around his shoulders, he embraced Joseph and thanked him. "It is beautiful." He directed his praise to me. "I am a carpenter by trade, but I know fine workmanship in cloth. Your mother is an artist."

"She is . . ." I took some comfort that Jesus spoke of her as if she was still among the living. Of course, he could not know everything because I had not given him all the details. Then, I thought, perhaps Jesus did know about the battle and the bandits. After all, he knew that I would be there, bringing Joseph's cup. "Yes," I concluded. "My mother is the best weaver in the world, some say."

Jesus ran his fingers along the hem of the cloth. "Yes. Of course she is."

"And," I blurted, "I'm almost done polishing the cup. I worked all night off and on. I'm afraid that, if we are leaving, something might happen to it. Please, sir, I want you to take the cup." I stepped forward and tugged the bundle to the front of my waist. "Before anything . . . before you go to Jerusalem."

Jesus shook his head. "No. You are the cupbearer, are you not?"

Emet shoved my wooden sword into my hand. "And other things. The other Nehemiah slept with a sword, they say."

Jesus nodded. "So he did. Cupbearer. Builder. Soldier. So I have a special assignment for you. Before Passover I will come to Jerusalem."

An excitement stirred in me at his words. The King was coming! Maybe he had not meant what he said last night about being tortured and killed. Maybe the one he referred to was not himself?

I asked, "When will you come, Lord?"

"You will know when I approach." The flock of birds rose from the mulberry tree and flew as one toward the sunrise. Jesus put his hand on my head. "Cupbearer, you will meet me there. Bring the cup to me then as you were instructed. Yes? There is only one right time to give it to me."

Chapter 30

On the way back to the Holy City, I made one attempt to ask my master, Joseph, what could possibly be waiting for me. Rousing himself from a deep reverie, he offered a wry smile. "I'm sorry, Nehemiah. I am thinking about a great many things right now. I will not let Lazarus or Jesus be assassinated when they come to Jerusalem. But right now I have to ponder who I can trust . . . and who I can't." Giving a cautionary gesture, he concluded, "You won't be disappointed. I promise."

With that, I reined my donkey to a halt until Joseph's horse was half a dozen paces in advance. Then I resumed following. I made no further attempt to unravel the mystery before the heights of the Temple loomed ahead.

After the storm the sky was fiercely blue, the air severely clean. A pale yellow sun still struggled to warm the landscape, but that day there was no wind competing against it.

We traveled the main highway running north to the Galil. Every half mile or so another converging stream of humanity poured in alongside us. Rivulets of tramping pilgrims coalesced into a river going to David's City. The Passover pilgrimage was already fully in motion. Those who had come from farthest away were the earliest en route—pious travelers from all corners of the world, seeking the Temple of the Almighty.

With the increased number of visitors and the lack of wind, the pillar of sable smoke from the sacrifices was twice as thick as I had seen it before. It towered far up into the heavens.

The sight reminded me of my mother's description of her home. It made me miss my mother and father worse than ever. It was so wrong for me to be here without them.

We approached the city by way of Damascus Gate, the same direction by which I had arrived with the caravan.

Dismounting, we left our animals in the care of a groom. As we passed through the gate, we were scrutinized by a hard-eyed Roman decurion. The Imperial officer had his full contingent of ten troopers lining the sides of the gate. Each was in armor and carried shield, short sword, and javelin.

"Taking no chances with rebels," Joseph muttered to me.

We stood on the main thoroughfare of the city. I thought we would follow it toward Joseph's home, but instead we took the first turning. We veered into the commercial district, the same part of the city as the burned-out remains of my grandparents' shop.

My stomach turned over, and I felt queasy. Did we have to go this way? It was an all-too painful reminder of my lost childhood, my missing family. I knew my grandparents weren't coming back to the Holy City until after Passover. There was nothing for me there now except sorrow.

"Come along," Joseph urged, seemingly oblivious to my distress. *But he's a good man, caring for his friends' safety,* I reminded myself. *I must not be too selfish about my own feelings.*

The Street of the Spice Merchants was one short row of shops before the Dried Fruit sellers, and then the Potters' stalls. Following that area were the Cloth Dyers. The Street of the Weavers was just beyond.

In the distance a dog barked. It was not an angry sound nor a fearful one, but a joyful noise of recognition. Instantly I was carried in my deepest longing to the last time I had seen Beni, my best friend: on the night of Zimri's attack. On the night when everything in my life changed, already some seven months in the past, a lifetime ago.

And then I saw him . . . or, rather, he saw me.

Bounding toward me in his singular stiff, plunging lope was Beni's woolly, black-and-tan mottled form. I had only a moment to shoot a bewildered, wondering look at Joseph and catch a glimpse of his smile in return before Beni bowled into me at full speed. Knocking me over, the herd dog planted his forefeet on my chest and licked my face. I bubbled with laughter, pushed him away, then pulled him back again.

For Beni to have made the journey all the way from Amadiya to Jerusalem could only mean—

I jumped up.

My mother, the hem of her robe lifted to her ankles so she could manage her limping run without tripping, dashed toward me, calling out my name. Coming up the street behind her were my father and brothers and Rabbi Kagba.

Mother swept me into an embrace, held me by my shoulders to look into my eyes, then crushed me to her again. All the while Beni danced on his hind legs around the scene, while passersby gawked.

"How? What?" I questioned, lifting my gaze to my father.

He knew exactly what I was asking. "We won the fight. But we had some injuries. Me"—he pointed to his head—"and Beni must have two of the hardest heads in Gan Eden. By the time we set out to follow, you were over the mountain."

Rabbi Kagba arrived, slightly out of breath and puffing.

"Nehemiah, how you have grown. I met your father searching for you and told him the direction you had taken. When we reached Zakho, your caravan had already left."

"And then," Father added, "an early snow closed the passes for a time and made us later still. But now, here we all are."

Mother on one side, Father on the other, and Beni, smiling in the way only herd dogs can grin, we entered the Street of the Weavers. Instead of the depressing ash heap I had seen before, a new shop rose in its place. The walls were up, the roof was on, and the hammering and sawing suggested the interior finish was progressing. A workman fitted the sliding panels on the street front that would open to display the wares to potential customers.

"We rented a house across the street," Mother explained. "It's small, barely big enough for us all, so your grandparents won't come up from Joppa until the new shop is complete. After Passover."

My teacher plucked at my elbow. He thumped his thumb against the bundle containing the cup. "Have you seen him?"

"Yes," I said. "And he is everything you told me . . . and more. He is coming here for Passover. I am to complete my mission then."

Joseph of Arimathea, who had not wanted to interrupt our reunion, spoke at last. "And I find I must order another prayer shawl. Nehemiah is right about Jesus of Nazareth. No man ever spoke like he does, or does the things he can do. I gave him the first shawl. He has promised to wear it at Passover."

Every day potential customers came to the place where our shop was being rebuilt. They asked the workers, "Where is it? The place where the world-famous prayer shawls once were sold?"

I heard the workmen answer, "Burned to the ground. Gutted. Being rebuilt, as you can see. But nothing to buy here now."

And the people went away disappointed.

There was nothing to be done. The work always took a little longer than one expected, the foreman explained to my father. So we were told we must be patient.

One morning, from the balcony of the rented house, Mama peered across the street as the workmen set the shutters of the new weaver's shop in place. "Oh! I can see it now. As it was . . ."

I was at the opposite window, playing with Beni. Papa was at the table going over papers with my three brothers. We all looked up to listen because Mama's voice was so soft we knew she was not speaking to us.

Wistful, remembering the glory of the old shop, she said, "I was too lame to go play with the other girls . . . not as lame as I am now. But I had such joy. I used to sit there in the window as a girl and weave and sing the songs of the loom, while the pilgrims came to listen on all the holidays."

Papa's face appeared pained. "Sarah, the new shop may be done before Passover."

She clucked her tongue, knowing it was impossible. "My loom is a thousand miles away. My father and mother are weaving for sailors in Joppa. My sisters are selling prayer shawls from their houses. And I have nothing to offer. Our prayer shawls . . . all the world once came here. Now even the sign is gone, and the shop is vacant for the first time since the days of the Maccabees. One hundred and sixty years of the forefathers of Boaz the Weaver. And it will not be ready when the pilgrims come."

My elder brothers exchanged looks with Papa.

He sighed. "Well, Sarah, you never know. There's always next year. And maybe a miracle. It could happen."

"We'll be back in our mountains . . . Gan Eden, among the flocks next year." She turned away from the window.

Beni left me and sidled over to my father to be petted.

For a minute, Papa's lower lip protruded slightly, as it did when he was in deep thought. Then he dismissed her melancholy, all business now. "I am sending these three sons to Joppa today to carry samples of raw wool, fabric, and a letter to the exporter. They must stay with your parents."

Mama limped to her chair and sat down. "Of course. My parents will welcome them. But will the boys come back in time for Passover? Or will our table in this house of exile be empty except for us few?"

Mama loved to cook for large crowds. Passover in the shepherds' camps back home had always been packed with joyful celebration. The thought that my brothers would also be absent made the holiday seem bleak and lonely.

Ezra asked me, "May I take your dog, Nehemiah? I'm training him, and we're getting on well. No fields around here to work him. Do you mind?"

Beni smiled and wagged at me eagerly, as if to ask permission. The city was not fun for him. Nothing much for a dog to learn here. Only Jerusalem's cats to chase and neighbors who complained about barking.

"All right, then." I felt left out. My brothers were going, and I must stay. There was still Joseph's cup, which I polished every day as I awaited the arrival of Jesus.

And so it was settled.

My brothers and my dog set out for Joppa that very morning. In the afternoon I wandered over to the shop and watched carpenters sand the cabinets.

A new, unfinished sign was laid out on the woodcarver's

bench. The carver carefully fashioned letters on the plank. Only one Hebrew word was so far engraved on the signboard: *BEIT*, which means "house."

I asked the woodcarver, "Will it be ready to hang before Passover?"

He laughed at my question and did not look at me as he lightly tapped the chisel to begin the next letter.

So it seemed that Mama was right. Nothing would be ready by Passover. The pilgrims would come, hoping to buy the most beautiful prayer shawls in the world to worship and pray and then as a shroud in which they would be buried. This year they would take away nothing. As their fathers and grandfathers had come generations before, they would come to the fourth shop from the head of the Street of the Weavers, but they would find an empty shell.

It was less than two weeks until Passover. I watched from the window of our rented house as the lanes of the city became glutted. The stalls of Jerusalem overflowed with goods. Drovers leading donkeys loaded with merchandise navigated through the crowds. Early pilgrims packed the narrow lanes and shopped for souvenirs. Fresh bedding and newly washed clothes hung like multicolored flags from the upper balconies of every shop and dwelling along the Street of the Weavers.

Across the street, stone masons and carpenters put finishing touches on the lower story of our rebuilt shop. Cabinets and shelves and countertops were fitted. Upstairs our residence was being painted. Papa had promised to pay the artist that very day.

Mama's leg was swollen and painful. She leaned against my

father's arm as we entered the building to inspect the work. The smell of clean sawdust and chiseled limestone hung in the new interior.

Mama ran her hands over the smoothly sanded countertop. "Beautiful. I can see a bolt of fine fabric laid out here. And, over there, stacks of prayer shawls on the shelves. Oh! My mother and father will be so pleased, Lamsa."

"Close your eyes." Papa led her to the opposite corner of the room, where something big was covered by a tarp. He pulled the covering away, revealing a brand-new loom. "Now look!"

The frame of the loom was painted with grapevines—like the heavenly loom she had once dreamed about in the wilderness of our mountains.

Mama gasped and clapped her hands together, then stroked the wood as though it were a harp. "Oh my! My! To work on such an instrument! But who will play this?"

Papa kissed her cheek. "My love, you know it is for you. We'll stay here in Jerusalem for a time. Rabbi Kagba says the new King of Righteousness will reign here. We will stay in Jerusalem. The great city of blessing. I have given instructions to our eldest son. With the help of my steward, he will return and tend the flocks. He is the heir and will rule the flocks in my place. I'll return from time to time to oversee his work. But now I am at an age where I want to return. Jerusalem must be our home and the home of Nehemiah now that Messiah will reign."

Mama wiped tears away. "My dream, Lamsa. My prayer— that Nehemiah could attend Yeshiva here in the city. We'll attend his *bar mitzvah* on the very mountain where Abraham offered his son Isaac to the Lord. There's time enough to prepare for our future. Now, this year in Jerusalem . . . and always!

How can I tell you what I feel?" When she leaned heavily on the countertop, I knew her leg was in great pain.

Perhaps my father had also seen how difficult it would be for her to journey back to our homeland. I wondered if that was perhaps a part of the reason for his decision.

The master builder swept his hand toward the steps leading to the upper story. "Sir, the main room upstairs is completed. A few weeks only and the bedchambers . . . ready to furnish. But now? The large upper room is ready—a beautiful room, as you commissioned, sir. The artist just completing the wall mural of Paradise, the garden of Eden from whence you come." He laughed. "A place I would like to dine, if I may say so."

Mama brightened. "Passover *seder*? Here? Jerusalem. Our first meal. Now that will be Paradise."

The builder bowed to her. "As you hoped. The upper room is indeed ready for the first supper, madam."

Papa replied, "As we prayed it would be."

The builder strode proudly to the stairway. "This way."

Mama eyed the steep steps with consternation. Her leg was not up to the climb. She bit her lip and hung back. "Lamsa, dearest, you go. And, Nehi, go up with him."

The builder, not comprehending the severity of Mama's pain, urged, "But the mural, madam. Ah, to see it is to drink the pure waters of Eden!"

She answered, "I'll wait here. Bask in the glory of our beautiful weaver's shop . . . imagine the shelves stocked with our handiwork. And, most of all, enjoy my new loom."

Papa and I followed the builder up the steps. There was no handrail, and the stairwell was narrow. We emerged into a room immersed in color and the scent of fresh paint and linseed oil.

The artist, a thin, paint-spattered old man, was cleaning his brushes when we entered. He glanced up and smiled at me with a mouth only half full of teeth. "This is the boy?" he asked my father. "The boy who rode the Great Hart and came from afar to Jerusalem?"

"Yes. Nehemiah, my son."

"Well then." He chuckled. "Well. Well."

The painting of Eden covered the west wall. Sunlight from the east streamed through the window and splashed the scene of ferns and trees and flowers in bloom beside a flowing brook.

I gasped. In the midst of the forest stood the Great White Hart. Steady amber eyes seemed almost alive. He gazed at me serenely. A deep wound over his heart oozed blood, to show his sorrow for the loss of Eden. Now, at the end of my journey, the great protector and companion who had carried me through so much danger was portrayed before me as if I was seeing him as he was.

And Joseph's cup was at his feet. Yes! Joseph's cup! I recognized the pattern of the engraving without question. The silver chalice stood on a boulder beside a brook so real I could almost taste the water. Grapevines curled around it, and clusters of grapes gleamed in the sunlight. But it was not wine that filled the cup. Water from the eternal spring and blood from the wound in the Great Hart's heart mingled together and filled the vessel to its brim.

"But how?" I looked up at my father.

The contractor said, "The view of the Temple Mount through the arched window is spectacular. I haven't seen a view so beautiful even in the palaces of the rich men."

Papa put a hand on my head. He gestured at the painting and then through the window at the Temple. "From the land of

Eden to Solomon's Temple Mount. It's been a long journey, eh, Nehemiah?" Clearly, Papa was pleased with the artist's vision. "The garden, as it must have been on our mountain, before all was lost. And now, here—in Jerusalem—all will be restored."

Papa fished for silver coins with which to pay the artist. A few small drops of red paint marred the new wood planks of the floor. The old man apologized and stooped to clean away the paint.

"Leave it," Papa insisted. "As if the blood of suffering flowed from your brush, all of creation groans as we wait in hope for the Redeemer. A few drops on the floor. A foretaste of all the feasts we will celebrate in this place. A reminder that the cup of sorrow will be followed by the cup of great joy! And we will begin our celebration of new life this Passover."

Chapter 31

Μy family and Rabbi Kagba worshipped together within the walls of the great Temple. Choirs and musicians and the prayers were almost drowned out by the clamor of buying and selling in the stalls of the merchants and moneychangers.

I scanned the faces of beggars and boys, hoping to find my Sparrow friends, who had taken me in on my first terrible night in Jerusalem. I did not find them among the throng.

I spent the week working to polish Joseph's cup. At last it was no longer a cup. As each layer of tarnish was removed, the intricate pattern of vine and leaf and cluster of grapes was revealed. It had become Joseph's silver chalice. Beneath my polishing cloth, the ancient gift was worthy of the coming King.

I showed it first to Rabbi Kagba. Tears misted his eyes. "Good job, my boy. Good job. At last I will see him with my own eyes. His hands will encircle this silver. The wine will reflect his face. And he will pour himself out with the wine as the *Havdalah* blessings are spoken."

There were rumors that Jesus had come as far as Bethany, that he slept beneath the roof of Lazarus and would enter Jerusalem soon. We did not know if this was true.

Joseph of Arimathea stopped by to tell us that the chief priest had met with Herod Antipas to discuss what steps must be taken if Jesus and Lazarus entered Jerusalem. The increased patrols of Roman soldiers and Herodian guards were evident. City officials were on edge. Rebellion and riots were a possibility.

Sabbath arrived. Though we could have walked to the Temple to celebrate, Mama's leg was worse than ever. We worshipped quietly at home. Rabbi Kagba led us in the same prayers I had heard on the lips of Jesus only a week earlier.

That night, when three stars shone in the sky, Sabbath ended. I asked the rabbi when he thought Jesus would come.

"Soon," the old man said. "As the Passover moon grows, the heavens once again give signs of his coming glory to us."

As everyone slept, I pocketed the chalice and tiptoed across the street to the new building. I climbed the stairs to the upper room. The aromas of paint and blooming night flowers mingled. I sat on the floor in front of Eden. In the darkness it seemed more than a painting. I felt I could have stepped into that perfect world. I might have dipped the cup into the brook and raised it to my lips.

The wound on the hart's breast seemed the color of wine. "Ah, we have traveled so far," I whispered. "So many wounds. So much heartache. And now, Jesus the King is coming! He will drink from this cup, and all things will be made new."

Over my shoulder, the moon rose in the east over the Temple Mount. I held the chalice up, toward the starry constellation of the cup, for the Lord of heaven to see it was clean and ready. "Here it is, my heavenly Father. I have done all you asked. I will give it to your King when he comes. Now, please, Lord, bless my family. Heal my mother's leg. Increase my father's work. His flocks and herds. The travels of my brothers back to Gan Eden. And . . . show me! Show me what I must do to serve your kingdom."

I crossed the street and went to bed, feeling certain that Jesus was very near to me. The tarnish of obscurity was washed away. The revelation was at hand. Somewhere, perhaps as close as Bethany, Jesus was also gazing at the stars and watching the Passover moon grow more full every night.

I closed my eyes and blessed the one from above who made the moon and the stars. And I blessed the one who had left heaven's glory to come down to earth to live among us. Jesus was his name. Certainly his eyes now looked up toward heaven from earth as if he were a man like all the rest of us. But he was not just any man.

I longed for the moment when Jesus would take this cup from my hand, lift it and bless it, and drink deeply from it. I fell asleep with this vision before my eyes.

Morning of the first day dawned. For the first time since I received it, I felt at ease leaving the chalice beneath the roof of my father, mother, and Rabbi Kagba.

At breakfast I said, "Papa, when I arrived, the shop and the house were in ruins. It was cold and snowy, and I was alone. Four link boys who live in the caverns beneath the Temple—they're called Red, Timothy, and two brothers, Obed and Jesse—gave me shelter and bread." I looked at Mama. "They told me my grandmother had fed them before the fire. Before she went away to Joppa."

Rabbi Kagba said, "A good and righteous woman. Repaid for her kindness when you were taken in."

"Oh, my dear boy. What shall we do?"

Papa reached for silver coins. "Some offering to help them during Passover?"

I shook my head. "I don't know if they're alive. The sickness took so many."

Papa replied, "And if they are alive, we'll repay them."

"Not money, Papa. They work very hard. I was thinking, maybe with our new building . . ."

Mama asked, "What?"

I looked through the window and imagined Passover next year when the weaver's shop was open for business and the shelves were filled. "I thought about it a lot in the night. When Jesus comes and is our King, the Temple will truly be a house of prayer as it was in the early days. Everyone in the world will come. Everyone will buy a prayer shawl from us. Mama, you will need help weaving. I thought that maybe, if the Sparrows are still alive, you could teach them to weave."

My suggestion was like a lamp, lighting every face around the table. Mama clapped her hands. "Oh yes! Yes! Glorious plan!"

"Ap-prent-ices." The rabbi drew the word out, pronouncing every syllable as if they were holy. "Fine! Fine!"

Papa studied me. "Lots of space. We'll have the builders add a room on the rooftop so your friends can sleep close to the stars."

Mama added, "As I did when I was a girl, dreaming of a bridegroom. Your father. Though I didn't know it was him I was longing to meet!"

"You'll have to find your friends," Papa said. "You know where the Sparrows live?"

And so it was settled. Leaving the cup wrapped beneath my pillow and sheathing my wooden sword, I set out to find the Sparrows.

As the sun beat down on Jerusalem, I passed the head of the Street of the Butchers. A butcher cleaned and carved chunks of meat from a slaughtered ox. Children hauled guts and fat to soap makers, hides to the tanners. The smallest children fanned away flies.

It was in the muck of the Shambles that I found the first of my four Sparrows.

"Hey! Hey, Nehemiah! Nehemiah!"

I turned on my heel and peered down the lane where every shop displayed haunches of sheep or goats and plucked chickens for sale.

"Nehemiah!" A boy's voice called to me once more, and I spotted the wild red hair of Red. His arms waved broadly. His face was beaming. He wore an apron, but it did little to protect his clothing from his task.

I raised my wooden sword and laughed. "Courage, Red!" I shouted.

He jogged to me and swept his hand over his filthy apron. "Still fighting the battle."

"You look like you've been in the thick of it," I teased.

"I've been hired to haul guts away to the knacker. Soap making. There's a need for every bit of an animal, you know. You learn things here. Even things you don't want to know."

"Well, brother, you're still alive," I said.

"So are we all." Red told me what I wanted to know. "Me, Obed, Jesse, Timothy."

"You made it through the sickness."

"Aye. Thanks to Lazarus . . . the famous Lazarus. You heard all about that, I suppose?"

307

"I met him."

"Well then. Lazarus spooned broth down my throat and Jesse's too, before he died. He'll remember me. Timothy and Obed never did get sick. But it swept through the Sparrows' camp. Almost as soon as you were gone, it started. Hey, did you find your family? I see somebody's rebuilding your grandfather's shop."

"All of them. Grandparents in Joppa. The rest—Mother, Father, my brothers—here in Jerusalem. And my family says . . . well, they wonder if the four of you would like to learn weaving."

By way of reply, Red removed his apron and flung it away. Leaving a wheelbarrow overflowing with entrails in the middle of the street, he took my arm. "Don't look back. It will do something to you, I promise. I'll never eat meat again. Not that I ever did. Enough of this. The boys are all at work. Not linking. But temporary like, for the holidays. So much work with all the pilgrims. Every crook in the city needs errand boys. Work like dogs, and they pay us like slaves."

Cheerful now, Red led me to the sheep pens where Timothy was hard at work scrubbing Passover lambs. Obed and Jesse shoveled manure.

Our reunion was joyful. The news that they were wanted as weaver apprentices was met with astonished jubilation. To become an apprentice was, after all, the goal of every Sparrow.

"I'll tell you the whole truth, Nehemiah," Timothy confided. "I know your father is a herdsman and all . . . no offense. But working here in the stock pens, I've grown to hate sheep."

Obed and Jesse agreed. "Me too."

Red confirmed, "And I hate everything that is inside a sheep."

"A torch for me, any day," said Timothy.

"And a loaf of bread," agreed Red.

"Me too," said the brothers, again in unison.

Red sprang the news. "But here's good news: Nehemiah's family is looking for apprentices. Weavers. Wool . . . not sheep, boys!"

Jesse's eyes widened. "How many apprentices? One? Two?"

"Four," I replied.

Red answered for all. "As much as we may hate sheep, I don't have anything against wool. Such as it is, off the sheep."

I clapped them on their backs. "It's settled, then. But my mother won't let you into the house if you don't wash."

They washed in a public fountain.

As we headed toward home, Timothy asked, "So, did you meet Jesus?"

"Yes. He even spoke to me," I told them. "And he's coming to Jerusalem."

Timothy twisted his mouth and jerked his thumb toward the Street of the Butchers. "See that carcass? That's what the rulers have planned for Jesus and his disciples if they enter Jerusalem at Passover."

Red concurred, "I heard the high priest's servant talking about it. They'll kill him. One way or another. They want him dead and gone."

The brothers piped, "Lazarus . . . dead too."

"Yes, Lazarus. Almost Lazarus as much as Jesus."

Red said, "The Sadducees don't believe in the afterlife. Lazarus turned their cart of steamy religious guts right over! They don't like hearing there's a heaven and a hell."

Timothy stopped as a squad of Roman soldiers marched by. "Especially not hell, I bet. Well, Romans—there's the proof it isn't getting better. Proof Jesus ought to keep his head down. The whole city is buzzing with rumors."

Jesus was all the talk of the city, it seemed.

🍃

As we walked through the crowds, I listened to the litany of the boys who had died and those who had lived by the miracle of Master Lazarus's kindness and that of his sister Mary and her servant, Tavita. The story of every painful swallow, hacking cough, and delirious nightmare was retold to me by my Sparrow brothers.

Once again I heard about the slow, horrible death of Lazarus as they had seen it.

The tears of his sisters.

Mourning for the passing of a good man.

Jesus coming too late.

Lazarus's rotting, putrid body in the tomb!

The voice of Jesus commanding death to retreat!

The stone rolled back and a smell far worse than bad meat left in the gut wagons of Butcher Street!

The presence of death seemed so close in my friends' eyewitness accounts that I could see it all. We passed the path that led to the Sparrows' cavern, but I hardly registered where I was.

Then we halted at the turning. Red paused in his narrative and glanced up at the sky. The report of Jesus commanding the shroud-wrapped body out of the tomb was only half told.

All four of my companions made puzzled-boy faces at one another. Suddenly a great noise like a flock of geese rose up from the east from outside the city walls.

"What's that?"

"Huh?"

"People. Lots of them."

"Listen! Cheering?"

I peered at the bright morning sky. An enormous flock of

birds darkened the sun as they flew toward the Mount of Olives. Gasping, I remembered the mulberry tree at the inn. I heard again in my mind the promise of Jesus as the birds had erupted suddenly from the tree. *"You will know when I am coming."*

At that instant two hundred Sparrow boys of the stone quarry gave a shout in unison. They tore up the paths, emerging from their dark poverty. "He is coming! Jesus is coming!"

Rags and blankets fluttered like flags in their grimy hands. They pushed and swarmed around us. I was caught up in the rush through the lanes.

"Come on! Hurry!"

"He's coming now!"

"Riding on a donkey!"

I did not question the truth that Jesus was approaching. We banged on doors and sounded the news.

Striving to outdo each other, we hammered on each portal, shouting the tidings, "Come and see! He is coming! Jesus is coming!" then raced to the next.

Colorful robes and blankets were snatched from the parapets of balconies to be waved in welcome as the common folk of Jerusalem joined in the rush to honor him.

This was the first day of the week. No work had been done on the Sabbath. No laundry had been washed. No shops had been open. No merchandise had been bought or sold. No fires were lit; no food purchased, until today. So the whole city was jammed with everyone making good all the things they had failed to do before the Sabbath rest and overflowing with pilgrims who had come for the Passover, now only days away. The city was ababble with voices speaking every tongue imaginable, shouting, laughing, singing, as if a competition had been decreed!

And into this glorious, riotous tumult, Jesus arrived!

The cry of "He is here" resounded from the city walls like the crashing of giant waves. Concentric circles of joy splashed every street and penetrated every shadow. Storefronts and houses were left unlocked and empty. We poured through the lanes and surged past startled Roman soldiers and growling Herodian guards.

Red and Timothy locked arms to keep from being trampled. "Stay close!"

Jesse and Obed linked to me. "Careful—stay on your feet!"

"Stay on your feet! Don't wanta get crushed!"

We burst into the light outside the walls.

"Blessed is he . . . ," shouted the crowds across the valley to the east.

" . . . who comes in the name of the Lord!" we bellowed back.

"Son of . . ."

"David!"

"Hosanna to the King!"

"Hosanna in the highest!"

Now the human flood was a river rushing on the road to meet the King. *Had it been like this when King David had danced for joy before the holy ark as it entered Jerusalem?* I wondered. Rabbi Kagba had taught me that when the ark containing the *Torah*, the very Word of Almighty God, arrived in Jerusalem, there was a mighty celebration.

Had it been like this on that occasion? Or was this greater still?

Palm branches stripped from trees were raised to welcome the Son of David.

All the poor of Jerusalem had light on their faces that day. It was well past sunrise, but it seemed that, all around me, every countenance shone with the blaze of dawn.

Here and there a Levite priest scowled or a scribe ducked into a doorway and slammed it forcefully to show his disapproval.

But not the people of the Land.

"He is . . ."

" . . . on the Mount of Olives!"

The faces of Pharisees displayed shocked anger and, I thought, fear of what was coming.

Who could resist such a force as Jesus?

We were carried down the road in the flood.

Just outside the eastern wall two tides met—heaping torrents of cheering, shouting people. The noise and the spectacle rivaled any ocean breakers I had seen at Joppa's shore. We who flowed out of the Holy City crashed into the current arriving from the Bethany road.

Red and Jesse snapped up palm fronds and waved them furiously. Red handed me one, and I shook it as if to make it seen back in Amadiya. "Look! There!"

"The Lord our Banner!" men shouted.

Down came the shirts and the tunics plucked from the wash lines. They fluttered to the ground with the colors of a thousand autumn leaves. They and a myriad of cloaks were spread on the ground before Jesus as the little donkey climbed the road to the Eastern Gate.

"Look! He comes!"

"Hosanna in the highest!"

"Hosanna to Jesus our King!"

As they came closer, we five scrambled up the embankment onto a boulder. From this vantage point I recognized Lazarus and the twelve disciples. Their faces beamed with pride and delight. And behind them was the old shepherd, Zadok, with Peniel,

Avel, Emet, and Ha-or Tov! Jesus' mother was surrounded by women who sang the song of David:

> "Give praise to the LORD, proclaim his name;
> make known among the nations what he has done.
> Sing to him, sing praise to him; tell of all his wonderful
>   acts."[1]

I waved my palm branch and shouted and laughed as he approached.

"Blessed is he who comes in the name of the Lord!"

The silver chalice left beneath my pillow came to mind as the crush of humanity parted for him. I could not turn back to fetch it! Oh, why had I not carried it with me as I had done every other day?

"I know those boys in the procession," I shouted to the Sparrows over the tumult. "Look there—it's Peniel! And Emet, with the little bird riding on his shoulder. And that one there is Avel . . . and Ha-or Tov, with the red hair! Their father is old Zadok!"

"Praise to the Lord!"

The song of the women was joined by the multitude. I roared the lyrics off-key, but it didn't matter. Every phrase was broken by gales of laughter as we sang.

> "He remembers his covenant forever,
> the promise he made, for a thousand generations,
> the covenant he made with Abraham,
> the oath he swore to Isaac.
> He confirmed it to Jacob as a decree,
> to Israel as an everlasting covenant."[2]

As the procession neared us, Jesus spotted me on the rock. He locked me in his gaze for a long moment. His eyes were filled with sadness.

How could he be sad at such a moment? The sight shook something deep within me. Was it because I had not brought Joseph's chalice to him?

I cupped my hands around my mouth and called, "I have your *Kiddush* cup, Lord! Don't worry. It's ready for you, all polished up! I'll bring it!"

I thought Jesus heard me. Was that a nod of acceptance? He turned his face to the walls and yawning gate. Then the moment was past.

The crowd closed on the road behind him, and Red jumped from the boulder.

Timothy studied me with new respect. "Hey, Nehemiah, I think he was looking at you. I mean, he seemed like he was staring right at you."

My smile faded at the haunting impression of sorrow. I answered quietly, "Yes. I think so too."

"Hurry up! Come on, boys. He's going into the city!" The flood of humanity swept toward the gates.

I locked arms with the Sparrows. We shouldered our palm branches like soldiers marching to war and followed the triumphal procession through the Eastern Gate and into Jerusalem.

"Who is he?" someone asked.

"It's Jesus, the prophet from Nazareth in Galilee," came the reply.

A litany of miracles followed.

"He fed five thousand with a few loaves of bread!"

"Free bread?"

"I was there in the field! Best bread I ever tasted."

"It was like Moses and the manna!"

"He turned water into wine at a wedding in Cana. Such wine—like nothing you ever drank!"

"We'll never be hungry or thirsty again with such a man as our King."

"I was deaf, but now I can hear!"

"I was blind, but Jesus gave me sight!"

"He brought a dead girl back to life in Capernaum. I know her mother, and the story's true!"

"Whoever heard of such a thing?"

"And surely you've heard of Lazarus?"

"He healed a paralyzed man who begged beside the well of my city for years."

"I've seen it. Lepers . . . completely restored!"

"I was lame and now . . . look. I can walk!"

The question on the mind of every man, woman, and child in the crowd that day was, "What can Jesus do for me?"

We clung to one another and fought to remain standing in the irresistible surge of seekers. I wondered how I could bring the chalice to Jesus with such a multitude surrounding him. Then my longing turned to my mother. If Jesus had opened the ears of the deaf and given sight to the blind, surely he could heal my mother's lameness.

We burst through the city gates and someone shouted, "This way! The prophet Jesus has entered the Temple!"

"Come on!"

"Let's see what miracle he'll do now!"

There was no chance for me to turn to the right or the left. No way I could go home and fetch the chalice or give my mother and father the news that the great Healer was at hand.

My friends and I were caught up, swept toward the Temple Mount in a relentless, dangerous current.

Lining the streets were Roman soldiers and Herodian guards. Their swords were drawn and ready as a warning that no rebellion would be tolerated. Faces were grim, mouths tight, and eyes fierce as they observed us. I thought, *They must also be fearful of what might happen.* If Jesus could feed his army with only a handful of bread, and heal their wounds, and even raise the dead, what chance did the armies of Rome have to oppose him?

A young man spit and taunted a Roman officer at the turning in the street. "Go back to your barracks and lock the door. Now you're going to see something!"

The soldier raised his short sword and growled, "I'll show you something, Jew!"

"Kill us, and he'll raise us up alive again. You can't fight that!"

The soldier's lips pressed tightly as he appeared to consider the miracles Jesus had performed over the last three years.

I saw terror in the eyes of our oppressors as we swept past them. We were two hundred thousand strong that day, and the soldiers were only a few thousand. And no matter how many of us or how few of them, I was convinced Jesus by his power *alone* could defeat every enemy!

I felt my wooden sword press against my leg. The inscription declared COURAGE. How brave I felt that day. The swords of mighty conquerors were nothing compared to the power of Jesus and the fierce love of the common folk who roared for him to be their king!

Red raised his fist and, in the fierce, breaking voice of a boy, proclaimed the thoughts of every Jewish man in the mob. "Hey, you Roman swine! If you kill us, Jesus will bring us back to life.

He will feed us and clothe us, and we will fight you again until you're all killed!"

We were still together when we reached the Temple Mount. Flocks of priests and Pharisees with scowling faces and crossed arms stood back indignantly as the throng swarmed into the courtyard crammed with booths of merchants and moneychangers.

The roaring of the human horde grew suddenly quiet. Instantly the pushing and shoving became still.

"There he is!"

"Look! It's him! Jesus!"

"He's talking to the overseer of the merchants!"

"What's he saying?"

"His face! Look how angry!"

"He's angry! Look at Jesus!"

I saw at once that something was wrong. A hush of expectance fell over us. Timothy and Red climbed onto the base of a column, then helped me and Jesse and Obed up.

A semicircle of Pharisees confronted Jesus. His disciples glared back at the Temple authorities. The moneychangers who converted secular currency into Temple shekels cursed and shouted at Jesus, "Who do you think you are?"

"What right do you have to tell us . . ."

"This is the way we've always done it!"

Those packed around me buzzed, "Those crooks! Jesus must have told them to get honest scales for a change!"

"What's Jesus saying?"

"What's going on?"

"Quiet!"

"Everybody shut up!"

"I can't hear what he's saying!"

Clinging to the pillar, we boys heard every angry word. And then, suddenly, Jesus picked up a moneychanger's table. He held it over his head and sent it crashing to the pavement. Coins flew everywhere!

Jesus roared in a voice that resounded in all the Temple courts, "It is written, 'My house shall be called a house of prayer,' but you have made it a 'den of thieves'!"[3]

People cheered as Jesus ripped into the merchants, over-turning their tables, opening the cages of the doves, and driving the crooks out.

I laughed and drew my wooden sword. "Courage! Look—he's wrecking the place. Look what Jesus is doing!"

A cloud of doves rose up. The air was filled with the flutter of their wings. Once again the vision of the birds rising from the mulberry tree came to my mind. The flock was free! Jesus had told me I would know when he was coming!

Well, he had arrived. The smashing and crashing of stalls and benches flying through the air was a certain sign of his zeal. Like a prophet of old, he was cleaning the scum from the pure waters of righteousness!

The mob surged forward, scrambling for loose coins. Startled guards, terrified that this was the beginning of a dreaded riot, retreated with the moneychangers.

"Come on!" Timothy leapt from the column.

Red shouted, "Let's go, boys . . . come on! Let's get something!"

I hesitated for a moment, then thought of my mother. I remembered the cup beneath my pillow. "I've got to go back, boys . . . to get my mother!"

I did not know if they heard me. They vanished into the crowd. I scanned the crush for a way out. As everyone moved forward, I jumped into a clear space, clambered onto a portico, and began to run the opposite direction.

Jesus was taking possession of the Temple Mount. I imagined Romans locking the gates and shutting everyone in . . . or out. I had to find a way to bring my mother to Jesus so she could join the multitude of those who would be healed!

I sprinted toward a broad gate that led to the causeway and the ritual baths. Traffic through that gate was thin, and I had a chance to escape.

Behind me the chanting of the people increased:

"Hosanna to the King!"

"Hail Jesus, Messiah!"

"Hosanna to the Son of David!"

When I emerged into the city, the flight of doves circled above my head. I laughed out loud and sprinted for home.

Chapter 32

*A*t my back, the voices of thousands acclaimed the arrival of Messiah. The Temple courts resounded like a giant coliseum filled with spectators, and still more pilgrims came.

I ran down the sloping street, pushing through the human tide that flowed inexorably up to enter the gates in hopes of seeing Jesus. Stretcher bearers carried the sick and the lame through the crush.

Panic seized me. What if my mother could not reach Jesus? Suppose I came too late and the way into the Temple was blocked? And what if the crowd gathered around him was too large for us to make it through?

Breathless, I came to the turning leading to the narrow Street of Weavers. The lane ahead was deserted.

"Mama!" I shouted. "Papa! Rabbi Kagba! Come—come quickly!"

Tools lay scattered in front of the new shop where the workers had dropped them. The door of the rented house was wide open.

"Papa, where are you? We must take Mama to the Temple! Jesus—it's him! He's here!" I flung myself into the house and stood panting as I scanned the empty room. "Mama!"

I dashed up the stairs, knowing they had gone without me.

Had I passed them in the crowds as I had hurried down to fetch them?

Disappointment turned to hope. What if they were already there? I stood at the top of the stairs for a long moment, then scrambled back to the ground floor and out onto the street.

All was silent except for a single blind boy, about my age, tapping the paving stones with his stick. He groped vacant air. His path was like a jagged crack in a clay cup—going nowhere. "Who's there?" the blind boy called. "Is someone there?"

I was still and silent, not wanting to be asked for help. I had to get away. Had to get back.

"I know you're there. I hear your breathing. Please, answer me."

I replied with an inward groan, "I'm Nehemiah. I've come back to find my mother. And my father and the rabbi too. To take them to Jesus, the Messiah, so my mother's lameness will be healed."

The boy cried, "Yes, the Healer! Oh, please, please, boy! They've all gone. Everyone gone but me. I can't find my way. They all ran past me, and now I'm lost. Please, take me to him!"

Impatience and panic gripped me. "Where do you live? Where is your family?" I stared up toward the Temple walls. A squad of soldiers tramped by at the head of the street.

"I live with the Sparrows in the cavern. I can't carry a torch, but they let me stay because my brother is there. They've gone, and I am lost. Please, Nehemiah, have pity on a poor, blind beggar. Lead me to Jesus, that I may be healed. Oh! What it will mean to me to see the color of the sky!" He leaned heavily against his stick. His free arm was stretched out as far as he could reach, the hand palm up like a beggar. His feet were pointed in the wrong direction. "If you don't lead me to Jesus, I'll never be healed. I have heard of him all these months. Though I have tried to find him, I always arrive too late. If you don't help me, guide me, I will be lost in darkness forever!"

I shook myself awake. I wondered if a blind boy could run. "Yes. Yes. Of course, I will. My family has already gone." I gazed at the boy's blue marbled eyes. "What is your name?"

"Hallelujah is my name."

From the Temple Mount I heard the crowds cheering for Jesus: "Hallelujah!"

"It's a good name! A great name for this day." Grasping his hand, I placed it on my shoulder. "Come on then, Hallelujah. We'll be the very last to enter the gates, I'm sure. Everyone is already there. I pray the gates are still open. I bet my mother is with Jesus even now. Even now he is healing the blind and the lame. She is among those who will dance today! And you will be among those who see."

And so, the blind Hallelujah gripping my shoulder, I turned back, forgetting to bring the chalice. Our progress was slow as every uneven flagstone caught the toe of the blind boy's sandal. We picked our way carefully up the steep street, coming at last to the broad steps.

He tested the ground with his stick, tapping, tapping as we walked.

I wanted to cry, "Hurry," but instead made myself speak his name in encouragement again and again:

"Hallelujah! Jesus is in Jerusalem!

"Hallelujah, Jesus will see you. And you will see his face today!

"Hallelujah, don't be afraid.

"Hallelujah! Jesus will heal you if only you have faith in him.

"Hallelujah! We will not be too late."

At last we came to the entrance of the Temple. The crowd seemed impenetrable. Ahead of us, as Jesus healed someone, we heard the repeated shouts of "Hallelujah! Blessed is the Son of David!"

A multitude blocked our way in through the gate. "Come on," I urged. "Hold tight. Hallelujah! We'll hug the wall and inch our way through the gate."

Slowly, our faces against the rough stone, we slid past the mob and emerged in the sunlight of the outer court.

Another loud shout of acclamation swept over us, echoing against the walls and pillars. I aimed for a column, thinking I could climb up and have a look. Using the boy's stick, I pried a path through the pilgrims and came to the base of a pillar at last.

"Here—put your hands on the column. Don't let go. I'll climb up and have a look." His unseeing eyes gazed upward as I clambered onto the base and searched the human sea.

"Hallelujah! There he is!" I cried. Jesus, wearing the prayer shawl my mother had made, sat at the top of the steps of the treasury where the offerings for the poor were given. He was surrounded by perhaps two hundred sick and lame and blind, who all waited their turn to be touched and healed. I spotted my mother in the very front of the supplicants. A circle of hundreds of observers fanned out, filling every space in the court.

Jesus placed his hands over the ears of a deaf-mute girl and, raising his eyes to heaven, proclaimed that her ears be opened and her tongue loosed.

With a cry of joy, the girl began to speak: "Mama! Oh, Mama! I can hear! I can hear!"

The cheers of the people drowned out the girl's voice. Her mother fell at the feet of Jesus and wept for joy.

"Hallelujah!"

"Praise God!"

"Blessed is our Messiah, who comes in the name of the Lord!"

I spotted the scowling Herodians mingling with sour-faced priests in the back of the porch.

"What happened?" Hallelujah grasped my leg.

I answered, "He is healing people! One after another."

He pleaded, "I must go to him. Please, find a way!"

But the crowd between the column and Jesus was so dense I could not see any way through.

And then I spotted Red and Timothy and the brothers standing on the base of a column near Jesus. I shouted, "Red!"

I saw him look up as he heard my voice. His head turned as he searched for me.

"Here! On the pillar! Red!"

He saw me, and his face broke into a broad grin. He waved and nudged Timothy, Jesse, and Obed. I saw his lips form the words, "There's Nehemiah."

Others turned to glance at me. I waved broadly and cupped my hands around my mouth. "I've got Hallelujah!" I called.

We were all participants in a great drama unfolding before our eyes.

"I . . . NEED . . . HELP!" I shouted.

Then I reached down and grasped the fabric of Hallelujah's ragged tunic. "Come on!" I commanded as, with all my strength, I pulled and hefted him up beside me.

"Hold on!" I positioned his arms, then indicated to Red and the boys the situation. How to get one blind boy through the human sea and near enough for Jesus to touch and heal?

My friends grasped the situation instantly. Timothy panto-mimed a boat sailing over the sea.

"Yes!" I agreed.

Red shouted to the crowd, "People, help us! We must pass our friend Hallelujah over your heads. He is blind and must be healed this very day!"

Hands reached out to receive the blind boy. Hallelujah fell into their arms, sailed over the human sea, bobbed like a little ship headed toward the far shore, where Jesus waited to receive him. Jesus stood and waded down among the sick to take him.

My mother sat on the steps at Jesus' feet. Taking Hallelujah onto his shoulder, Jesus smiled and waved at me. Then he placed his hand on my mother's head and spoke quietly to her. She grasped the fringe of the prayer shawl that she had made so many months before.

Jesus swung Hallelujah down to the ground beside him, then spoke to my mother once more.

I saw her lips move. "Yes! Yes! Thank you, Lord!"

What had happened? Something was instantly changed. She wiped away tears and tested her lame leg. Then she took one step and another, climbing the stairs with ease.

The crowd roared, "Hallelujah!"

Jesus' lips were curved in a smile as he pointed toward me.

I saw her look up. She squinted, trying to find me, and nodded slowly. She laughed as she spotted me hanging from the pillar like a monkey.

"Nehemiah!" she cried and then turned to descend the steps without fear. "That's my boy!" That's when I knew for certain something miraculous had transpired. Her gait was strong and steady. There was no trace of pain in her expression.

And then, Jesus, Son of David, took the face of the blind Sparrow in his hands. His eyes searched the eyes of the boy, and then he kissed each eye with the tenderness of a father saying good night to his son.

I did not hear the words Jesus spoke to the boy, but in an instant, the eyes of Hallelujah were opened, and the people went wild with joy.

A strong man grasped me, and I found myself being passed from hand to hand above the heads of the people. My mother embraced me when I reached the steps. "Oh, Nehemiah! My leg is healed! Oh, look what he has done!"

From every corner of the Temple Mount children were passed hand over hand until a chorus surrounded Jesus. Timothy, Red, Jesse, and Obed joined Ha-or Tov, Avel, and Emet. My friends embraced me. A hundred other children joined us as Jesus touched and healed everyone who had come to the steps.

"Hosanna to the Son of David!"

"Hallelujah! Sing praises to our King!"

"Blessed is he who comes in the name of the Lord!"

There was no silencing the crowd.

Moments later the chief priests and teachers of the law, with the Temple guards around them, elbowed their way to the platform where Jesus stood.

Caiaphas, the chief priest, raised his arms, demanding silence. The people obeyed and a hush fell over us, not because anyone was afraid, but rather because we did not know how anyone could object to the miracles happening before our eyes.

Caiaphas's face was hard and cruel as he challenged Jesus, "Do you hear what these children are saying?"

Jesus' voice was clear and pleasant as he replied, "Yes. I hear them. And have you never read, 'From the lips of children and infants you have ordained praise'?"[1]

The captain of the guard stepped forward and demanded, "All right, the show is over. Break it up and go back to your places. By order of the Sanhedrin, the Temple gates will be closed until morning."

Jesus was surrounded by his disciples and escorted out before I had a chance to thank him.

Papa and Rabbi Kagba found us. My mother walked from the Temple that day without a limp and without pain for the first time. Red, Timothy, Jesse, Obed, and Hallelujah came home with us to the Street of the Weavers.

Over dinner my mother asked Hallelujah, now that he could see, if he might like to become a weaver of prayer shawls. And that is how there came to be five apprentices.

It was Rabbi Kagba who brought the chatter of excitement back to reality that evening.

"When I was a young man and saw the signs in the heavens that foretold the birth of a King in Israel, I came here from afar with other men who had also read the signs. What we found at the news of the newborn King was not joy among the rulers of this city and this nation, but envy and murder in their hearts. Can we believe that anything has changed?"

My father leaned forward and searched Kagba's face for an answer. "You're right. Of course, you're right. Jesus gave every miraculous sign today—from the healing of my Sarah and giving sight to this boy, Hallelujah—but it wasn't enough for the high priest or the Herodians."

The rabbi answered, "They will try to kill him, just as they did when he was a baby."

Mama gasped, "Oh no! Please say it can't be!"

Rabbi Kagba replied, "Even though Jesus has done all these miraculous signs in their presence, they still will not believe in him. This fulfills the word of the prophet Isaiah, 'Who has believed our message and to whom has the arm of the LORD been revealed?'[2] For this reason they won't believe because, as Isaiah says elsewhere, 'He has blinded their eyes and hardened their hearts, so they can neither see with their eyes, nor understand with their hearts, nor turn—and I would heal them.'"[3]

I asked, "Please tell me why. What does it mean? Every good thing that happened today, and every day with Jesus!"

The rabbi addressed me patiently. "Isaiah saw Jesus' glory and spoke about him. Even now, I have heard that many among the leaders believe in Jesus. But, because of the Pharisees, they won't admit their faith, for fear they'll be put out of the synagogue."

"Like they did with Peniel, who was born blind," I said.

Mama added, "They love the praise of men more than praise from God."

"True," agreed the rabbi. "So true."

My father, a man of action, asked, "What can we do? How can we help him?"

It was Timothy who came up with the answer. "Jesus needs spies who can tell him what they are planning."

Red had an idea. "Link boys? Us Sparrows are nothing but poor beggars in the eyes of the rich rulers."

"They think we don't have ears to hear their plots," Jesse agreed.

Hallelujah added, "They talk in front of me about important matters as if I am made of stone. I might have been blind, but I still had ears."

Obed agreed. "When we carry the torches and lead them through the city, they continue discussing whatever the council discussed in privacy."

My father snapped his fingers. "Of course! You boys! You can do it. Information—this is the way we can help protect Jesus."

After supper, I went out with the five Sparrows, hopefully to carry torches for exalted rulers who traveled the city after dark.

We waited on a corner just outside the Chamber of Hewn Stone, where the religious rulers met to discuss the matter of Jesus and his followers. Lamps burned within. Their meeting continued for long hours.

By and by the door opened and light pooled on the pavement. A solitary figure slipped out. For a moment, I thought I recognized him as one of the twelve close friends of Jesus, the disciple called Judas Iscariot.

A voice from within the hall addressed him. "You should at least think about it . . . as a patriot, eh? We know you are a patriot above all. Remember what was said tonight. It is better for one man to perish for the sake of our entire nation."

"I will," the man answered. "Yes, I promise I will . . . at least think about it."

I hoped that the fellow would hire us to link for him so we could learn more, but he deliberately turned away from the light of our torches and vanished into the shadows.

We had heard that Jesus and his band had returned to stay at the home of Lazarus in Bethany. I decided it was impossible that one of Jesus' closest friends would be here tonight, so I put Judas Iscariot out of my thoughts.

Timothy hissed to Red and Hallelujah, "You two, follow him! See where he goes. Report back to Nehemiah's house."

They sprinted into the darkness in pursuit.

Minutes passed. Suddenly the great doors gaped wide, illuminating the square with light as pompous men and their servants and scribes flooded out.

"Here they come." Timothy clutched his torch and thrust one into my hand. "A link, sirs?"

I followed his script. "A link?"

"A torch to light your way home?"

Two pompous, red-faced men hailed us. And three others called for Jesse and Obed. We had struck gold!

Timothy whispered eagerly, "We've got Caiaphas and his father-in-law, Annas! High priest. Hold your torch high and forward. He likes the shadows pushed back."

The two men barely acknowledged us. They spoke to one another as though we had no brains or ears to hear them and no voices to repeat what they said.

Caiaphas declared, "Herod Antipas is as eager as we are." Then he commanded us, "Guide us to the palace of Herod Antipas."

Annas said, "This is getting us nowhere. Look how the whole world has gone after Jesus."

Caiaphas snorted. "They'll be a rabble. Murder us in our beds if we don't put a stop to them."

I held my torch high in imitation of Timothy. He knew the route to the palace by heart. He glanced at me and raised his eyebrows as the conversation of our customers spilled out a treasure of information.

Caiaphas tugged his beard. "It was Lazarus. The last straw. There will be no stopping Jesus unless Lazarus is dead. They all come to see Lazarus!"

"As much as Jesus, I think."

"Our assassins have failed. Time and again. No one can get near him."

"I say we start with Lazarus. Silence him and all the glory fades. Then we discredit Jesus. Say it was all a great hoax."

"Gamaliel and Nicodemus oppose us."

"We question Jesus in matters of the law, and he manages to outsmart us every time. A clever fellow."

"He turns every point back on us—a verbal sword in the heart."

"A real sword would put an end to his clever talk."

"We can't get anyone near enough. He is surrounded by bodyguards. Fanatics. His disciples would die for him."

"Die *with* him, you mean."

"We'll have to arrest him by night. When the people are asleep and unaware."

"A trial. With judges in attendance whom we know will vote with us."

"We can bribe witnesses. We will see to it that those in the council who favor Jesus are delayed . . . distracted . . . prevented . . . from attending our next meeting."

I glanced over my shoulder to see Caiaphas smile. "And then there's the traitor in Jesus' own camp."

"We can't be sure of him."

"I think we can. He will turn. He is disillusioned already. Not well liked by the others, I hear. I tell you, he will do whatever we tell him."

Timothy nudged me as we reached the steps of Herod's estate.

Silently I put out my hand to receive our payment. The coins dropped in my palm. Neither of the rulers looked at our faces. They continued to talk over us as they pulled the bellrope.

Annas declared, "Lazarus is a problem. He must die and remain a dead man."

"Herod can see to that. His court is filled with assassins."

The gates swung open for the conspirators. We stood rooted with our torches high as the two gained entry, and the portal slammed shut.

Timothy and I pivoted on our heels and jogged to the next street. "Don't say anything," Timothy warned. "Every shadow hides an informant."

And so we hurried home to the Weavers' Street. One by one the others returned. We gathered in the lower room with my parents and Rabbi Kagba, and each of us gave our report of the murderous treachery that grew more fierce as the hours passed.

That night I heard Rabbi Kagba's footsteps pacing on the rooftop above the little room where I slept with five Sparrows. From north to south and back again the old man tramped. I knew he was worried about what was coming. So was I. I remembered the stories of the old man who had once been young.

Thirty-three years before, Rabbi Kagba had lain awake beneath the stars of Jerusalem with a dozen other great men from the East. The worry of imminent doom had raced through his mind and made him rise and pace and wonder what was to be done.

The slaughter of all the baby boys in Bethlehem and the escape of only one to Egypt had taught him something. The nightmare of murder had not been mere imagination to be brushed away with the morning light. Though the death of only one was the goal, the lives of many might be lost in the battle. It was indeed possible that men could accomplish evil so profound that the human heart could hardly comprehend it.

In Ramah, the cry of Rachel weeping for her children resounded even now. Jesus, sole survivor of the wrath of demon kings and princes, had grown up to become the Redeemer they hated and feared. He had returned to banish them from their dark thrones. The murderous creatures that ruled the hearts of rulers now made plans to finish what the soldiers of Herod the Great Butcher King had begun. "Jesus must die," they hissed. "And all those who follow him."

A vision of massacre played in my mind.

The moon shone through our window, bathing the sleeping Sparrows in silver monochrome.

I sat up as Rabbi Kagba descended the stairs and called softly to my father from the landing, "Lamsa! Wake up, Lamsa."

I heard the padding of my father's bare feet toward the rabbi. "You too?" he asked. "I can't get it out of my mind either. What shall we do, Rabbi?"

"I'm certain tomorrow they'll kill Lazarus to prove Jesus is a charlatan. That's their plan, Lamsa."

"Yes," Papa agreed. "I am sure of it. Murder, perhaps on the road tomorrow."

I sat up and untangled myself from the blankets. Standing, I carefully picked my way through the heap of legs and arms and slack-jawed faces.

Poking my head out the door, I croaked, "Papa? Rabbi Kagba? I'm awake too. Dreaming, but awake. A nightmare, really. We should go. Bethany. Go right now, I mean. Tonight. Ride to the house of Lazarus in Bethany. Warn Lazarus he should not return to Jerusalem in the morning."

Kagba studied me from the shadows for a long moment.

"Yes, Nehemiah, my thoughts exactly. What do you say, Lamsa? I think your boy has summed it up."

My father clasped my arm. "There's treachery in the camp, I think. Red and Hallelujah followed their man as far as the city gates. The Eastern Gate. The road to Bethany. Nehi, would you recognize the fellow if you saw him again? I mean, if he is one of the disciples of Jesus?"

"It was dark, Papa. I think so. But I can't say for sure."

Kagba interrupted. "The point is Lazarus. A good man. They will kill him first. His life, returned from the land of the dead, is a cause for them. They want Lazarus back in his tomb to stay. I say we ride to Bethany tonight. And Nehemiah must come with us."

Papa nodded. "The moon is almost full. The road will be illuminated. All right, then. Dress quickly. If we leave now, we'll be in Bethany before sunrise."

Chapter 33

As the Sparrows slept, I dressed quickly. My father saddled the horses below in the courtyard. I removed Joseph's cup from beneath my pillow and held it in the light. Gleaming silver seemed to glow from within.

For a moment I considered carrying it with me to Bethany, then thought better of it. Hadn't Jesus told me I must carry the cup for him until he was ready to take it from me in Jerusalem?

I held the cup close to my cheek, remembering the righteous men who had drunk from it. With a kiss I rolled it in its protective fleece, then returned the bundle to its hiding place beneath my pillow.

Mama's sleepy voice called to me from her bedchamber. "Nehemiah?"

I stood in the doorway of her room. "Yes, Mama."

"From the beginning I knew God had some special task for your life."

"Yes, Mama."

"And so you are in God's hands. You are the light in my life. Please—after what you boys saw tonight—be careful of wolves in the flock."

Wolves. Did she mean the man I had seen leave the council who looked so much like Judas? "Yes, Mama, I will. I don't think the fellow is a follower of Jesus. I'm almost sure. None of those men could betray him."

"But if it was, he will be desperate to keep his betrayal a secret."

"Don't worry."

"I'll try. I'll keep praying," she answered quietly.

Papa saddled his big bay and Kagba's strong mule for the journey. My father climbed onto his saddle, then reached down, grasped my arm, and swung me onto the bay's back. I hugged his back, grateful for his warmth. "All right, then," Papa said. "Angels go with us, and angels stay with those who remain behind."

The *clip clop* of hooves was the only sound as we rode through the deserted streets of the city.

Pilgrim fires winked on the slopes of the Mount of Olives. It was as though the stars had fallen to earth. The moon hung low in the west and cast our long shadows before us.

We did not speak as we rode. Our thoughts had turned from the elation of yesterday to the dangers of the coming day and tomorrow. We were united in our focus on two goals. First, to warn Jesus and Lazarus of the threat we had heard from the lips of the high priest himself. The second was somehow more troubling to me: to be certain that the informant I had seen at the door of the council was not a member of Jesus' inner circle.

The sky had only begun to lighten as we rode through the vineyards of Lazarus. A single light shone from the wall above the gatehouse of his estate.

Crickets chirped. A night bird sang from the brush. I smelled wildflowers and the scent of my father's leather jerkin. How could our desperate mission seem so peaceful?

As if he heard my thoughts, Rabbi Kagba said in a hoarse voice, "I have longed to see him as a man. To speak with him and kneel before him. But once again I come to warn him of danger. More than thirty years. The stars are the same."

Papa said, "As if no time has passed, eh?"

"Perhaps no time has passed. God's ancient promises exist outside of time."

My father said, "It seems there is always a battle between good and evil. Will it ever end?"

"The devil has a long memory, Lamsa. He remembers the perfection of Eden. He caused the fall of man and the curse of death upon what was a perfect world. On that day, God promised that a Savior would come and crush the head of the serpent."

"But doesn't it also say the serpent will strike the Savior's heel?" Papa replied. "A wound to our Redeemer. What does that mean?"

The rabbi motioned to the constellation of Ophiuchus. The stars depicted a fierce battle between a man and a serpent. "Look there in the sky! The outcome is certain. The stars are unchanged; God's promise is unchanged. Satan has feared this hour, and we are alive to see it. We are witnesses to the coming of our Redeemer. The serpent's head will be crushed, but our Savior will be wounded. Yes. Yes. We cannot be surprised. Not a fatal wound, but a wound all the same. The Devil does not believe what God has declared in his Word and etched in the stars, eh? Working in the lives of evil men, the Dark Prince of this world believes that the wound he inflicts on our Savior will be fatal. But it is written: in the end, the innocence of Eden will be restored. The outcome is certain, so we must do good and never fear."

The gates of Lazarus's estate loomed above us. Papa rang the bell.

An aged gatekeeper called down, "Who are you, and what do you want?"

Papa stood in the stirrups. "Please summon your master, Lazarus. My name is Lamsa. I come from beyond the two rivers where Eden once existed. And my son, who is known by Jesus, is with me—Nehemiah, cupbearer to the King. And here is Rabbi Kagba, one of the Magi who first paid homage to Jesus and then warned his mother and father of the danger of Herod's plots when Jesus was only a baby. We have come to bring news and warning once again."

The servant mumbled, "Daylight in an hour. Still early. Though the house is already stirring." He left his post, taking the lantern with him.

Long minutes passed. I felt the chill of the early morning.

After a time, the gates groaned open. A woman's voice welcomed us. "Come in, come in! Hurry!"

By the light of the gatekeeper's lamp, I recognized Mary, the beautiful sister of Lazarus. Her clear brown eyes smiled up at me. She was wrapped in a warm shawl. Her oval face was framed by thick, dark, wavy hair. Her teeth were straight and white.

The aroma of baking bread made my stomach growl.

"Welcome, Nehemiah. Are you hungry?"

"Yes, ma'am."

"Breakfast's almost ready." She reached up to help me slide off the horse. "And welcome, Lamsa and Rabbi Kagba. The Lord told us to prepare a meal for you—that you would be coming to break bread with us this morning."

I bowed deeply to Mary in unison with my father and Kagba.

The rabbi spoke first. "I'm glad he expected us."

Papa added, "We rode from Jerusalem with urgent news for your brother."

"Yes. *Shalom* and welcome." She took my hand. "Come along. They're waiting for you to join them at the table."

Nothing surprised me anymore. If Jesus had foretold our arrival, surely he knew why we had come.

❃

We entered an inner courtyard, open to the sky. Lazarus's sister Mary asked us to wait there for a moment, saying she would return to fetch us soon.

Seated on a stone bench beneath a fig tree was a pair of clean-shaven strangers. By their expensive clothing, they were wealthy men. They surveyed us. One whispered to the other, who shook his head.

Beside me, I felt my father stiffen. He made no move to speak to the foreigners, nor did they greet us.

Rabbi Kagba murmured, "Greeks. Here to see Jesus?" He shrugged. "Who knows how far his fame has spread."

On the opposite side of the terrace was a scalloped, two-tiered fountain. Rabbi Kagba and my father used the waters to wash the dust of travel from hands and faces. I needed it to scrub away the sleep.

In a couple of minutes Mary came back. She was accompanied by a servant, who carried a tray of food to the other visitors. Mary ushered us into a large dining room. Beneath a wall mural depicting a waterfall dropping into a verdant valley sat Jesus. Surrounding him were his closest disciples and a number of others, including Lazarus and the shepherd Zadok. About twenty in all. The meal of hot bread and dried dates and figs was already in progress, accompanied with quiet conversation. I spotted the man named Judas Iscariot, seated between Andrew and John. Grabbing my father's hand, I squeezed it and received a reassuring press in return. This fellow Judas looked very, very like the man I had seen at the council, but still I could not be sure.

My attention was diverted by another drama enacted immediately after we entered the chamber. Rabbi Kagba's body trembled, and his eyes brimmed with tears.

Jesus rose and strode quickly to him. Seizing my teacher's arms with both hands, Jesus said, "Welcome. Welcome, my friend."

Dropping to his knees, Kagba said, "My Lord, I hoped . . . I have waited . . . thirty years and more I have cherished . . ."

Instead of lifting Kagba immediately, Jesus knelt alongside him. "And now you're here," he returned, smiling. "Thirty years is a long time to hope without seeing. Please, come and join us. And you are Lamsa of Amadiya," Jesus said, greeting my father while assisting Kagba in rising. "Welcome. You must be proud of your son. Welcome, cupbearer."

Jesus indicated places immediately to his right, beside Zadok. With some jostling, the others moved aside.

"Judas," Jesus remarked.

Breaking off a conversation with Andrew, Judas looked up. I stared at him. For a fleeting instant there was something furtive in his expression . . . or had I just imagined it?

"Yes, Lord?"

"We have not taken the offering for the poor to the Temple. Would you see to that right away? If you've finished eating, that is."

"Of course."

"For the Sparrows," Jesus added, patting me on the shoulder. "This time, all for the Sparrows."

Judas frowned. I saw his jaw clench as if he were about to protest, but he ducked his chin, nodded curtly, and strode from the room.

Zadok was a big man. When he stood to make room for us,

his head of bristling white hair seemed to almost touch the ceiling while his brawny shoulders were wider than the table. An ancient scar running from an eye patch down across his cheek showed where someone had tried to split his head in two. But it was his remaining eye, intense and searching, that held me captive, as it did Rabbi Kagba.

"I know you!" Kagba said.

"As well you should, Kagba of Tarsus," Zadok rumbled. "It was to my house you came. You and the others. Your gift. Myrrh, wasn't it? Strange choice, that. Burial spice for a newborn."

All the other discussion ceased. Everyone knew an important reunion was taking place.

Zadok explained, "You know the tale. When the Master here was naught but a babe, learned men came to worship him: Perroz. Gaspar. Melchior and Balthasar from Ecbatana. And Kagba here. They brought gifts and a warning."

"It was Melchior who dreamed it," Kagba said, emotion making his voice catch in his throat. "We warned Joseph to take Mary and the baby and flee into Egypt—to our people in Alexandria. But we—" He stopped abruptly, then seized Zadok's wrists. "Your wounds! We never dreamed Herod would . . . could be . . . was so . . ."

"Ruthless?" Zadok supplied. "Aye."

Both men sighed heavily.

Zadok's shoulders shuddered. He swallowed a deep breath, as if attempting to rid himself of painful memories. "Slaughtered the babies, did the Butcher King. My babies among them." He indicated his ravaged features. "I tried but failed."

"We did not know." Kagba pleaded for forgiveness.

"You brought the warning," Zadok returned. "In those days, no one was safe . . . just like now."

Those words signaled an eruption of many voices in confirmation.

"He's right!"

"Another Herod—the same demons!"

"Worse, even. Roman soldiers make no pretense of caring about Jews."

"It is even worse than you know," my father contributed. "Listen to my son."

Silence fell again as I retold the tale of how the Sparrows carried out their spying missions and what we had overheard passing between the high priest and his father-in-law. "And I heard someone . . . offered money to betray Jesus."

"One of us?" Simon Peter bellowed. "Name him! Point him out!"

"No, I . . . it was dark. I can't," I concluded.

Lumbering to his feet, Peter said, "You must leave here, Lord. You and Lazarus. You must go today."

Several of the disciples jumped up, waving their arms and repeating Peter's words.

"Simon," Jesus said sternly, "sit down. Sit down, all of you." When the uproar had subsided again, he continued. "Listen." Clapping our host on the back, Jesus taught, "A man, just like friend Lazarus here, planted a vineyard. He rented it to some share-croppers and went away. At harvest time the owner sent a servant to receive his share of the crop. But the tenants beat the servant and drove him away empty-handed.

"A second messenger was treated the same way. A third they clubbed almost to death and threw him out. So the vineyard owner said, 'What shall I do to get what belongs to me? I'll send my son. They will respect him.'"

The silence of anticipation made me feel as if the very walls leaned inward to listen. The painted spray of the waterfall, so real and lively a moment earlier, appeared frozen in midair.

Jesus continued, "When the tenants saw the son arrive, they plotted together. 'This is the heir,' they said. 'We'll kill him and take the vineyard for our own.' And they did."

"Ah, no!" Zadok groaned.

"What will the vineyard owner do now?" Jesus asked. "Won't he come and execute those thieves and murderers and give the vineyard to others to tend and enjoy?"[1]

"But, Lord—" Peter protested.

"Haven't you read," Jesus said, interrupting the rising protests, "where is it written about the cornerstone, Rabbi?"

Kagba licked his lips as if his mouth had difficulty working. "The Psalms. One hundred eighteen."

Indicating approval, Jesus quoted, "'The stone the builders rejected has become the cornerstone; the Lord has done this, and it is marvelous in our eyes.'[2] Now I agree that Lazarus must flee. He must leave here today. But I . . ." Jesus' jaw tightened. The lines of his face took on the appearance of chiseled stone. "I must and I will attend Passover . . . in Jerusalem . . . this year. Do you understand?"

There was no further debate. At last it was Zadok who responded, "Lord, we do not understand, but we obey."

Dawn broke. I was reunited with Zadok's sons Ha-or Tov, Avel, and Emet while the grown men discussed the dangers of Jerusalem.

Avel leapt onto an upturned barrel, waved his wooden sword, and growled, "Oh, that I was a grown-up! They wouldn't get past me."

Emet piped up. "David was a boy when he killed Goliath."

Ha-or Tov agreed. "But Goliath was right there. Out in the open. Standing in a field. The assassins of Herod Antipas lurk in the shadows. You heard what Nehemiah said."

"So where will Lazarus hide, do you think?" Emet asked.

I answered, "They aren't telling. And they shouldn't tell."

Zadok appeared at the stable door and crooked his gnarled finger. "You've done good, Nehemiah. Now the sisters of Master Lazarus have asked to speak with you. Details. You know these women. They want to hear it over again in case you left out a word or two."

I followed the old man into Lazarus's house. The servants busied themselves with preparation for the journey of their master.

I heard them discuss who would go with him and who would remain behind.

I felt the cold eyes of Judas on me as I passed. I was still troubled by the similarity between Judas and the man I had seen outside the Chamber of Hewn Stone. Though I could not say Judas was the man who whispered treason, there was something in his manner that made me glance at him, then look away swiftly lest he see suspicion in my face.

I climbed the stairs to the chamber of Master Lazarus to give my report once again to his sisters. I stood in the partially open doorway as Martha selected tattered clothes for their brother to wear in order to hide his wealth from possible bandits along the way, and Mary packed his traveling garments in a leather bag.

Lazarus sat at his desk and sorted which documents he would take and which he would leave behind.

"Today, they said?" Martha worried. "Kill you today?"

Lazarus nodded. "But you mustn't be afraid, sister. Never

again. Though they may kill the body, I have seen with my own eyes what glory awaits us all."

Mary held a cloak up to the light. "This one, I think. And you can purchase more when you arrive."

Martha's brow furrowed. "If you arrive . . ."

Mary scolded, "The strongest servants travel with him. They have fine new swords and know how to use them. Our brother will be safe. Why else would we receive such news and—" She glanced up and saw me there. "Nehemiah. Come in. Come in."

Lazarus motioned for me to sit beside him. "It's no accident you heard what you heard. Tell my sisters so they will know everything."

"Yes, sir." I repeated the events. "So we carried torches for Caiaphas and Annas, you see. I think they are as afraid of Master Lazarus as they are of Jesus."

Mary stooped and brought her face very close to mine. "A plot to take his life."

I answered truthfully. "Today they have set everything in motion. We guided the priests to the palace of Herod Antipas, but they made their plans along the way. They spoke over our heads as if we were stones. They said they would see to it that your brother would be killed this very day."

Mary stood and spread her hands. "Yes. So you must not delay, brother. You ride out this morning, or they kill you today."

Martha added, "And no one must know where you've gone, or when you're coming home."

Lazarus nodded deeply and placed a hand on my head in blessing. "Thanks be to God for your sharp ears, boy."

I replied, "The Sparrows of Jerusalem love you, sir. For what you did for them when they were dying. All of them wish you well, and they would have done the same to warn you. I know they pray for your safe escape."

Lazarus snapped up the satchel and carried it down to where horses and two strong, ebony-skinned men waited for him.

The courtyard was suddenly crowded with men, women, and children—followers of Jesus and servants of the great household. I spotted my father and Kagba near the gates. I knew my father was not pleased that Lazarus was riding out in broad daylight and that so many knew he was going. How long would it be before the Herodian assassins were on his trail?

Lazarus embraced his sisters.

Jesus stepped from the house into the light. "I have prayed that you will be safe, my friend," Jesus said. "There is much for you to accomplish."

Lazarus implored him, "Come with me, Lord! I beg you. Ride with me to safety. The Greeks have offered you refuge in their own land. Then, when the day is right, you can return."

Jesus clasped his friend's hand, then stepped back as Lazarus and his companions mounted up. "It's time for the Son of Man to be glorified. You are a planter, so you already know this: unless a kernel of wheat falls to the ground and dies, it remains only a single seed. But if it dies, it becomes a great harvest. 'Anyone who loves his life will lose it, while anyone who hates his life in this world will keep it for eternal life.' As hard as it is, my servants must follow me, and my father will honor the one who serves me."

Lazarus cried, "I'm leaving only because you command it. I beg you to come with me!"

"What would you have me say?" Jesus asked. " 'Father, save me from this hour?' What's about to happen is the very reason I came. So I say, 'Father, glorify your name.' "

Then a voice like thunder came from heaven: "I have glorified it and will glorify it again."

All of us who gathered there heard it. Many said it had thundered, but I knew we had just heard heaven speak.

Jesus looked up at Lazarus and said, "Those of you who heard the words know the truth. It's time for judgment on this world. It's time for the prince of darkness to be driven out. You can depend on this: when I'm lifted up, I'll draw all men to me."

Behind me I heard murmuring. Turning, I saw a man I did not recognize speak to Judas. "What's he mean?"

Judas challenged Jesus, "We've heard from the law that Messiah will remain forever, so how can you say, 'The Son of Man must be lifted up'?"

The stranger asked, "Who is this 'Son of Man'?"

Lazarus saluted and rode out.

Then Jesus said, "While you still have light, walk in it. The man who walks in the dark does not know where he's going. Put your trust in the light while you have it, so that you may become sons of the light."[3]

"Bah," I heard Judas's companion mutter. "He speaks in riddles."

On the road, Lazarus spurred his mount into a gentle lope as he rode through his vineyards. The gates were closed.

When we turned back to where Jesus had been standing, he was gone.

Chapter 34

My father, Rabbi Kagba, and I rode out from Bethany shortly after the departure of Lazarus. I glanced over my shoulder to see Ha-or Tov, Avel, and Emet raise their wooden swords in a salute: "Courage!"

We approached the boundary of Lazarus's vineyards.

Kagba sighed. "We have done what we could do. I hope it is enough."

I asked, "Where do you think Master Lazarus has gone?"

My father replied, "If it were me, I would ride east. Twenty miles from Bethany to cross the Jordan. Twenty more and he'll make Medeba, in the kingdom of Nabatea. He'll be safe there. Another day's ride to Petra. Neither Herod nor Pilate have authority there."

I said quietly, "Papa, I wish Jesus had gone away with Lazarus. Or maybe gone to a ship and sailed away with the men from Greece."

Kagba interjected, "I must search the Scriptures. I have not read that, as a grown man, Messiah would flee from those who seek his life. He will defeat his enemies, not run from them. Since he and his family stayed in Egypt until the death of Herod, the prophecy, 'Out of Egypt I called my son' has been fulfilled.[1] But now the hour has come. Jesus will turn and fight the brood of vipers."

My father added, "If Jesus showed he was afraid of them, who would believe he was the one we have been waiting for? He must come to Jerusalem for Passover. The whole city expects Jesus to claim the throne of his father David and claim his rightful place as true King of Israel."

Kagba looked very weary. "There will be many who'll die for him. The Romans will not let go of their dominion over the Holy City without a fight."

My father said, "And that's why Caiaphas declared that Jesus will die for many."

I asked, "Papa, do you think Jesus and his disciples will come again to the Temple? Today?"

"Yes," Papa said. "He will come. And today his enemies are waiting and prepared for him. It will be a day of conflict."

I leaned my face against Papa's back and let the gentle motion of the horse lull me near sleep. Even as I rested, my mind replayed every nuance of the high priest's malicious plot. I thought of Joseph's cup and considered with amazement that Joseph, like Jesus, had been hated and falsely accused. I whispered the promise Joseph the Dreamer had spoken: "What men intend for evil, God intends for good."

The morning sun rose behind us and warmed my back. Mid-morning we reached the summit of the Mount of Olives. Thousands of pilgrims had pitched their tents on the slopes surrounding the city. It seemed as though all of Israel was stretched out before us.

When we arrived home in Jerusalem, the Sparrows were already out among the people. They gathered facts and rumors we could use to help protect Jesus.

My mother prepared a wonderful meal. We ate together and told her everything that had happened in Bethany.

"Do you think Jesus will come back to Jerusalem today?" Mama danced as she carried a plate of chicken to us. "I want to thank him. There was no chance to thank him properly for what he's done for me. Look!" She strode across the room and back. Spreading her arms wide, she declared, "See? Never before! Never in my life!"

"He'll come. Yes," Papa said, but there was no joy in his voice, only admiration. "A man of great courage."

"And resolve," my teacher concurred.

Papa broke the bread and spoke the blessing. "David against Goliath. Yes, Jesus is coming back. He will celebrate Passover here in Jerusalem."

I finished lunch and bounded up the stairs. Taking the cup from its hiding place, I examined it in daylight once more. Had I missed anything?

The sun flashed on the silver-etched vines. For an instant I saw the face of Jesus among the vineyard looking back at me. And then I saw him as a little boy holding up the cup of blessing. He had the saddest eyes, yet the kindest eyes I had ever seen.

I saw the little boy pour out the wine of the *Havdalah*, saying farewell to Sabbath. Like a mirror, the wine held his reflection. He lowered the candle to the wine. Three wicks but one holy flame. He paused as light filled the surface, and then he extinguished the flame. His face vanished from the vines in the blink of an eye, and the cup seemed to be just a cup again.

I held cool metal to my cheek and closed my eyes. "He poured himself out," I said, but I did not yet know what it meant. "Father, I never asked before now . . . but if I ask, will you show me? What did Joseph see when he looked into this cup?" I asked quietly, knowing that I had at last come to the end of my task. Soon the chalice would be passed to its rightful owner.

I peered into the bowl, hoping for an answer. I gasped at what appeared.

In the sunlight I saw clearly one streak of bronze-colored tarnish inside the cup, below the rim. How had I missed it? The image seemed like a crown of woven thorns. Had it been there yesterday? It seemed as though the discoloration was a part of the metal.

Dread set in as I attempted to rub it away. No matter how hard I scrubbed, the circle of thorns did not fade.

Wind stirred. I heard a child's voice whisper. Was it my own voice? Or the voice of the boy? As I gazed at the tarnish, the child spoke the prophecy the Lord had spoken when Adam sinned and the innocence of Eden was lost: "Cursed is the ground because of you. . . . It will produce thorns . . ."[2]

Suddenly I knew, like Joseph the Dreamer, I was seeing a vision of what was, what is, and what was to come.

One after another, a new, more horrible stain appeared, then disappeared inside the chalice—each image more terrible than the last:

The hand of a traitor filled with silver coins.

A lash tore the flesh of a bloody back!

Spikes pierced a man's hands and feet.

Three Roman crosses stood on a hill.

Lightning flashed.

The earth quaked!

Cries of suffering erupted as Joseph's cup seethed and roiled in a blood-red sea of evil unlike anything the human mind could comprehend.

I flung the cup away and fell to the floor. Darkness in broad daylight swirled around me. Was I dreaming? I begged to awaken.

And then, peace.

※

I don't know how long I slept.

I opened my eyes and saw a mother weeping, her head turned in agony to the sky, as she embraced the dead body of her innocent child! She beat her breast and would not be comforted.

I asked, "Who is she?"

I heard a voice reply, "She is Eve, weeping for her children."

Last of all, I saw the gaping mouth of an empty tomb.

It was set in a place I recognized—the newly cut tomb of Joseph of Arimathea!

Then the vision vanished.

I remembered again Jesus pouring out the wine for *Havdalah*. I had seen his face shining in the liquid as the flame of the candle was extinguished. I understood. Jesus was the light. He was the candle. His blood was the wine of blessing and redemption. He was the promised Redeemer who would call us forth from the tomb. Jesus would open wide the gates of Eden for us to return home.

I groped for the chalice and drew it to me as I curled up on the floor. Opening my eyes, I saw reflected sunlight on the silver where the cross had been. The inside of the cup was spotless— clean and untarnished.

I lay there for a time, trying to take it all in. At last, I sat up and cradled the chalice in my hands. One last time I examined it. "Clean. Worthy of the Lamb of God who takes away the sin of the world."

I stood and wrapped it in the fleece, then replaced it under my pillow.

Outside my window I heard the voice of Red call to me, "Nehemiah! Are you up there? Wake up! Jesus has returned. He's teaching at the Temple. Hurry!"

The instant I stepped onto the street, Red clapped me on the back and sprinted away. I followed, as over his shoulder he grinned with excitement. "Hurry up! We can't tell your mother or she won't let you come. There's going to be trouble, I think!"

"What's happened?" Close on his heels, I got the story in shouted bits and pieces as we dodged through the throng.

"Big crowd. Jesus teaching. Priests and Pharisees come along and . . . it's like a contest of riddles. Them asking questions I don't understand, and him answering with answers I don't understand. But I think he's winning. Some of the men in the crowd cheered when Jesus called the Pharisees 'blind fools'! Can't you run faster? It's really good. They're boiling over. Want him arrested! His disciples are looking like they'll fight, and about ten thousand common folk will join in if they try to take Jesus away!"

I laughed, not knowing why. There was nothing funny about such news, but I did not want to miss the riot if the confrontation came to blows. "Hurry, then!" I shouted as we dashed through the souk.

Shoppers turned away from haggling and followed after us.

Crossing the causeway, we ran up the steps and entered the Temple. Red was a master at weaving through a packed crowd.

I half suspected he may have been a skilled thief to supplement his income, but today he had only one goal: to get close enough to witness the battle of wits between the teachers of the law and Jesus of Nazareth.

On the treasury steps, the enemies of Jesus gathered around him in a half circle like a pack of wolves. What may have begun as a quiet attempt to discredit him had exploded into red-faced shouts of outrage:

"Jesus! Blasphemer!"

"Who do you think you are?"

"Are you more righteous than us?"

"How dare you accuse us before the people!"

Red led me to the other boys, about the third rank back from the bottom step. Together we snaked through and inched our way onto the stairs. Through the press of spectators and accusers I saw Jesus, unperturbed, as he answered their rage.

" . . . You give a tenth of your income, but you don't do the things that really matter . . . like justice, mercy and faithfulness. You should have practiced those without neglecting the other. You blind guides! You strain out a gnat but swallow a camel."[3]

A man I had seen with the high priest shouted, "You ignorant, Galilean fraud! You law breaker! Blasphemer! You heal on the Sabbath and call your violation mercy!"

Jesus answered, "Woe to you, teachers of the law and Pharisees, you hypocrites! You clean the outside of the cup, but inside it is full of greed and self-indulgence. Blind Pharisee! First clean the inside of the cup, and then the outside also will be clean!"[4]

The people cheered and laughed at Jesus' words.

The uproar increased among the Temple officials. "Are you calling us unclean?"

Jesus bore into them. "Shame on you, teachers of the law!

Pharisees! You are like whitewashed tombs, which look beautiful on the outside but on the inside are full of dead men's bones and everything unclean. You look good to people on the outside, but inside you're packed with hypocrisy and wickedness!"[5]

Another shout of approval from the people.

Red nudged me hard. "Aren't you glad you didn't miss this?"

"Not for anything." But my heart pounded. My eyes were wide as I saw Temple guards and Herodian soldiers standing ready to draw their swords and slaughter anyone who made a wrong move.

Jesus did not draw back. "Judgment is coming on you, hypocrites! You build elaborate tombs to honor the prophets and you decorate the graves of the righteous. And you say, 'If we had lived in the days of our forefathers, we wouldn't have joined in, when they shed the blood of the prophets.' But the truth is this: you're the offspring of those who murdered the prophets! Fill up the cup, then, with the measure of your forefathers' sin! You snakes! You brood of vipers! How will you escape being condemned to hell? Therefore, I am sending you prophets and wise men and teachers. Some of them you'll crucify. Others you'll flog in your synagogues and pursue from town to town." Fixing his eyes on Caiaphas, he continued, "And so on your heads will come all the righteous blood shed on earth. Every bit, from the blood of righteous Abel to the blood of Zechariah. The same Zechariah whom you murdered between the Temple and the altar. Listen to me: all this will come upon this generation!"[6]

At a signal of the high priest, the soldiers drew their weapons. The people grew quiet and nervous. Many in the back left the scene.

"You are a lying prophet." Caiaphas shook his fist in Jesus' face. "Destruction will come upon you, not us. All the evil of the ages be heaped upon your soul, and not upon the people!"

Jesus shook his head slowly. Sadness filled his eyes. "O Jerusalem! Jerusalem! You who kill the prophets and stone those sent to you. How many times I wanted to gather your children together like a hen gathers her chicks under her wings. But you weren't willing. Look . . ." Jesus' gaze wandered over the magnificent buildings of the Temple Mount.

The eyes of the throng followed, even the high priest's.

"See," Jesus continued, "your house is left to you desolate." Jesus then parted the crowd. "I tell you, you won't see me again until you say, 'Blessed is he who comes in the name of the Lord.'"[7]

The outrage at his proclamation was so fierce and incoherent I could no longer hear what anyone said. I expected the soldiers would rush in and arrest him on the spot.

Instead, Jesus walked through the people and out of the Temple grounds. His disciples came behind him. Scowling, Peter, James, and John walked backward with their hands on their swords.

Avel spotted me and the Sparrows and called, "Come on, boys! Follow us!"

I wormed my way out of the crush with Timothy, Jesse, Obed, Red, and Hallelujah. We left the Temple with the band of Jesus' followers.

Judas pleaded with him, "But this is the Great Temple! Say the word, and the people will fight for you to be their King!"

I heard Jesus answer sadly, "Do you see all these great buildings? I'm telling you the truth—not one stone here will be left on another. They'll all be thrown down."[8]

Jesus was silent as we left the city through the Eastern Gate. His followers continued to chatter and cheer themselves about the battle of wits that had just taken place. They congratulated each other for being on the right side. After all, hadn't Jesus spoken the harsh truth in a way that no one had ever dared speak before?

There was an arrogant jubilation among the men as they discussed in detail the shocked expressions on the faces of the opposition and their escalating rage.

Peter blustered, "But you notice, they were afraid to fight us! They didn't use their swords, did they? Afraid of what the people would do."

"A victory," James asserted. "They'll back down, you'll see."

Thomas shook his head. "I'm not so sure. But the priests and Pharisees were on the defensive. That much is certain."

With a sideways glance, I saw Judas scowling. He of all the men did not approve of the outcome. "We should've fought them," he said. "I think we missed our chance today. That's all."

It was a short distance to the Mount of Olives. Jesus went to a quiet garden, spread his cloak, and sat down. It had been a long day.

"Lord," Matthew asked, "you say the stones of the Temple will be thrown down. When? And what will be the sign of your return? And what signs will there be for the end of this age?"

I joined the Sparrows as we climbed onto the low branches of an ancient olive tree.

Others in the group gathered around Jesus with an eagerness to hear what he had to say about the end of Jerusalem. Would he call down fire from heaven? Maybe tomorrow? Or before the end of Passover?

Jesus kept his gaze fixed on Jerusalem as he spoke. "Make sure no one fools you. Many will come using my name, claiming, 'I'm the Messiah.' They'll deceive many. You'll hear of wars and rumors of wars, but see to it you aren't alarmed. These things will happen, but that still won't be the end, not yet. Nation will rise against nation and kingdom against kingdom. There will be famines and earthquakes all over the world. But these are just the beginning of birth pangs—the labor pains of the end of the world."

Red nudged me and whispered, "Sounds to me like he's saying the end of the world is a long ways off."

Jesus now turned his eyes on his followers. "You must know this too: you'll be handed over to be persecuted and put to death. And you'll be hated everywhere because of me. When persecution comes, many will turn away from the faith. They will even betray and hate one another."

Near the back of the circle I watched Judas stand and walk away. He went to a boulder and looked out across the valley at the Temple.

Jesus briefly glanced at him as he spoke. "Many false prophets will come on the scene and will deceive many people. Wickedness will grow so big that even love will turn cold."

Then Jesus looked right at us boys as we perched in the tree. "But he who stands firm to the end will be saved. And this good news will be preached to the whole world. There will be witnesses in all nations . . . and then . . . *and then*," he emphasized, "the end will come."[9]

Avel stroked the sparrow on Emet's shoulder, then smiled up at me. "He's talking to us, boys."

I nodded.

Jesus continued, "There'll be great tribulation, unlike anything ever, from the beginning of the world until now, and never to be equaled again."

My stomach churned as he described the terrible days that will come before the end of the world.

"The sun will be darkened and the moon will not give its light; the stars will fall from the sky, and the heavenly bodies will be shaken. At that time the sign of the Son of Man will appear in the sky, and all the nations of the earth will mourn. They'll see the Son of Man coming on the clouds of the sky, with great power and glory. And he will send his angels with a loud trumpet call, and they will gather his elect from the four winds, from one end of the heavens to the other . . . when you see these things, you know that it is near. Right at the door.

"I tell you, the generation that sees these things will not pass away until all these things have happened. Heaven and earth will pass away, but my words will never pass away.

"No one knows about that day or hour, not even the angels of heaven, nor the Son, but only the Father. As it was in the days of Noah, so it will be at the coming of the Son of Man. Before the Flood, people were eating and drinking and marrying up to the day Noah entered the ark. And they didn't know what would happen until the Flood came and took them all away. That's how it will be at the coming of the Son of Man. Two men will be in the field. One will be taken and the other left behind. Two women will be grinding with a hand mill. One will be taken and the other left. So pay attention! Keep watch! You don't know what day your Lord will come . . ."[10]

Jesus spoke to us for a long time about his final return to Jerusalem and the end of the world.

The sun sank low in the western horizon as his teaching finally came to an end, and the last of our questions were answered. I knew he was not only speaking to us that day, but to those who would come after us. There were some among us who listened with disappointment.

"When the Son of Man comes in his glory, and all the angels

with him, he will sit on his glorious throne. All the nations will be gathered before him, and he will separate the people one from another as a shepherd separates the sheep from the goats. He will put the sheep on his right and the goats on his left. Then the King will say to those on his right, 'Come, you who are blessed by my Father; take your inheritance, the kingdom prepared for you since the creation of the world. For I was hungry, and you gave me something to eat. I was thirsty, and you gave me something to drink. I was a stranger, and you invited me in. I needed clothes, and you clothed me. I was sick and you looked after me. I was in prison and you came to visit me.'

"Then the righteous will ask, 'When did we do these things for you?'

"And the King will reply, 'I tell you the truth: whatever you did for one of the least of these brothers and sisters of mine, you did for me.'"[11]

The sun was setting, but I felt he spoke to me. "Even if all you have to give in my name is a cup of cold water, you will not lose your reward."

He finished teaching us and said quietly, "As you know, the Passover is in two days. And the Son of Man will be handed over to be crucified."[12]

Some among the women began to weep quietly. Other disciples argued with him. The one named Judas turned his head and narrowed his eyes as he studied Jesus. It was right then that I was sure it had been Judas whom we had seen outside the door of the Chamber of Hewn Stone.

Jesus and Judas locked eyes with a hard look. I knew there was no event to come that would surprise the Lord. The Cup of Joseph, which I had believed contained such hope, had taken on a new and tragic meaning.

A heaviness hung over us all as Jesus departed for Bethany with his disciples.

I returned to Jerusalem with the Sparrows to await my final instructions from the Lord.

Chapter 35

$\mathcal{I}$n the morning I awakened to my mother's voice outside in front of the new shop. She was singing to the rhythm of her loom shuttle:

> "He is mighty.
> He is mighty!
> May he soon rebuild his house.
> Speedily, speedily,
> and in our days!"

I sat up from my bed.

Hallelujah was already at the window. "Listen to our new mother sing!" Hallelujah said with awe in his tone. "Look! Look!"

Red rubbed his face. "Hallelujah, what's happening?"

I did not wait for Hallelujah's reply. I rushed to the window, and the other boys crammed in around me. A crowd of people twenty deep was in front of the new shop. There was my mother, singing and weaving, as the brand-new sign was being hung above the door by a workman on a ladder.

> "He is distinguished;
> he is great.

He is exalted!
May he come soon
and rebuild his house.
Speedily, speedily,
and in our days, soon!
God, rebuild.
God, rebuild.
God, rebuild your house, soon!"

For a moment the early-morning sun glinted on the red and gold gilded letters of the sign.

"What's it say?" asked Timothy, who could not read.

Red demanded, "Does anybody know what it says?

The brothers chimed in, "*BEIT.* 'House.' I can't read the rest."

"The first word is *house*," I agreed.

Hallelujah shook his head in wonder. "What colors are those? Somebody tell me the names of the colors on the sign."

"Hallelujah, look! Red is the color, just like the color of Red's hair."

"And gold is the color like the sun."

Hallelujah breathed a long sign of approval. "Ahh . . ."

Timothy asked me, "But what's the sign say, Nehemiah? You can read. Tell us!"

I was lost for a moment in the words of the song as my mother sang. The crowd grew larger as her voice drew them. "Rebuild! Rebuild."

I answered, "The letters in gold on the new sign spell *BEIT TALLITOT.* 'House of Prayer Shawls.'"

Someone in the crowd called, "House of Prayer. But where are the shawls?"

Another cried, "I have come all the way from Cyprus and

was told by my brother to bring him one like our grandfather bought from this shop. But where are they?"

As Mama's song came to an end, my father stepped forward, smiling. He raised his hands high to silence the questions. "The House of Prayer Shawls is once again open! Look! The most beautiful *tallitot* in the world will be on the shelves and available this afternoon."

All heads turned to scan the Street of the Weavers. At the bottom of the lane, I spotted my three brothers with a string of a dozen donkeys loaded with baskets. Ezra was in the lead. Beni panted at his heels.

I shouted, "Ezra! Beni!"

My dog barked and ran ahead. Ezra waved. "We've got them!" he shouted. "Father sent us to Joppa and to the house of every relative to collect them. Look—we've brought them!"

A cheer went up from all the people. We boys rushed from the rented house to swarm around my brothers to help unload the cargo and carry prayer shawls, *Shabbat* tablecloths, and scarves to fill the shelves.

"Sometimes miracles happen," Papa said as Mama embraced him. He instructed my elder brothers to wash and eat and then return to help stock the shop for what would surely be a rush of customers.

My mother clasped Papa's hand and bounded up the stairs of our new home.

At Ezra's command, Beni lay obediently outside on the threshold like a sentinel.

I followed Mama and Papa upstairs.

"The Lord has rebuilt," Mama whispered. They stood before the painting my father had commissioned for our large room above the shop. "The flowers. The Great White Hart. The colors in the water. Perfection, Lamsa. As it must have been . . . our mountains as they were when Eden was still there."

While Jerusalem boiled with religious and political turmoil, Mama spent the day furnishing the room as my brothers worked organizing the inventory downstairs. Papa told her the upper room must be ready for Rabbi Kagba to preside over our first supper, which would be the Feast of Unleavened Bread and the beginning of Passover.

Papa and Rabbi Kagba gathered the young Sparrows, who had never experienced a proper Passover meal.

"There is no leaven in this house . . . nothing to clean out," Rabbi Kagba taught. "Leaven represents sin in the heart of men. Like a spot of yeast goes through all the dough, a little bit of sin will spread through a man's heart. That's why for the Feast of Unleavened Bread we sweep our houses and clean out every crumb. In the same way we sweep our lives clean of every crumb of sin." The old man leveled his gaze on us. Red blushed as he asked, "Boys? Have you any sin in your life? Confess it now and sweep clean your inner house. Make your heart ready for the coming of the Lord. For he truly is coming!"

Red blurted eagerly, "Oh, Rabbi, I can tell you! I am crammed full of leaven and that's a fact. Stale bread, that's me. Feed me to the birds! I'm so full of yeast and sin like no boy you ever met. My fare has been stolen bread and apples and such at least once a week from the souk. If I counted the dried apricots I have crammed in my pockets. There's never, never enough to eat and so . . ."

Rabbi Kagba put a hand on Red's arm. "And so, your heart you have swept clean. You will never steal so much as a single apricot again. And now, my boys, we begin new life in a brand-new house."

Papa concurred. "So, boys, that is why we have not broken bread in our new house before now. No crumbs of leavened bread. We have reserved sharing our first supper in the upper room for this Passover . . . the Feast of Unleavened Bread."

As workmen carried furniture up the steps, I sat on the window ledge and watched. Mama stood before the painting with her arms crossed, head tilted, and chin slightly raised like a little girl in awe. She studied every detail, each brushstroke and color of Eden. Leaning very close, she gazed into the hart's amber eyes and asked me, "Is this what he looks like up close, Nehi?"

"Yes," I replied. "When I look at him, it's like seeing an old friend. Mama, he is waiting for Messiah to redeem the world, just as we are."

Mama hung red curtains she had woven around the window, framing the glory of the Temple Mount. A long table of polished, striped acacia wood was the centerpiece. She had been weaving the fabric for red and gold cushions for many weeks. Now the pillows were covered, and I helped her carry them upstairs.

"When Jesus is King," she said with satisfaction, "my dream is that he may one day eat supper with his disciples right here in our upper room. I would cook for him and, with strong, steady legs, climb these stairs and place the steaming platters in front of him."

I did not tell her the sorrows I had seen in my vision, or what Jesus had said about being crucified. I think she would not have believed me anyway. Who could imagine such a thing coming true? She would have said my vision was only a bad dream brought on by exhaustion. She would have said that Jesus was just telling another parable. Perhaps he only meant to teach us something important.

But I was certain of what I had seen, and I couldn't guess what the lesson of such a parable could be.

Mama gathered us boys, and calling the Sparrows her sons, we went to the potter's shop together. After what seemed like hours, she selected and purchased new dishes, matching clay cups, serving platters and trays, painted with vines and clusters of grapes. Red, Timothy, Jesse, Obed, Hallelujah, and I helped carry the crockery home in a cheerful procession. The boys had eaten from broken shards of pottery, but never from unbroken plates.

Red declared he would feel like he was the richest boy in the world if only he could ever eat one meal from such finery.

My mother gazed at him with amazement. "Well, it's all for you! This Passover! Such a meal we will share here!"

So the room was ready for our first supper.

The Day of Preparation dawned. The Sparrows and I rose early and went with Papa and Rabbi Kagba to select a lamb. I never liked this part of the Passover tradition. The choosing of an innocent, perfect lamb for sacrifice always seemed a sad thing to me. Even in our mountains, where lambs from my father's flocks were plentiful.

In Jerusalem the stock pens were crowded with tens of thousands of lambs born and raised in Bethlehem. They were set aside for the very purpose of dying as sin offerings.

Papa knew what was good and best and better among the pens of milling sheep. He examined them all and finally picked an animal from the lambs that had not yet been washed. It was his intention that the Sparrows would learn to wash it and brush it, using the day to prepare it for slaughter. By the end of that time, the boys would be attached to it.

In this way they would learn the hard lesson that the sin

of all men required the atoning death of a gentle and beautiful creature that knew nothing of sin. It was a hard lesson to learn. I knew that firsthand. I recalled vividly the sadness and shock I'd experienced when the innocent lamb had died in my dog Beni's place. It was far different in my mountains, when we lived our days with the sheep, than simply purchasing a chunk of meat in the city marketplace.

While Papa taught the Sparrows something about the care and feeding of lambs, Rabbi Kagba and I set out together to draw water from the well to wash it.

Hand-over-hand I helped pull up the bucket and pour it into the ceremonial jar. Rabbi Kagba balanced it on his shoulder, and we headed back toward home.

We had just turned the corner of our street when I spotted Peter and James walking toward us.

I waved. "*Shalom!* Peter! James!"

"Look!" Peter's brooding face broke into a smile. "It's Nehemiah and the rabbi."

"*Shalom,*" Rabbi Kagba greeted them. "Is everything well with your master?"

"Aye." Peter nodded. "Jesus sent us to find you—that is, I think he meant you. He told us to come to the city. He said a man carrying water would meet us and . . . we're to follow you."

My teacher's eyes misted with emotion. "The first supper . . . ah, yes. So it will be as I dreamed it would be. Come along, then. Follow us."

My father knelt in the dirt as we approached. The boys stroked the baby lamb and spoke kindly to it as boys often speak gentle words to small, dumb creatures. The lamb was sitting across Red's lap. It laid its head against his shoulder and closed its eyes.

Papa stood as Peter and James approached. "*Shalom*, brothers. Is your master well?"

"He is well and sends his greetings."

"Jesus is coming into Jerusalem for Passover?" my father asked. "In spite of everything?"

"He is," James replied. "With the twelve of us."

Peter added, "The teacher asks if the room is ready so he can eat Passover with his disciples?"

My father's face lit with understanding. "I have just the place for your master. The upper room in my new house. Everything new and ready—no meal ever before eaten there. Please, if you will do me the honor. I'm unworthy that Jesus should enter under my roof, but if the Lord will only come and bring his disciples here to my new house, you'll see. New dishes and cups. Please, yes, the table is ready. The room is prepared. If Jesus will eat the first supper here beneath the roof of my house, then my house and my family will be blessed forever. "

"He told us you would say that." James's eyes were somber, not like a man looking forward to a celebration. "Yes. Jesus will come to your house for dinner this evening."

My thoughts flew to Joseph's silver chalice. Not only would I present it to Jesus tonight, he would take his first drink from it in the upper room of my home!

Peter said to me, "And he told me, 'Nehemiah will have the cup ready.' I don't know what cup he means, boy, but I suppose he knows . . . and you know, Nehemiah?"

I nodded but did not speak. Peter's gruff voice and wild looks somehow always caused me to lose my voice.

My father embraced James. "You can't imagine the joy! After my wife was healed—she would walk a thousand miles to fix a meal for Jesus. It's her dream to feed him. Well, that's a woman for you. And her prayer! She mentioned it again only this morning." He mimicked my mother's voice, "If only I could cook a meal for Jesus!"

Peter said, "I heard she's a good cook."

Papa exclaimed, "Such a cook she is! But I promise if she never cooked another meal, she wants only to cook supper for Jesus. Could there be such an honor? Serving Jesus his Passover supper as he prepares to enter into his kingdom?"

"Why am I surprised?" Peter asked. "So, it's settled. I suppose it was always settled. We just didn't know the details—upper room of the weaver's shop. Thank you very much. Tell your wife thanks as well. And now Jesus has sent us fishermen to select a lamb. I'm not very good at it. I get attached to the little things before I carry them home."

Papa put a hand on Peter's arm. "No, please. I am a shepherd and the son of a shepherd. This morning I selected the best lamb of the flock from Bethlehem. My boys are washing its fleece right now. What an honor it would be if Jesus and his close friends would accept the lamb I had intended to be offered for my family. If Jesus would accept the sacrifice from my hands for his good and the good of his friends, even though I'm not worthy for him to enter under my roof, then I'll be doubly blessed!"

The arrangement pleased everyone and sent my mother spinning with joy. Jesus the Lord, her Healer and Redeemer, was coming to bless her upper room by breaking bread there.

A steady stream of pilgrims flooded the shop to purchase prayer shawls as Mama prepared the supper for our special guests.

My three elder brothers manned the counters for two hours

and then the shop was closed as preparation for Jesus' arrival continued.

It was mid-afternoon when Mama brought me in to the back room. Everything smelled of clean woolen fabric, fresh paint, and newly sanded wood. The shelves were stocked with fabrics made famous by the weavers of my family. I felt proud.

Mama opened the chest and, with a wave of her hand, motioned for me to come and see. "Nehemiah, these are the very best prayer shawls and *kittels* I ever made on my loom. Ever in my life. Sometimes something extraordinary happens, you know. When you pray or sing or create or just live, and God pours his love through us into something. So every year from our far mountains, from the place where Eden once was, I sent something special I had made to my sister for safekeeping. That is why these were saved from the fire that took everything. God saved them for this night, you see. These were never offered for sale. How could I sell such things? But I thought I saved them for special occasions in our own family. Like your *bar mitzvah*, or your wedding someday. Everything here. Ready for the most holy moments in our lives. Or one day, when perhaps I might have a grandchild of my own. And here . . ." She held up a man-sized *kittel*, the white robe worn by a bridegroom for his wedding. Later the robe he wore at his wedding would become the garment a man wore for his burial.

But that night, I knew Mama thought only of the wedding feast of the Messiah, not his death and burial. "So, Nehemiah, what do you think? For Jesus, the bridegroom of Israel?"

The light glistened white as snow on the fabric. The detail on the border was like a grapevine and clusters of grapes. "He will like that one, yes. I think so, Mama."

I tried not to think of the use of the *kittel* as burial clothes.

It seemed too ominous, considering what Jesus had said about his death.

"Yes, Mama. I remember how you sang when you made this one. And this too." I wondered if she had something special for me.

She retrieved a smaller white *kittel* and held it up for me to see. "I made this one for your *bar mitzvah*. Also grapevines. See? And *Kiddush* cups all around. I did not know what was about to happen. I just thought it was right for my son, Nehemiah, named after the cupbearer. You see? You should wear it tonight, I think."

I accepted it, excited, fearful I might make some mistake, and thankful I had lived to see this day. Did she see the nervousness in my eyes?

I focused on the exquisite prayer shawls. Running my fingers over the fabric, I traced the blue thread of the fringes. I remembered my mother patiently knotting one strand after another by the lamplight in our camp.

Removing the stack, she laid them out on a bench. "And all of these—they're the special ones. I want you to take them upstairs and put one at the seat of each of the disciples . . . and one for Jesus, as our gift."

I knew that Joseph of Arimathea had given Jesus one of the special prayer shawls Mama had made, and Jesus wore it often. But my mother's heart was so eager to give something extra. Her face beamed like a hopeful little girl's as she asked me to help her choose. I embraced her, telling her there never was a woman like her, so talented and so kind.

Together, we selected the most beautiful *tallith* for Jesus to wear. It was the one she had named "Joseph's Coat of Many Colors."

"Of course," I said, certain the Holy Spirit had guided my mother's hands in the weaving and her heart in the naming.

The twelve shawls selected for the disciples were all different but of equal beauty and intricacy. But there was one gift that troubled me deeply—the twelfth *tallith* meant for Judas Iscariot.

I carried the precious gifts to the upper room and laid them at each of the seats. I only prayed that I was wrong about Judas . . . that somehow he would prove to be a true friend of the Lord.

She came up to inspect the room. As she stood before the painting of Eden, her eyes welled. "Eden. Like this house must be reborn. Beauty for ashes. Out of the ashes of my childhood, now the Lord has blessed me with this honor. Yes. Beauty for ashes in every life. My son as the cupbearer. My house rebuilt. Jesus coming here tonight for the first supper. I am blessed to have prepared it for him. What more could any woman ask?" She kissed my forehead. "I'm proud of you, Nehemiah. You have come a long way and suffered much to come to this night. Now go and wash and put on your wedding garment. The bridegroom of Israel is on his way."

While I washed and changed into my new clothes, Mama took her place at the loom again and began to sing at the window. I smoothed the fabric of my *kittel* and studied my reflection in the bronze mirror. I looked very grown-up.

The sun was almost down when I carried Joseph's silver chalice from the rented house, through the shop, and up the stairs of our restored home. The lamps and candles were already lit. *Matza* bread, wine from the vineyard of Lazarus, and all the ritual elements of the Passover meal were in place.

As the service progressed, Mama would carry the steaming platters of the feast to serve the guests.

Only the cup had yet to be placed in Jesus' hands, and all would be fulfilled.

I was alone in the upper room. The sense of holiness was heavy, a tangible weight of anticipation in the atmosphere. Through the window the buildings of the Temple were bathed in golden sunlight.

With a glance toward the painting of the great wounded hart, I unwrapped the chalice and held it up to the light. The golden light of Jerusalem reflected in the polished silver.

I was ready for my task as cupbearer to the King!

My teacher had taught me the meaning of every blessing that would be recited over the wine in Joseph's cup. This night, Jesus would bless and drink the four traditional cups offered at Passover from the chalice. Each cup of wine represented God's plan of redemption for Israel and for all of mankind through the Messiah.

Suddenly my mother burst into song with the rhythm of her loom. I knew then that Jesus and his disciples had turned the corner and were coming up the street!

Peering out the window, I saw sunlight glint on the lettering of the sign above the door and read the words HOUSE OF PRAYER.

My mother sang as the loom boomed like a drum:

> "He is pure,
> he is unique,
> he is powerful,
> he is wise,
> he is King."

In my white robe, I stood at attention behind Jesus' seat, Joseph's chalice in my hands. My heart pounded with excitement as I heard the door open.

My mother continued with great joy:

"He is awesome,
he is Redeemer!
He is righteous!"

I tried to remember all the rituals of the Passover cup I had been taught. I stammered as I rehearsed what I had learned about the chalice of the Messiah. Would I be worthy when the moment came? Would I remember to say and do what I was supposed to do?

Mama's lilting voice added:

"Take this cup,
the cup of sanctification.
Take this cup.
I will bring you out of bondage.
Take this cup.
I will deliver you.
Take this cup.
I have redeemed you!"

Tears streamed down my cheeks as I realized the moment I had longed for was at last upon me. The ancient silver chalice, which had held so much suffering and pain, was polished like new inside and out. Jesus would soon stretch out his hands to take the cup, drink from it, and then offer it back for all to drink who came to his table.

Everything fled from my mind as I heard the bell above the door, and Jesus entered the House of Prayer.

Mama announced his arrival in song.

"He is the Omnipotent God!
Rebuild! God, rebuild your house soon!"

I heard Jesus greet my family downstairs: "*Shalom! Shalom!* Thank you for taking me in. Well done, good and faithful friends."

And then . . . I heard his footsteps on the stairs!

My mother sang,

> "He is holy.
> He is compassionate.
> He is all righteous!
> Oh, God,
> rebuild your house soon!"

Chapter 36

'Twas only nine that evening as I sat on the stairs leading to the upper room where Jesus ate with his disciples. Judas, the betrayer, stood and stumbled out, almost tripping over me as he fled from the light into the darkness.

After the door slammed, I heard Jesus speak the words we later learned by heart.

Some believe he was addressing his followers, but I am certain Jesus spoke the first words directly to his Father.

The eyes of the Son raised heavenward and fixed on a throne, a holy altar, on mighty, outstretched hands that had governed galaxies and worlds, and ordained kingdoms and the lives of men and angels. "Blessed are you, O Lord, King of the universe who created this fruit of the vine I offer to you."

Jesus reached higher, stretching upward, until the chalice penetrated heaven. "Take this cup." He spoke with tenderness to his loving Father.

All time stood still in that moment. There was no time, no day or night, only eternity. The walls and ceiling of the chamber dissolved, and suddenly I saw the faces of all who had lived before and multitudes who would live in years to come. They gathered with us around the table, waiting eagerly to drink from the silver cup Jesus offered.

All who called on the Name of Jesus were brought together in that moment, in that place forever and ever.

Jesus offered the cup to all. "Drink from it, all of you. This is my blood of the covenant, which is poured out for many for the forgiveness of sins. I tell you, I will not drink from this fruit of the vine until that day when I drink it anew with you in my Father's kingdom."[1]

The chalice floated from hand to hand, and the precious contents were shared by all—first by Jesus' closest friends and then passed along.

I reached eagerly for it and looked deeply into the red wine. Again I saw my own reflection in the mirror of liquid. I was no longer a boy, but a man grown strong and courageous. I raised the cup to my lips and whispered, "Amen." I tasted the wine, closed my eyes, and smiled.

I found myself watching the flocks on a distant mountain illuminated by a golden light. The Great White Hart stood beside me. Eden restored. Not of this earth, I knew.

Not of this time.

I passed the chalice to another. I did not know who took it from my hand.

I heard Jesus' mother begin to sing,

> "I love the LORD, for he heard my voice;
> he heard my cry for mercy.
> Because he turned his ear to me,
> I will call on him as long as I live."[2]

All of us lining the stairs and those who supped in the room below joined in Mary's song.

"For you, LORD, have delivered me from death,
my eyes from tears,
my feet from stumbling,
that I may walk before the LORD
in the land of the living.

What shall I return to the LORD
for all his goodness to me?
I will lift up the cup of salvation
and call upon the name of the LORD."[3]

When all in the house had tasted from it, the empty cup returned to me. I held it close to my heart as if embracing an old friend. We had traveled many miles together to this holy moment and to this room where past and future became one eternal present.

Was I still to be cupbearer to the King? I peered over the top step. Tears misted my eyes as Jesus stood and wrapped himself in his seamless robe. He held me gently in his gaze for a long moment and nodded.

I wrapped the cup in my cloak.

"Come," he said, "follow me. The moment is at hand. We will go now to the Mount of Olives and pray."

Thus the first part of my journey came to an end.

But, in truth, it was only the beginning.

Notes

Part One

  1. Psalm 42:1, adapted from NIV

Chapter 1

  1. Psalm 42:1, adapted from NIV

  2. See Matthew 24:27.

Chapter 2

  1. Psalm 23:1–2 ESV

  2. Psalm 23:3 ESV

  3. Psalm 23:4 ESV

Chapter 3

  1. Numbers 24:17 ESV

  2. Isaiah 7:14 ESV

Chapter 6

  1. Esther 7:2

  2. Read the story in Genesis chapters 37 and 39 through 45.

Chapter 8

  1. Luke 2:35, adapted from NIV

  2. Deuteronomy 6:4

Part Two

  1. Psalm 91:1, 13

Chapter 9

  1. Psalm 91:13

  2. Psalm 91:1

  3. Psalm 50:15

  4. Psalm 72:13

  5. Proverbs 20:13

  6. Isaiah 55:1

Chapter 13
1. Psalm 42:1, adapted from NIV
2. See Genesis 50:20.

Chapter 16
1. Genesis 12:1 KJV
2. Isaiah 40:26 KJV
3. Isaiah 40:31 KJV

Chapter 18
1. Malachi 1:6, adapted from ESV

Chapter 19
1. Isaiah 49:6 ESV

Chapter 22
1. Isaiah 61:1
2. Isaiah 53:5

Chapter 23
1. Matthew 12:39 ESV

Part Three
1. John 12:35–36

Chapter 26
1. Luke 16:19–31, adapted from multiple versions
2. Jeremiah 1:4–8, adapted from NIV
3. Exodus 3:5

Chapter 27
1. Matthew 18:6–7, adapted from multiple versions
2. See Matthew 18:21–22.
3. Luke 17:6

Chapter 28
1. See Luke 17:11–19.
2. See Psalm 91:11.
3. Luke 17:20–21, adapted from NIV and NKJV
4. Luke 17:22–36, adapted from NIV
5. Psalm 91:3–4, adapted from NIV

Chapter 29
1. Luke 18:9–14, adapted from NIV and NKJV
2. See Luke 18:16–17.
3. Luke 18:18–30, adapted from NKJV
4. Luke 18:31–33, adapted from NIV
5. Psalm 75:8, adapted from NIV and NKJV
6. Isaiah 51:22 ESV

7. Isaiah 53:2 NKJV
8. Isaiah 53:5 NKJV
9. Isaiah 53:6, 10 NKJV
10. Isaiah 53:12 NKJV

Chapter 31

1. Psalm 105:1-2
2. Psalm 105:8-10
3. Matthew 21:13 NKJV

Chapter 32

1. Matthew 21:16, adapted from NIV
2. Isaiah 53:1
3. John 12:40

Chapter 33

1. Read the story in Matthew 21:33-44.
2. Psalm 118:22-23, as quoted by Jesus in Matthew 21:42
3. Read the story in John 12:25-36.

Chapter 34

1. See the prophecy in Hosea 11:1.
2. Genesis 3:17-18
3. Matthew 23:23-24, adapted from NIV
4. Matthew 23:25-26, adapted from NIV
5. Matthew 23:27-28, adapted from NIV
6. Matthew 23:29-36, adapted from NIV
7. Matthew 23:37-39, adapted from NIV
8. Matthew 24:2, adapted from NIV
9. Read the story in Matthew 24:3-14.
10. Matthew 24:29-31, 33-43, adapted from NIV
11. Matthew 25:31-40, adapted from NIV
12. Matthew 26:1-2, adapted from NIV

Chapter 36

1. Matthew 26:27-29
2. Psalm 116:1-2
3. Psalm 116:8-9, 12-13

Authors' Note

$\mathcal{J}$ esus clearly believed in the power of stories. He told parables—stories—to stretch the minds and transform the hearts of his listeners. We, too, believe in the life-changing power of stories, and that's why we're passionate about writing fiction.

In every work of our fiction, there is truth, based on research, and there is imagination, based on our minds and perspectives. We weren't here on this earth as Jesus walked among the people, but through the verses of Scripture and our imagination, we have portrayed to the best of our ability what he might have said and the way in which he might have said it. *Take This Cup* is how we imagine the events might have happened for young Nehemiah and his family, for Joseph of Arimathea, for the Sparrows of Jerusalem, for the boy Hallelujah, and for all the other characters in this story whose lives, bodies, and hearts were transformed by Jesus. It also traces the path of the legend of the Holy Grail and how we imagine the cup might have passed through the hands of ordinary people, such as Nehemiah, changing their hearts and life paths.

There are many legends about Joseph of Arimathea, the wealthy Jewish man who asked for permission to bury Jesus' body properly after his death. It is said he used the Holy Grail—the cup that Jesus used during the Last Supper—to collect Jesus' blood while he was being crucified. Then, afterward, it is said that Joseph traveled to England, bringing the cup with him. Which of the legends are true, and which are just stories? None of us is likely to know until we enter the realm of heaven, where the desires of our hearts will be met and our questions answered.

But can lives, bodies, and hearts truly be transformed today while we are here on earth? With Jesus, *anything* is possible! Through *Take This Cup,* may the Messiah come alive to you . . . in more brilliance than ever before.

Bodie & Brock Thoene

About the Authors

*B*ODIE and BROCK THOENE (pronounced *Tay-nee)* have written over sixty-five works of historical fiction. That these best sellers have sold more than thirty-five million copies and won eight ECPA Gold Medallion Awards affirms what millions of readers have already discovered—that the Thoenes are not only master stylists but experts at capturing readers' minds and hearts.

In their timeless classic series about Israel (The Zion Chronicles, The Zion Covenant, The Zion Legacy, The Zion Diaries), the Thoenes' love for both story and research shines. With The Shiloh Legacy and *Shiloh Autumn* (poignant portrayals of the American Depression), The Galway Chronicles (dramatic stories of the 1840s famine in Ireland), and the Legends of the West (gripping tales of adventure and danger in a land without law), the Thoenes have made their mark in modern history. In the A.D. Chronicles, they stepped seamlessly into the world of Jerusalem and Rome, in the days when Yeshua walked the earth. Now, in the Jerusalem Chronicles, the Thoenes continue that journey through the most crucial events in the life of Yeshua on earth.

Bodie, who has degrees in journalism and communications, began her writing career as a teen journalist for her local newspaper. Eventually her byline appeared in prestigious periodicals such as *US News and World Report,* the *American West,* and the *Saturday Evening Post.* She also worked for John Wayne's Batjac Productions and ABC Circle Films as a writer and researcher. John Wayne described her as "a writer with talent that captures the people and the times!"

Brock has often been described by Bodie as "an essential half of this writing team." With degrees in both history and education, Brock has, in his role of researcher and story-line consultant, added the vital dimension of historical accuracy. Due to such careful research, the Zion Covenant and Zion Chronicles series are recognized by the American Library Association, as well as Zionist libraries around the world, as classic historical novels and are used to teach history in college classrooms.

Bodie and Brock have four grown children—Rachel, Jake, Luke, and Ellie—and eight grandchildren. Their children are carrying on the Thoene family talent as the next generation of writers, and Luke produces the Thoene audiobooks. Bodie and Brock divide their time between Hawaii, London, and Nevada.

www.thoenebooks.com
www.familyaudiolibrary.com

Thoene Family Classics™

THOENE FAMILY CLASSIC HISTORICALS
by Bodie and Brock Thoene

Gold Medallion Winners*

The Zion Covenant
Vienna Prelude*
Prague Counterpoint
Munich Signature
Jerusalem Interlude
Danzig Passage
Warsaw Requiem*
London Refrain
Paris Encore
Dunkirk Crescendo

The Zion Chronicles
The Gates of Zion*
A Daughter of Zion
The Return to Zion
A Light in Zion
The Key to Zion*

The Shiloh Legacy
In My Father's House*
A Thousand Shall Fall
Say to This Mountain
Shiloh Autumn

The Galway Chronicles
Only the River Runs Free*
Of Men and of Angels
Ashes of Remembrance*
All Rivers to the Sea

The Zion Legacy
Jerusalem Vigil
Thunder from Jerusalem

Jerusalem's Heart
Jerusalem Scrolls
Stones of Jerusalem
Jerusalem's Hope

A.D. Chronicles
First Light
Second Touch
Third Watch
Fourth Dawn
Fifth Seal
Sixth Covenant
Seventh Day
Eighth Shepherd
Ninth Witness
Tenth Stone
Eleventh Guest
Twelfth Prophecy

Zion Diaries
The Gathering Storm
Against the Wind

Jerusalem Chronicles
When Jesus Wept
Take This Cup

THOENE FAMILY CLASSIC ROMANCE
by Bodie Thoene

Love Finds You in Lahaina, Hawaii

THOENE FAMILY CLASSIC AMERICAN LEGENDS
Legends of the West
by Brock and Bodie Thoene

Legends of the West
Volume One
Sequoia Scout
The Year of the Grizzly
Shooting Star

Legends of the West
Volume Two
Gold Rush Prodigal
Delta Passage
Hangtown Lawman

Legends of the West
Volume Three
Hope Valley War
The Legend of Storey County
Cumberland Crossing

Legends of the West
Volume Four
The Man from Shadow Ridge
Cannons of the Comstock
Riders of the Silver Rim

Legends of Valor
by Jake Thoene and Luke Thoene

Sons of Valor
Brothers of Valor
Fathers of Valor

THOENE FAMILY CLASSIC CONTEMPORARY
by Bodie, Brock, and Luke Thoene

Icon

THOENE CLASSIC CONTEMPORARY
by Bodie and Brock Thoene

Beyond the Farthest Star

THOENE CLASSIC NONFICTION
by Bodie and Brock Thoene

Little Books of Why
Why a Manger?
Why a Shepherd?
Why a Star?
Why a Crown?
Writer-to-Writer

THOENE FAMILY CLASSIC SUSPENSE
by Jake Thoene

Chapter 16 Series
Shaiton's Fire
Firefly Blue
Fuel the Fire

THOENE FAMILY CLASSICS FOR KIDS
Sherlock Holmes &
The Baker Street Detectives
by Jake Thoene and Luke Thoene

The Mystery of the Yellow Hands
The Giant Rat of Sumatra
The Jeweled Peacock of Persia
The Thundering Underground

The Last Chance Detectives
by Jake Thoene and Luke Thoene

Mystery Lights of Navajo Mesa
Legend of the Desert Bigfoot

by Rachel Thoene

The Vase of Many Colors

THOENE FAMILY CLASSIC AUDIOBOOKS

Available from

www.thoenebooks.com

or

www.familyaudiolibrary.com